GREETINGS

In 1936 S C H (Sammy) Davis was to become President of the Club. Among his many accomplishments, as a competition driver and journalist, could be added those of cartoonist and artist. He had been a student at the Slade School of Art and presented the Club with this drawing as the basis of its 1936 Christmas card.

A PORTRAIT of the Vintage Sports-Car Club 1934-2014

The almost timeless scene outside the Radnorshire Arms in Presteigne High Street in October 2008, which the Club had first visited in 1939. An Austin Seven and a Bugatti, no doubt having recently completed the road section as indicated by the lack of mud, wait patiently while their drivers have probably gone into the hotel to report their arrivals, have their mileages checked and to sign on.

(Roger McDonald)

A PORTRAIT of the Vintage Sports-Car Club 1934-2014

Thomas Pellow

First published by The Vintage Sports-Car Club in 2015

The Vintage Sports-Car Club
The Old Post Office
West Street
Chipping Norton
Oxfordshire
OX7 5EL

www.vscc.co.uk

Copyright © Thomas Pellow 2015

The moral right of the author has been asserted

All rights reserved.
No part of this publication may be reproduced, stored in a retrieval system, or transmitted in any form or by any means, without the prior permission of the publisher. The reproduction of any part of the text or any of the illustrations in whole or in part is forbidden without written permission from the copyright holders.

ISBN 978-0-9542876-9-6

Designed and printed by Quorum Print Services Ltd, Cheltenham
www.quorumprint.co.uk

Typeset in Abode Garamond Pro

Contents

Acknowledgements	vii
Infancy. 1934–1939	1
Renaissance. 1945–1955	43
The Club that Carson built. 1956–1972	107
Russell Road – The Early Years. 1973–1983	141
The Golden Jubilee Year. 1984	163
Russell Road – The Later Years. 1985–1997	177
Chipping Norton and beyond. 1998–2014	217
Appendices	261
Bibliography and Sources	269
Index	273

Acknowledgements

The need for the story of the Vintage Sports-Car Club to be recorded, as it approached its 80th birthday, emerged from a conversation with Mike Stripe, the then Club Secretary. His predecessor, Peter Hull, had written of the early years in his "History of the Vintage Sports-Car Club", as published in 1964. This covered the years up to 1953 in some detail and those up to 1964 in outline. Nearly fifty years later it was evident that an update was due.

A small editorial board was appointed to oversee the project – John Staveley, the Editor of *The Bulletin*, together with Gary Clare and Tony Hartnell, both of whom had served on the Club's main Committee. On a sunny August day, with a soundtrack of hard worked engines and squealing tyres in the background, we met in the office beside the Prescott start line to discuss the proposed outline of the book. Since then they have stayed in contact with its progress, up to the stage of final proof reading when they were joined by Derek Howard-Orchard. Any errors that may still remain are, of course, the responsibility of the author.

Tony Hartnell was to prove invaluable in his candid comments on the early drafts of the Chapters as they gradually appeared, while in the closing stages of finalising the text David Filsell, with over fifty years of active membership of the Club, was to prove himself a painstaking and informed copy editor. His sometimes astringent comments and concern for detail greatly improved the text. The late David Venables, long-time Deputy Editor of *The Bulletin*, likewise provided guidance, encouragement and expertise.

Acknowledgements

Finding photographs to illustrate the decades of Club activity, across the wide range of motor sport disciplines involved, would have been a daunting task without the continuing support of Roger McDonald. Access to his archive, the McDonald Collection, made a pleasure out of what could so easily have become a problem, while his memories of many years of VSCC membership guided and illumined my research throughout. It would all have been so much harder without his unstinting support.

Ted Walker, of Ferret Fotographics, has also been most generous in his support, particularly in providing images of the rarely photographed early years. Pictorial coverage of the fifties and sixties has been greatly enhanced by access to the photographic collection of Max Hill, as kindly made available by his son, Keith Hill. In bringing the story up to date thanks must also go to Peter McFadyen.

All of the cartoons have previously appeared in *The Bulletin*, and appreciative thanks are due to those who drew them, with such insight into the workings of the Club and indeed into the minds of its members. Cartoonists tend to hide their talents behind pen (or should they be pencil ?) names. Thus it has proved hard to identify them so that they might be approached direct about the re-use of their work – but despite such enforced lack of contact my gratitude to them is no less real. The penultimate illustration in the book is a reproduction of the Club's 2013 Christmas card, for which thanks go to Richard Wade.

To prepare a manuscript such as this requires access to earlier published sources, and the loan of a complete run of the post-war *Bulletins* has proved crucial in this respect. Along with the run of the Club's Newsletters as housed in its library at Chipping Norton they have made the task possible, while the support of the Club's librarians in finding my way around a range of printed and other archival material has greatly aided the process. Sincere thanks are due to Ian Ferguson, the Librarian, and his colleagues Derry Aust, Andy Butcher, Cosmo Davies, Roger Edmonds, Nigel Hall, and Paul Spencer for the ever friendly welcome that underpinned their expertise and support. One of the challenges, when faced with a pile of historic *Bulletins,* is to stay on task and avoid being distracted as one stumbles across interesting articles while searching for something completely different. Fortunately help was at hand in the shape of the on-going Index produced by New Zealand member Clive Taylor, the updates being emailed to the Library and myself over the course of the months.

Acknowledgements

On my multiple visits to Chipping Norton I frequently found it necessary to pause and ask a question of one or other of the Club's staff. Thanks go to Steve Allen, Andy Conway, Gill Batkin, Sally Duckett, Andy Halstead, Gemma Price, James Taylor and Richard Winchester, all of whom, at some time or another, have put up with my interruptions with good grace, and have provided the information being sought. Nor must Mike Stripe be forgotten, for he was in at the very beginning and contributed some of his views on the work of the office to the final Chapter before leaving the Club.

A Club is an amalgam of its members, and so many of these have made contributions to this book. Interviews with several of the Presidents who have guided the Club over the years have proved particularly illuminating. Especial thanks go to the late Bruce Spollon, Roger Collings, Roger Ballard, Tony Stephens, and the present incumbent, Tim Kneller.

Others who have helped in a variety of ways, both great and small, include the following:

Jim Adams, Angela Cherrett, who along with Thelma Grose, provided information on the eventual inclusion of ladies at the Marshals' Dinner; Peter Clews, Tim Cork, Anthony Costigan, David Crouch, Alan Couper, Ray Edge, Malcolm Elder, with his delightful insights into the winter driving tests over the years; Mark Garfitt, Julian Ghosh, Hugh Girvan, Tony Griffiths, Tim and Rebecca Gunn, David Hinds, Julian Hunt, Martin Jelley, Neil Murray, together with Bob Wimmer who followed him as Competition Secretary, for their "insiders" memories; George Shetliffe, Mike Sythes, Mike Tebbett, and especially to Paul Tebbett who was generous in his considerable help relating to the Welsh weekend; Chrissie Tebbett, Mark Walker and Dick Wilkinson.

Well aware of the fallibilty of memory my apologies to those who, inadvertently, I might have missed out.

Finally my thanks go to those involved in the process of turning what started out as a collection of pencilled scribbles into a finished book; the ever tolerant Sandra Brown for her patience and keyboard skills, to Don Millar for providing accompanying computer expertise, and to Peter Minnis and his helpful staff at Quorum Print Services.

Infancy
1934–1939

By the early nineteen thirties, in parts of England at least, the worst effects of the depression that had followed the Wall Street crash of 1929 were beginning to lift. Particularly in the South and Midlands unemployment was starting to fall and evidence of recovery was to be seen in the emergence of new consumer based industries and a house building boom underpinned by low interest rates. The National Grid, completed in 1933, provided some of the stimulus for the new manufacturers and markets that were starting to emerge, and especially for the spread of electrically powered domestic appliances – radios, gramophones, vacuum cleaners and electric cookers – which all reflected a new age. Expanding industries, making anything from artificial textiles to motor cars, demonstrated a growing confidence and along with this went a rise in disposable income – but such was almost entirely confined to the south.

J B Priestley, novelist and playwright, set out to explore the divided country that he was to write about in his book *English Journey* of 1934. In the previous autumn he had travelled across the land by coach, train and taxi (for by his own admission he was a hopeless driver) to find that in addition to the "old England" of comfortable cathedral cities, market towns and rural by-ways and the sharply contrasting industrial areas where the staple industries of iron, steel, coal, ship building and textiles still struggled with ongoing depression and the blight of endemic unemployment, a "third England" was starting to emerge. He identified "a new post-war England of arterial and by-pass roads, of filling stations and factories that looked like exhibition buildings, giant dance halls and cafés, bungalows with tiny garages". Within it dwelt an aspirational population which, as part of its rising standard of living, sought increased mobility and the freedom that motoring could bring; often linked to an enthusiasm to read and learn more about it.

Magazines evolve, and so it was with the *Cyclecar* started by the Temple Press shortly before the First World War; which next was to become the *Light Car and Cyclecar* before settling down in the thirties as the *Light Car*. It reflected the evolution of such essentially basic vehicles, inclusive of Austin Sevens from 1923, followed by Morris Minors five years later. These and similar cars were becoming increasingly affordable and desirable, and it was to their owners that the *Light Car* looked for the bulk of its market.

Many of its readers belonged to one or more of the wide range of motoring clubs that were springing up, details of which were listed, catalogue style, in several pages of the magazine at the end of each year. In addition to the names and addresses of their secretaries and annual subscription rates, each club's entry concluded with details of the principal competitive events that they organised or hoped to organise – almost all of which were trials. On mainland Britain races for clubmen were confined to Brooklands (Donington was not opened to cars until 1933, with Crystal Palace following in 1937) although sprints, speed trials and sand races found some support. But it was in trialling that the bulk of amateur sporting motorists were to be found while increasingly vehicle manufacturers were taking an interest in this branch of the sport to the extent of funding semi-works trials teams. So it was entirely in keeping with the spirit of the times when the following letter appeared in *The Light Car* of 5th October 1934.

A Club for the Not-so-Rich

"A number of fellow-enthusiasts and myself have for some time been contemplating the formation of a club for light cars of not more than, say, £50. The owner of a by-no-means-new Austin Seven for instance, may tune it until it will reach a speed of 65–70 mph, but even so such a car would stand little or no chance in an ordinary club trial against more modern cars. For this reason membership might well be limited to cars made before, say, January 1, 1932. This date would, of course, be advanced by 12 months each year.

We would be glad to hear from anyone interested, particularly those living in or near London, or in the South of England. And we would like their views on the name of the Club; how often trials should be held; amount of subscription; and so on.

B H Nicholson
C P L Nicholson
Walton-on-Thames"

(As if to stress the basic nature of the appeal an editor of the magazine inserted "Rolls Owners Need Not Apply" alongside the text).

In mid-November *The Light Car* was able to report on the initiative of the Nicholson cousins.

> The Vintage Sports-Car Club
> "At a meeting held at Harrow on Tuesday October 30th, a club for owners of middle-aged cars was formed. The title of "The Vintage Sports-Car Club" was adopted and it was decided to limit membership to owners of cars which were manufactured before January 1931. It was further decided that owners of home-built cars would be accepted at the discretion of the Committee, providing that either the chassis or engine was manufactured before 1931.
>
> An informal run to a point on the Brighton Road is being held on Sunday November 18th, and anyone interested is cordially invited. Particulars may be obtained from the Secretary, Mr. C P L Nicholson, 7 Abercorn Mews, London NW8, from whom full particulars of membership may also be obtained."

Motor Sport also commented on the formation of the Club, suggesting that this had taken place a week earlier on 23rd October, so evidently the embryonic Committee was busy holding its meetings at weekly intervals during this formative time. The *Autocar* likewise reported on the Club's emergence, its brief report containing reference to a crucial shift.

> "An interesting new venture has been started under the title of the Veteran Sports Car Club (*sic*), the idea of it being to get together people who own cars manufactured before 1931, 30-98 Vauxhalls, three-litre Bentleys, and such like. The Secretary is C P L Nicholson, 7 Abercorn Mews, NW8."

Quite what the Nicholsons, Bruce and Colin, must have felt about the change in emphasis that had been so quickly worked upon their initial idea is not recorded, but almost certainly the young Cecil (hereinafter referred to as "Sam") Clutton – aged only twenty-six at the time – was heavily involved. A sixth generation family member of the well known firm of surveyors and estate managers, his motoring interests had been instilled by his father Lt Col J Clutton, the owner of a 16hp Fafnir dating from 1910. Sam Clutton was to become a quite outstanding member of the Club and key to many of its early developments. His early involvement followed directly on his response to the invitation that had appeared in motoring magazines asking those interested to write for details of the Club. This he had done and was promptly invited to the next meeting in early November at which he was co-opted onto the Committee. From the start he showed he was a man who liked to get on with things. As he was to write many years later:

> "… quite soon the Club was in the throes of political (not to say matrimonial) in-fighting. One faction of the Club saw it as a home for tired Austin Sevens and the other was 30-98 Vauxhall and Bentley minded. The issue was further confused by one important member getting shacked up with another's wife, and I seemed to be the only person who was on speaking terms with all members of the committee. So it fell to me to organise a meeting to get the situation rationalised at which the RAC Competition Secretary very sportingly took the Chair. Happily it was the 30-98 faction which emerged in control."

Despite something of a take-over and this modification of their original idea, the Nicholsons remained loyal and supportive of the emerging club. Colin (C P L Nicholson) was to remain its Secretary from 1934 into 1935, when the post was taken over by another founder member E T (Ned) Lewis, who originally had been the Competition Secretary, while Bruce (B H Nicholson) was to become Treasurer in 1935, taking over from Clutton who had briefly held that post earlier in the year. Although shifts in roles and titles within the committee were rapid and numerous it retained sufficient focus so that by the end of the first year it had settled on a badge, a set of published rules, and significantly, had revised the name of the Club.

In 1930 the Veteran Car Club had been founded for the owners of cars built before 1905. (This date was to change to 1916 some twenty years later, and then again was changed to 1918). One of the trio who had met in the Old Ship Inn, Brighton, had been S C H (Sammy) Davis – well known journalist, illustrator and above all racing motorist, inclusive of his membership of the select band of Bentley boys who made such a name for themselves at Le Mans in the 1920s. Involving himself in the nascent beginnings of the younger Veteran Sports Car Club he, no doubt, was able to point an informed finger at the problem. The Committee minutes of 16th November reported that:

> "The question of a new name was raised, the grounds being that the present name is too similar to that of the Veteran Car Club and the Company of Veteran Motorists. No suggestions were forthcoming but it was agreed that the name of the Club must be altered."

A letter from Bill Boddy (not yet a member at that stage) was read out containing a number of suggestions and then discussed.

The Committee returned to the problem at its next meeting where Colin Nicholson proposed that the name remained unchanged. However, Ned Lewis replied that the name "The Vintage Sports-Car Club had been suggested to him and moved that it was a better name than the present one". The proposal was seconded and carried *nem com* so that Sam Clutton (in his already readily identifiable style) was able to write to *The Light Car* with the following announcement, published in late November.

> "It appears that a certain amount of confusion has arisen over the recently formed and already flourishing Veteran Sports Car Club. It's that hard worked word Veteran that's done it. People have been writing palpitating post cards to the founders saying please can't they think of a different name because we already have the Association of Veteran Motorists, the Veteran Car Club, the Veteran this, the Veteran that and what-have-you. The upshot of all this is that the title of the Vintage Sports-Car Club has been provisionally adopted. I say provisionally because in the unlikely event of anyone hitting on a better name it might be adopted."

Infancy

Clutton's optimism as well as his writing style shines through. The "flourishing" club he referred to had but a few dozen members at this stage and had yet to run an event.

Motor club badges mattered far more in the 1930s than they do now, – if only because badge bars sit uncomfortably with modern aerodynamics and safety requirements – so to design one for the new club was something of a priority and discussed almost immediately at Committee. Most probably Colin Nicholson, as Secretary, had come up with the original idea and (as the Minutes report) "after much discussion and experiments with drawings it was decided to adopt the "V" design with the St Christopher plaque as the Club badge". At the Committee meeting of 12th December 1934 he was able to report that an order for one dozen badges had been placed with the firm of Caxtons who – on receipt of £3.12.0d (three pounds, twelve shillings) would proceed. For unexplained reasons ("innumerable difficulties have conspired to make the delay") it was not until well into 1935 that the first badges actually appeared. Quality has been defined as "fitness for purpose" and by this measure the name of the Vintage Sports-Car Club has proved ideal. Coupled with the dominant "V" of the Club's principal logo its image and identity have been ensured. However, if their badges may have been delayed, members were at least provided with a small (3"x 4") booklet from the outset, telling them about the Club they had joined. Its cover of pale blue card bore the badge, and in eight tiny pages set out the Rules of the Club. Rule 1 named the Club while Rule 2 defined its objects:– "… to provide competitive events for owners of cars five years old or more and social events for the members". Rule 3 allowed specials into the Club from the very beginning: "In the case of home-built cars either the chassis or the engine must comply with the age limit, but in any case applications for membership shall be at the discretion of the committee." Wisely, the committee has retained such power of veto over the ensuing years.

The subscription for 1935 was set at ten shillings annually in the case of driving members (ie those with vintage cars) or five shillings annually in the case of associate members and was required to accompany any application for membership. Again the committee was concerned to guard the door for "three adverse votes are sufficient to cause the rejection of an application for membership." There were nine on the committee at this time, comprising the Secretary, Assistant Secretary, Treasurer, Press Secretary and Captain. Together with the President and Vice President this left but two ordinary members to make up their number. The final page of this brief membership booklet gave a clear idea of how the committee expected the Club to develop:-

Points granted towards annual aggregate awards

Social runs Attendance, 1 mark (also given in all other events).

Scavenge Hunts Starters 1, Finishers 1, Marshals 2
1st place, 2 extra..........................total 4

Treasure Hunts and Timed Main Road Runs with Special Tests ..
Starters 1, Finishers 1, Marshals 2
1st place, 4 extra..........................total 6
2nd place, 3 extra..........................total 5

Trials Starters 2, Finishers 5, ...total 7
Marshals 7
Principal award, 15 extra..............total 22
Premier award, 10 extra................total 17
2nd class award, 5 extra..................total 12

Speed Events Starters 3, Marshals 3
Fastest time of day, 25 extra..........total 28
Class winners, 15 extra................total 18
2nd place in class, 10 extra.............total 13
3rd place in class, 5 extra...............total 8

Clearly the founding fathers did not expect that by its 80th year the Club would be able to offer a programme that included five race meetings, five hill climbs, four sprints and three driving test meetings, in addition to rallies and tours, but without a single scavenge hunt or treasure hunt in sight, nor that most of the cars qualifying for membership would be well over seventy five years old, let alone five.

The first social gathering of VSCC members took place on 18th November, with a small party assembling to watch that year's London to Brighton run – as then organised by the RAC. Afterwards they went out to tea together, all fourteen of them, no doubt discussing their brand new club and (at that stage) its somewhat unrealistic hopes to hold a trial every month. Its next event was to be a Scavenge Hunt on December 16th – a form of competition popular in the 30s but now deservedly lapsed. Tasked with collecting an unlikely collection of items – which might range from a lady's garter to a Whitworth spanner of an unusual but specific size – competitors had a time limit within which to return with their spoils. Details of this, the first competitive event held by the VSCC, remain lost in time for no record of it survives. But for the Club a more important happening during the last month of that year (which had seen the introduction of a new Road Traffic Act, the 30mph built up area speed limit, compulsory Third Party insurance and the building of the first ERA) was the election of seven new members to the Club. One of these was T W (Tim) Carson who, together with Sam Clutton, was to prove absolutely central to its development in the years ahead.

1935. The first season

The Club wasted no time in getting underway in 1935. A brief notice had appeared in the motoring press at the beginning of January advertising an Invitation Trial, while a more detailed announcement was to follow in the *The Light Car* of 18th January.

> Vintage Sports-Car Club
>
> "The first trial of the recently formed Vintage Sports-Car Club will be held on January 20th, starting from the "George and Dragon" Marlow at 1.15pm. The route, which will be approximately 50 miles in length and will include several of the well known Chiltern trials hills and an acceleration test, will finish at Amersham. The event is, of course, open only to owners of cars constructed or registered prior to January 1931 and entries close today … They should be sent to the Competition Secretary Mr E T Lewis, 12 Butler Avenue, Harrow, Middlesex."

As a foretaste of things to come the Austin Seven Car Club also had a short entry in the same magazine:

> "The Club will support the Vintage Car Club's (*sic*) trial on Sunday next … Members will meet at the "Ace of Spades" Great West Road, Middlesex at 11.00am. All Austin Seven members will be welcome."

A week later the report duly appeared:

> "Anyone who visited the "George and Dragon" at Marlow on Sunday last for the start of the Vintage Sports-Car Club's Chiltern Trial might well have thought that he had been transported back several years, for the

entry was liberally sprinkled with such cars as 12/50hp Alvises, 30-98hp Vauxhalls, 3-litre Bentleys and so on. By special arrangement with the RAC the trial had been opened to non members of the Club provided that the cars they entered were at least five years old, and an interesting feature of the event was the banning of competition tyres. This incidentally made some of the hills very difficult and many found Crowell quite unclimbable. Actually this hill caused a considerable hold-up, although a large part of the delay was due to the failure of a non-competing modern car! Two competitors slid down the side of the hill but fortunately without serious damage, and darkness had fallen before the whole entry got clear. With three exceptions however everyone checked in at the finish. As a result of the trial, incidentally, the Club membership has been more than doubled."

The first competition event organised by the VSCC did not have an outright winner for, as is still current practice on the long distance trials run by the MCC (Motor Cycling Club), the awards were categorised. Premier (First Class) awards were won by H P Powell (Amilcar), W H Green (Riley), B H Nicholson (MG), C Clutton (Frazer Nash), and G Shaw (Austin Seven) – while among the nine Second Class Awards were T W Carson (Vauxhall), C P L Nicholson (Austin), and H P Bowler (Bentley). Thus the "two factions" of the Club were each represented; on the one hand by an Austin Seven and an MG, (these appropriately driven by the two cousins from whose initiative the Club had come into being) and on the other by a Bentley and a Vauxhall. Many of these drivers were to become forces within the Club. Harold Powell was a well known triallist with the MCC and shortly became a VSCC Committee member, Harry Bowler was to become its competitions secretary and eventually President – while Sam Clutton and Tim Carson together provided the crucial leadership that was to carry the Club forward so successfully in its formative years.

After so strong a start an entry of only fifteen cars for the next trial, held near Haslemere in Surrey in mid-March, was very disappointing, while that for the Buxton Trial in May was even smaller. Donald Munro in a 4½-litre Invicta was the winner of the March event with Harold Powell (Amilcar) and Sam Clutton (Frazer Nash) gaining first-class awards, while to swell the field for the Derbyshire event the Frazer Nash Car Club was invited to take part. Even so the entry remained small and evidently it was a very informal event for the morning concluded with competitors having to choose between tackling a trials section on Eyam Bank or repairing to the nearest pub for lunch.

Motor Sport reported that the votes were "unanimously cast in favour of the latter" which no doubt helped create a sufficiently benign atmosphere to allow two trialling gate-crashers, in the shape of Maurice Toulmin (well known trials driver of the MG Cream Cracker team) and 'Porky' Lees (who later was to become a core member of the Northern Section of the VSCC), to be welcomed into the group and take part during the afternoon. Of the "serious" competitors Powell's Amilcar made the best performance, while Anthony Powys-Lybbe (Alvis) and Sam Clutton (in his Anzani-engined Frazer Nash) both won Second Class awards.

The trialling aspirations of the Club were beginning to look rather tattered and the committee's concerns needed to be conveyed to the membership. After a short time in the post of Treasurer Sam Clutton had become Press Secretary to the Club and, effectively, made himself the main communicator within the membership as well as with the outside world. In September 1935 a duplicated sheet was sent to all members, written in the bouncy, self-confident and outspoken style so typical of him.

>   Vintage Sports-Car Club
> "There are so many things about which circulars will shortly have to be sent to Members that the Press Secretary has been instructed to do one very large one altogether. You thought the Press Secretary never did any work did you? Actually we hope that something of this sort will recur at intervals, as a sort of Club *Bulletin*."

As indeed it did, with Clutton as Editor setting its tone right through until the early 1950s. This first *Bulletin*-cum-*Newsletter*, like so many of the early ones, was undated but with hindsight it can be seen as Volume I, No 1 of the long series that has followed. It continued:

> "Our next show should have been a reliability trial on October 20th, but as this is rather close to the North-West London Trial on the 19th, and in view of the poor support which trials have received lately, we have decided to cancel it and run a Treasure Hunt instead. This will take place in North London, starting at 1.15 and ending up for tea at the Barn, Bayfordsbury, near Hertford. It won't be the brain-twisting sort, but more of an excuse for an afternoon's motoring and foregathering afterwards. The entry will be 3/6d (three shillings and six pence) per car and the prize will be two thirds of the total entry money. Please send a card to the Secretary …

...saying if you are likely to turn up. If only members would co-operate in these small ways it would so enormously help the running of events.

Incidentally, when writing, do also give your views about reliability trials. It's pretty obvious that those so far haven't given much satisfaction, and unless we can hit on something that pleases most people things will become exceedingly difficult. After all, our club really has tremendous possibilities if only it can get over these inevitable teething troubles, and it's worth a 1½d stamp to help things along."

Another and different type of teething trouble related to object 2 of the Club's rules ... "to provide ... social events for members". There had been a proposal to hold a dinner dance on November 16th but, presumably due to lack of interest, this had been postponed and in the second *Bulletin* circulated early in the month there was promised:

"... a less formal party next Saturday. In the afternoon a map-reading contest will take place starting at 2.15pm from the Middlesex Arms at the junction of the Barnet by-pass road and St Albans Road. Intending competitors should arm themselves with the following junk (1) Ordnance map of Watford No 106, Scale 1" to the mile. Price 2/6d on cloth (2) Ruler in eighths of an inch (3) Protractor (4) Torch. Entrance will be at 2/6d (two shillings and sixpence) per car and tea extra."

Alas no report of the event has been discovered – but if indeed it did take place, and small as it probably was, it would have been the Club's first ever navigation rally.

The earlier *cri de coeur* asking for members' views on trialling had however been heard. The Club responded by promising a trial that would "give large and small motor cars as even a chance as possible, and the course will not be of a damaging nature".

The December trial, held near Guildford, attracted forty-three entries, about half of whom were members from invited clubs. Typical of trials of the period it included a stop-go, an acceleration and a reversing test as well as a selection of observed sections – the whole affair jointly organised by Tim Carson, then into his second year of committee membership and LTC (Tom) Rolt who had joined the committee during the year. The invited clubs did well, with the overall winner in an MG Midget – while the top vintage award (open only to VSCC members) went to T G Brooks in his

Infancy

Spencer-Brooks Special (essentially a 14/40 MG) in first place. The ever-present Sam Clutton was second, this time in a 30-98 Vauxhall.

Earlier in the year the Club had held its first speed event. A quarter of a mile of gently curving loose surfaced drive through Aston Clinton Park in Buckinghamshire led up to the Howard Park Hotel, a course that had been used by various clubs for speed trials for several years. Four other clubs had accepted invitations to take part, prominent among them being the Frazer Nash contingent. Forty eight cars were to compete, ranging in size from 750cc Austins to the 4½-litre Invicta of Donald Munro of the host club, the engine of which had only been reassembled on the morning of the event. Despite this he went on to make the fastest time of the day by a vintage car. Lt Col J Clutton, Sam's father, had opened the course taking 44 secs to drive up in his 30cwt Fafnir of 1910 (This stately car, which later was to inspire the formation of an 'Edwardian' class within the VSCC, like many a great lady was of questionable age. Sam Clutton writing of it in various articles referred to it as being of 1909/10 vintage and also as dating from 1911; 1910 thus seems a reasonable compromise). Fastest time of the day was made by Rupert Instone's GN Martyr in 18.7 secs, considerably helped by its solid back axle on the deteriorating road surface, while his nearest rival Arthur Baron in a supercharged 1½-litre Bugatti was but a tenth of a second behind and might have been faster had he not had the misfortune to break a valve on his final run. Amazingly three Frazer Nashes tied for first place in their class, resolved by a run off.

Tim Carson had a trying day and was vocal in his disapproval of the rough track surface. His 30-98 Vauxhall lost a headlamp while his Carson Special (based on another 30-98) shed its exhaust. Clutton however fully approved of it all for in the September circular-cum-*Bulletin* he pointed out with characteristic lack of diffidence that "if you were at the Speed Trials on August 31st you will agree that they were a huge success. If you weren't there I'm just telling you". Come Christmas, via the second *Bulletin* published, he was able to look back over 1935, the first full year of the Club's existence, and to look forward to S C H (Sammy) Davis's acceptance of the Presidency for the coming year.

> "This cannot fail to have a most beneficial influence on the Club's future, while not only his great reputation, but also the fact that he owns two Vintage Sports Cars makes it very difficult to think of anyone who could perform the office of President more appropriately than he."

In the Autumn the Club had numbered seventy three members, with Bentley and Frazer Nash dominating among the cars owned but with some extremely interesting "other makes" to keep them company. *The Bulletin* went on to state "in fact we are getting very reasonably proud of the famous cars which belong to the Club". Several were then listed, inclusive of Sammy Davis's 1897 Bollée "Beelzebub" (the oldest car in the list) and his 1929 Le Mans Aston Martin, Col G M Giles's 1913 Bugatti "Black Bess" (4 cylinder, 5-litre, OHC and chain drive – and said to do 80mph in second) Harry Bowler's 1926 3-litre Bentley "which seems to crash through a reliability trial and win races at Brooklands with equal facility", and among the specials Barbara Marshall's Anzani-GN. Also named among the specials was Tim Carson's, based on a 1921 Vauxhall 30-98 but with the chassis inverted and fitted with a front axle from a 3-litre TT Vauxhall.

Cars of this ilk could frequently be found outside The Phoenix Inn on the London Road at Hartley Wintney in north east Hampshire which, as *The Bulletin* stated, "you will doubtless remember is the country headquarters of the Club and presided over by Tim." Here the saloon bar would be crowded with members, both at weekends and on the regular "second Thursdays of the month" gatherings that were soon established and which continue to this day.

While the walls of the bar were resplendent with racing photographs and motoring prints and the air full of heated discussions as to the relative merits of Bentleys, Bugattis Vauxhall 30-98s and the like, outside on the forecourt, the real things could be found. Here Carson, who specialised in Vauxhalls, did his own trading while Tom Rolt and John Passini ran the Phoenix Green Garage on the corner; distinguished by its Rolls-Royce breakdown truck that had started life as a 1911 Silver Ghost with landaulette body.

The Bulletin promised that after Christmas a members list would be produced and that the committee was planning the calendar for 1936 in which "there are to be three Speed Events and three Reliability Trials…" and that it was "busily searching for a really seductive hill for a speed hill climb. There is still a little jugglory (*sic*) about fitting in dates but the next event will definitely be a Chilterns Trial on February 16th."

First place in the award for the highest aggregate marks gained during the year went to Donald Munro, while Clutton came second and Harold Powell third. To round off the year came the up-beat message: "And so we have come to the end of our first season.

Infancy

Every new club has to face a lot of difficulties and we have had our fair share, but it really seems that the worst of them have been overcome, and that we can look forward with every degree of confidence to a prosperous 1936."

The 1936 season

If the optimistic *Bulletin* of Christmas 1935 pointed forward to better things to come this was to prove true enough for the Club – which did manage to run its promised three trials and three speed events during the year – and more generally for the recovering economy in the south of England. However, in the north circumstances were still very difficult (it was in October 1936 that two hundred men from Jarrow, where 70% of the citizens were unemployed, set out to march to London to draw attention to their plight) while internationally, with the remilitarisation of the Rhineland and the beginnings of the Spanish Civil War came the dawning realisation that war almost certainly was on the horizon. Not surprisingly there was something of hothouse escapism in the noise and often rowdy behaviour to be found in the bar of the Phoenix.

The Annual General Meeting of the Club, held in London in mid January, was a decorous enough affair and significant for two decisions taken. The original intention had been to make cars of over five years of age automatically eligible for driving membership, this date advancing annually by one year from the original cut-off of 31st

The closing page of the November 1936 Bulletin *ended with the following tale:*

A	(an inexperienced motorist) Who is that?	B	(an experienced motorist) It is a policeman.
A	What is he doing?	B	He is waiting to summon us if we go too quickly.
A	Who pays him?	B	We do.
A	Oh … and who is the other man?	B	It is a Road Scout.
A	What is he doing?	B	He is warning us not to go too quickly lest we be summoned by the policeman.
A	Who pays him?	B	We do.
A	Oh … and what is that?	B	It is a horse.
A	What is it doing?	B	I think it is smiling.

December 1930. However, the AGM came to a clear decision to keep to the original date. The other decision taken was to create a new class of membership for the cars built between 1905 and 1915. (Later this was to be raised to 1918.) At this time the Veteran Club catered for cars built before 1905 (it too was later to lift its age limit to 1918) so that many significant cars built early in the century had no appropriate club in which they could find a home. Lt Col J Clutton's Fafnir had shown members the appeal of such vehicles and the Edwardian Section (the actual name was to come later) was accordingly formed.

The Committee itself was settling down. Under the chairmanship of the new President, Sammy Davis, Lt Col Clutton was elected as its Vice Chairman with E T (Ned) Lewis its Honorary Secretary, a post he had held in the previous year. Sam Clutton continued as Press and Assistant Secretary, as well as *de facto* editor of *The Bulletin*. The Nicholson cousins continued to serve – along with Harry Bowler, H W and R C Dawkins and Harold Powell – while Tim Carson became the Club Captain.

With the Annual General Meeting out of the way the Club could get on with its principal business "to provide competitive events …for the members". The first of these was the Chiltern Trial held on a miserable Sunday in mid February. After days of hard frost a sudden thaw made for fog throughout the day and for very slippery observed sections that caused many failures. The trial was divided into two classes with Crowell, the hill that caused so much trouble in the previous year, omitted for cars of over 2-litres as being too narrow. Another narrow lane was to cause a long delay when, due to navigational error, two competitors were to meet head-on. New to the list of VSCC award winners was Marcus Chambers (later to find fame racing HRGs at Le Mans, and as the British Motor Corporation's Competitions Manager in the 1950s) who won the over 2-litre class in a 4½-litre Bentley. He was fastest on the acceleration test and also impressed by being fastest on the manoeuvring test in his far from nimble car. The only first class award in the class was won by another competitor who was likewise to become a notable member of the Club – A S (Anthony) Heal in a 30-98 Vauxhall. The under 2-litre class went to J H Allason in a Frazer Nash, despite having come to a stop on the manoeuvring test with petrol starvation.

The second trial of the Club's year also took place in poor weather, drizzle falling throughout a March Sunday on the increasingly slippery Sussex hills. The entry also was a disappointment – only ten taking part. Don Kirkman, in an Alvis 12/50, had built a cantilevered style structure at the back of his car on which his bouncer did

Infancy

what bouncers do – at a time when there was great debate in trialling circles as to the legitimacy of such devices as fixed rear axles, knobbly tyres and body extensions as aids to traction. Although achieving the only "clean sheet" on the trial, Kirkham did not in fact win, for thanks to an outstanding performance on the acceleration test, Clive Windsor-Richards in a 30-98 took the Premier award. There was then a long wait before the third trial of the year, the Gloucester Trial in late November. This took the then not unusual format of being a "follow-my-leader" trial in which both competitors and marshals travelled together in a queue from hill to hill, and were sometimes joined by members of the public wishing to get in on the fun. This time the winner was in a 12/50 Alvis, Dennis Clapham taking home the Vintage award.

Back in March, the day before the poorly supported Sussex trial, several prominent members of the Club had been further north – up in Leicestershire at the relatively new road racing circuit of Donington. Here the inter-club team competition for the Stanley Cup was to be held and Harry Bowler, Tim Carson and Marcus Chambers were to represent the VSCC; the first involvement of the Club with racing. They had a mixed day. Carson's Special suffered a variety of mechanical problems, while Marcus Chambers' 4½-litre Bentley threw a connecting rod, but Harry Bowler redeemed matters by winning a race in his widely campaigned 3-litre Bentley, and the cup for the best vintage sports car performance of the day.

1936 was a wet year and the first of the Club's own speed events, back at Aston Clinton Park in mid May, was heavily watered by both a thunderstorm and prolonged heavy rain. Also the gravel surface of the drive began to break up badly and was pitted with potholes. As a result it was to be abandoned as a speed venue shortly afterwards. However, the VSCC event went ahead.

Of the sixty one entries fastest time of the day and a course record (amazing in view of the surface) was put up by A F P Fane in his single seater supercharged Frazer Nash in 16.7 secs. Among other notable competitors were John Bolster – at that time driving a Vauxhall 30-98 – and Stirling Moss's mother, Mrs Aileen Moss, in her Marendaz Special. Best in the vintage classes was the 1923 GN-based Sumner-JAP driven by R A C Sumner who took 19.3 secs on his best run, while Marcus Chambers managed 30.7 secs in a 1907 7-litre Renault. He was however beaten in the Edwardian class by a car that was to become closely associated with the Club, and particularly with Sam Clutton, the 1908 12-litre Grand Prix Itala, driven on this occasion by its then owner, J S Pole. The sheer variety of machinery seen at VSCC meetings was certainly established early on, while the informality of such speed events was demonstrated by Fane leaving the start line in a felt hat and removing it further up the course.

Finding venues for speed events was to become the challenge for the rest of the year – and the first honours were to fall to Tim Carson. After exploring drives and pleading with owners all over the area around the Phoenix he eventually persuaded Sir Denzil and Lady Cope, who owned a large estate a little to the north, en route to Reading, that part of their drive might be used. Permission was granted on condition that members of the public would not be admitted and so a third of a mile of the smooth gravelled drive at Bramshill, inclusive of a fast bend, became a sprint course for the day. Very much a Phoenix affair, John Passini was Secretary of the meeting and among the entrants was Tom Rolt who drove their 1911 Rolls breakdown truck in the Edwardian class. It was a day of incessant rain, conditions badly delaying the proceedings that were run virtually single handed by Carson, so that the sixty or so entrants could only have one run each. Fastest time of the day was made by S S Brocklebank in a 2.3-litre Bugatti, while only 0.6 secs behind came Sumner in the Sumner JAP to make the best vintage performance. The Edwardian class (then named the Veteran class)

July 1936 – a wet and murky day – while in the gloom Col G.M.(Eric) Giles leaves the starting line at Bramshill in "Black Bess", the 1913 5-litre chain driven Type 18 Bugatti. This was the second of three three speed events organised by the Club that year, the first of which, at Aston Clinton, was also marred by poor weather.

saw Clutton, now in the Itala, the winner, with Eric Giles in the 1913 5-litre Bugatti "Black Bess" second, a little way behind. Among others who finished well up in their classes were several drivers who were to become well known in vintage circles. They included Ivo Peters (railway photographer *par excellence*) and arch enthusiast Miss Midge Wilby, both in Frazer Nashes. The unlimited vintage class saw Vauxhalls in the top places driven by Tom Plowman, later to distinguish himself and his car at Montlhery, and Anthony Heal, of the well known furnishings firm in Tottenham Court Road, who actively supported the Club over many years and briefly was to serve as its Secretary. Drying out, externally at least, the competitors who gathered in the Phoenix that evening ensured record takings at the bar.

Finding a venue for the proposed October sprint event became the next challenge, and this time it was Clutton who made the discovery. As part of the building boom that took place in the south east in the mid to late thirties, a new estate was under construction at Littlestone-on-Sea near New Romney in Kent. The service road, running close to and parallel with the sea, without camber was eighteen feet wide and well constructed of concrete; ideal for a straight line sprint. At least October 10th dawned dry and sunny, in contrast to the weather at the earlier speed events, although the wind was strong and very cold. Both competitors and spectators were grateful to the local authorities who, in the carefree days before drink-driving legislation, had granted all day licences to the hotels and inns of the area, which were well patronised. Of the fifty competitors, fastest time of the day over the half mile course was made by John Lemon Burton in a T51 Bugatti, who crossed the finishing line at 125 mph, while Arthur Baron, also Bugatti mounted, was quickest of the vintage entrants. Sumner, another likely contender in his JAP engined special had a difficult day, shedding a chain.

In the over 3000cc Open and Vintage class 4½-litre Bentleys dominated, Forrest Lycett just pipping Marcus Chambers – in doing so winning the award presented by Tom Plowman for the fastest unlimited sports car. By coincidence it was the trophy that Lycett himself was to present to the Club for its annual aggregate award, and which has become its most coveted piece of silverware, was that year to be won by Marcus Chambers.

It had been a tense and edgy year for the nation, with three Kings occupying the throne consequent upon the abdication of Edward VIII, while the RAF was re-arming in anticipation of war. (Hurricanes had first flown in 1935 while Spitfires were to do so in 1936.) It was also the year in which the infant VSCC found its feet. Sammy Davis as President gave it respectability among the motoring fraternity, while Forrest Lycett as the new Vice President added weight to its growing reputation. Not least among the new members welcomed into the Club in the autumn *Bulletin* was "Mr W Boddy, the well known authority on vintage motors who at one time ran that excellent paper *Brooklands* and now writes extensively for *Motor Sport*." VSCC events have always been well covered on its pages while Bill Boddy, who was shortly to become its Editor, was later to be responsible for a number of initiatives within the Club and proved a friendly and constructive critic over the years. Although for the second year running the committee had failed to convince members that they might yet enjoy a dinner dance at least the Club's Christmas card was to find great favour. This was drawn by the President himself who, before his exploits at Le Mans and Brooklands and a successful career as a motoring journalist, had trained as an artist at the Slade School of Art. His sketch of a fast approaching twin cylinder air cooled single seater captured the optimism found in the Club – and as Clutton was to put it in the penultimate *Bulletin* of the year "The Club Christmas card, with an exclusive drawing from the pen of our President is just about the very best thing ever and one member has ordered 200 on the spot! (6 pence each or 5 shillings a dozen)."

1937 – A year of development

Seventy of the then one hundred and fifty members of the Club attended the 1937 Annual General Meeting, held at a restaurant in Baker Street. Sammy Davis was confirmed in his role as President, again to be supported by Vice Presidents Lt Col Clutton and Forrest Lycett. The key role of Secretary was to have been filled by E T Lewis but *The Bulletin* had to report that "Ned Lewis was booked to continue the Secretaryship 'til the very last moment when he was suddenly ordered up to Manchester (poor devil) on a newly acquired job … Let us hope that he will find such solace as may exist in his depressing domicile". (There being no club members from that city at the time and few in the north Sam Clutton's as ever forthright views very probably caused little offence, but although tongue in cheek he almost certainly meant what he wrote.)

The vacancy was to provide a crucial turning point in the history of the Club. Excellent Secretary though Ned Lewis had proved to be he was followed by Tim Carson who stepped into the breach that January day and was to become arguably *the* key figure in its development over the following third of a century. Although little over thirty years old at the time (he had been born in Ireland in 1906 and then educated at

Charterhouse) he already had an excellent motoring pedigree. By the age of 14 he had obtained a motor-cycle driving licence and on his 2 speed 225cc New Hudson mount rode to Brooklands and never looked back. As well as competing in sprints and hill climbs he eventually lapped the Weybridge circuit at 87mph on a 1914 V twin Harley Davidson, cementing his interest in older sporting machinery, while once he had graduated to four wheels, and particularly Vauxhalls, he later took a Class D record of 96 mph at Brooklands. He is said to have owned approaching a dozen 30-98s over the years, as well as a wide range of other cars of character. Kindly and unflappable, he had proved himself an effective organiser at Bramshill and this ability served him well both in running the Phoenix and also the Club, helped by his quiet Irish blarney which no doubt aided his motor trading. The VSCC has long been a club of powerful personalities and Carson obviously learnt to handle them well from the outset with a mix of diplomacy and confidence. His son Terry, by his first wife Fee, quotes his father as saying "I generally let everyone have their say … and then do what I think."

Also continuing to serve on the committee was another outstanding character in the shape of Sam Clutton who, although three years Carson's junior and still in his twenties, had already put his mark on the Club. As *Bulletin* Editor he quickly established a house style reflective of his own informed, amusing, candid yet often provocative manner. Busy building his own career within the family firm, pressure of work forced him to stand down from the editorship for a short time in 1937, when it was taken over by Watkins Pitchford. Clutton therefore believing he would not have to write a report of the Donington meeting as held later that year was rather taken aback when asked to do so. Accordingly his report on the day started thus: "I take back all the nice things I said about the Press Secretary in the Editorial of the last *Bulletin*. The man is a complete swob and I hope his rabbits die."

Although he could be maddening, his boundless energy and deep love of fine machinery shines through whatever he wrote and helped the Club to establish a clear stance as to its position on the worth of vintage sports cars. In March 1937, before standing back from the editorship of *The Bulletin* for just three issues, and in the first of those to be produced in printed magazine format, he set out his stall:

Space Expected to be Filled by Editor
"And so, with its eleventh number, *The Bulletin* blossoms forth in magazine form, more worthy of our ever-gathering prestige.

The occasion may not be altogether inapt to attempt an analysis of those almost intangible qualities which make a Vintage sports car so different from practically anything available today. The appeal of a Vintage machine is, I think, twofold.

On the one hand there is the easy assurance of a relatively large engine working at conservative revs, and moderate output. On the other – perhaps the most important aspect – there is that intimacy between car and driver which is fostered by absolute positive and accurate steering, a close-ratio gearbox, aided only by a clutch stop and controlled by a sturdy vertical lever, and the 'all-in-a-piece' road holding characteristic of the best Vintage years.

Modern sports cars (*soi-disant*) seem to divide themselves into four classes. Most popular in this country is the buzz-box of loathsome repute. A small car is reluctantly propelled by a tiny engine working at very high speed and volumetric efficiency. Although the total weight is preposterously high (there is one 850 machine in sporting form which weighs over 15 cwt) all components are cut down to the narrowest margin of safety and the result is incessant unreliability and the constant sense of mechanical strain that is so exhausting on a long journey. The short chassis is excessively prone to pitching and tossing, and to avoid this the suspension has to be damped to such a point as would shake the back teeth out of an ostrich. The buzz-box, then, principally offends in the way it performs.

Next comes the Anglo-American sports-bastard in increasing popularity. Apart from its redolence of mangel-wurzles the engine does its part very nicely; but what then? Enormous tyres are largely responsible for the advent of the exaggeratedly low-geared steering that entirely precludes any possibility of correcting a skid, while the control afforded is about as positive and solid as a jellyfish. Weight distribution is upset by a forward engine mounting and hopelessly spongy springing completes the homicidal ensemble, with its general impression of an animated feather-bed. Add to this a long, tenuous gear lever, waving like a lily in the breeze, blancmange-like coachwork, with fittings made of sour milk or desiccated coconut, and the picture is complete.

Fortunately, the remaining two types, even if in a minority, are still the 'real thing'. Lagonda, Aston Martin, HRG and Bugatti, to name those which come most readily to mind, retain most of the finest characteristics and traditional construction of the Vintage years while incorporating the best modern improvements.

An altogether new breed relies on light metals and special chassis construction in conjunction with independent suspension. The engines also are lighter, and are able to do their work at fairly moderate speeds and output. BMW and Delahaye may be counted as the pioneers and as a logical development of the older school. The only thing one perhaps regrets is that by their very lightness and the abundance of pressed parts the sturdy construction and hand finish of components (which, while of no very positive value in itself, is nevertheless an endless source of pleasure to the mechanically fastidious) is necessarily absent.

But then, we are a club of relatively poor men, and it will be many years before such machines as those mentioned in the last two classes come within the range of the purses of most of us.

And so it is, though the uninformed and uncomprehending may scoff that the sole attraction of a Vintage sports car lies in a childish love of noise and discomfort, that there are positive attributes in our cherished mounts that cannot be found in any of modern construction.

Let them laugh!"

Hard though it is to comprehend today vintage sports-cars could be bought very cheaply in the 1930s. In those early years of "motoring for the masses" a four seater Austin Seven or Morris Minor made far more sense for most families than did say a 3-litre Bentley, being lighter to drive, easier to house and using far less fuel. At the same time mass production was taking the market away from those manufacturers who had relied on hand built machines, while the Americanisation of attitudes that required motor cars to be cheap, comfortable and, above all, easy to drive compounded the problem. A rhyme that appeared over the name of E Wrigley in the June 1937 *Bulletin* surely summed up the views of most of the membership, chiming in with the Clutton perspective.

> "Changed at twenty down to first,
> Wondered why the motor burst?
> Gave him quite a nasty turn,
> Buzz-Box owners live and learn."

Cars in which engineering mattered, along with the dynamics of handling, roadholding and driving enjoyment, were largely going out of fashion. But not for the members of the VSCC whose numbers were still rising and who – despite the anomalies of the agreed cut-off date – for example 12/50 Alvis were built on either side of the divide – again voted to keep the last qualifying date for membership at December 31st 1930.

By June there were some two hundred and seven members of the Club and the membership list of the time clearly shows the balance of their preferences. There were 33 Bentleys, 17 Vauxhall 30-98s, 12 Bugattis and 10 Alvis 12/50s among the cars listed. At the other end of the size scale came just 2 Austin Seven Ulsters, 2 Austin Seven specials and 1 Morris Eight. The Club that the Nicholson cousins had set out to found had simply not come to be, although they both remained members at this time, albeit as Associates rather than full Driving Members. A similar bias was to be found in the home addresses of the membership; it was very much a home-counties club. Virtually 90% lived within easy reach of London with just under twenty further afield. Of these five were to be found in Lancashire including Ned Lewis now living in Manchester and Kenneth Neve, who also was to feature strongly in the future of the Club. There was but one member in Scotland (with an Alvis 12/50) one in Eire (with the singleton 8hp Morris) and the first trans-Atlantic member in the shape of H B Evans of Newton Highlands, Massachusetts, USA – an associate without a listed car. Little could he have foreseen the multiple appearances of Model A Fords on the trials scene towards the close of the century.

The Club certainly had achieved much in its short lifetime. In his June editorial Clutton, writing immediately before handing over to Watkins Pitchford, summed up the progress made:

> "It is impossible on handing over not to look back at the miraculous advances the Club has made during the two and a half years of its life.
>
> We had around thirty members at the time of the successful first Chiltern Trial in January 1935, organised in frantic haste by Ned Lewis, when

it was discovered a fortnight from the day, that the promised organiser had done not one thing about it. Another landmark was in August 1935 when, at Aston Clinton, we had the first of the several successful speed trials that now stand to our credit. That, too, was organised by Ned Lewis, together with Alan Whiddington. Few can have any means of knowing the enormous amount of work Ned did to put the Club "on the map" in its early days.

That evening also saw the small beginnings of our now flourishing pre-war Class, as the course was opened by Col Clutton on the 1910 Fafnir, which was at that time the only car in the Club manufactured between 1904 and 1915. Now we have fifteen such machines, nearly all with long and inspiring histories that, put together, would make an epic in motoring literature …

So it has gone on, till now we can claim over 200 members, between them owning cars that cover every phase and facet of that virile period of motor manufacture which lasted through the decade up to the end of 1930. Now, never a competitive meeting goes by without one of our members proving the supremacy of his machine over its modern successors, despite its long years of service, while the alarming pace at which new members continue to flock in suggests that, for some years at any rate, we shall have little need to alter our age limit.

Beyond all this there is, throughout a very large part of the Club a strong esprit de corps, which one cannot help attributing in a large measure to our headquarters, the Phoenix, and the welcome accorded by Tim Carson to any members that call there, whether in or out of licensing hours.

We may not, as a Club, have much time for social events, but the unorganised weekend gatherings at the Phoenix are worth any number of dinners, dances and boiled shirts.

Anyway, no one wants to go on reading at length what they already know, but until one looks back in detail one is apt not to realise what a very remarkable Club we have."

For the third year running the trials season began in the Chilterns, the relatively small entry of twenty four all turning out, but having to spend an hour or so in the George and Dragon at Marlow while waiting for the start, which did not happen until well after the time specified in the regulations. No-one is recorded as grumbling, least not the landlord, so they were able to tackle some very muddy hills with at least much initial bonhomie. This was perhaps a good thing as the early sections were very nearly unclimbable, made more so as competition (ie knobbly) tyres, in accordance with club rules, were not permitted.

It was also the final trial in which foot holds and extensions on the rear of Alvises were allowed, two of which in the hands of D D Clapham and G G Levy, gained awards. A first class award went to Watkins Pitchford – a committee member and soon to become Editor of *The Bulletin* – who went particularly well on the special tests in his Frazer Nash, *Motor Sport* recording that the car looked "decrepit". In sharp contrast was the very smart and recently re-built 1922 supercharged Targa Florio Mercedes that was driven on the trial by C W P Hampton.

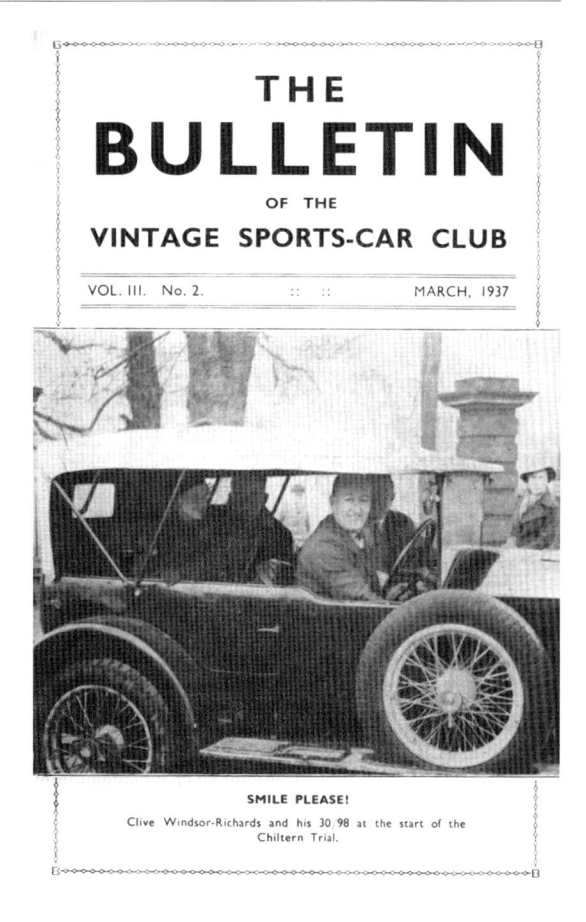

Clive Windsor-Richards with his crew about to leave for the start of the 1937 Chiltern Trial, hood up as was his usual practice. The trialling dress code of the day: Suits, collars and ties for the gentlemen, hats for the ladies. The March 1937 Bulletin *was the first to have a photograph on its front cover.*

Mid-April saw a return to Sussex where the trial was jointly organised with the mid Surrey Automobile Club and the City and Guilds Motor Club. Making a change from the more usually successful makes of trials machinery the main club awards went to a 1½-litre Lea Francis driven by A L Denyer and a 2-litre Lancia Lambda in the hands of Aubrey Birks.

Infancy

The trials season was to be rounded off by another visit to the Cotswolds in late November, the principal awards going to Eddie Wrigley in his 12/40 Lea Francis and Midge Wilby driving a Frazer Nash.

Not all the non-speed events involved off-road motoring – or not quite. Another map-reading contest had been organised by Marcus Chambers on what turned out to be a very wet Sunday in late January. "It was a marked success despite rain beyond belief" reported *The Bulletin*. Rupert Watkins Pitchford's Frazer Nash was seen completely bogged down in a farmyard with minimum operative transmission but he suddenly re-appeared later in the day resplendent in a minute Ford saloon. Who can blame him for not wishing to grapple with fettling chain-drive under such wet and muddy circumstances?

However, the speed events of 1937 all took place on hard surfaces rather than on the deteriorating gravel drives of earlier years. Although in a demonstration rather than in competition the Edwardians were the first out in April; Sam Clutton driving the 1908 Itala and R G J (Dick) Nash in the 1912 15-litre Lorraine Dietrich "Vieux Charles Trois", scurrying around the newly opened two mile circuit of the Crystal Palace.

The first of the Club's competitive events that year was on the familiar territory of Littlestone, where speed trials were held in May. The weather was excellent, there was a good entry and *The Light Car* reported that it was among the most successful events the Club had ever held. *Motor Sport* confirmed this, approving of the "high ratio of laughs a minute". One of these was caused by Noel Sissons who managed to persuade his Bentley to leave the start line in reverse. Another mishap befell Forrest Lycett driving an Alfonso Hispano-Suiza who, on returning to the paddock, was in all probability not at all amused when a back wheel fell off. Sam Clutton was later to drive the car back home, and for the second time in the day the car was again to shed a wheel. Despite such mishaps, Lycett nevertheless emerged as the handicap winner of the 'pre-war'/Edwardian class. He was also to win the unlimited capacity sports car class in his 4½-litre Bentley, so obviously had chosen the safer of his vehicles to transport him back to town. Fastest time of the day was made by Gerald Sumner in the unlimited racing car class, driving the 10½-litre Delage which had held the Land Speed Record in 1924, breaking the course record and crossing the finishing line at 127 mph. The racing car class of up to 3000cc was won by John Bolster driving the then named "Bolster Mary". The excellent ribbed concrete surface played host to its visitors until nearly

7pm, for so large was the entry that it took until then before everyone had managed to complete their runs. Alas it was to be the VSCC's last visit to this seaside sprint course for the building development, the *raison d'être* for the road, then reclaimed it for its intended purpose.

Seven weeks later came a club "first" in the shape of a circuit race meeting, jointly organised with the Bugatti Owners Club, with which the VSCC has enjoyed a long and fruitful relationship. Donington Park had been developed in stages during the thirties, being extended several times, so that by 1937 it was a well established and popular venue. Harry Bowler acted as Clerk of the Course, Clutton started the races from the running board of his new Bentley coupe – a three litre model that while capable of 90mph required a gallon of fuel every fifteen miles – while Anthony Heal provided a knowledgeable commentary. It was a dull cold day but despite this the meeting was seen as a great success. The majority of the races were of only three laps each and among the winners were Marcus Chambers in his 4½-litre Bentley, a car driven to another victory later that day by Mrs Fee Carson. C W P Hampton, who drove both his 2.3-litre T43 Bugatti and 1½-litre Mercedes, was the star of the meeting coming away with a pair of victories, a second and a third place, while the longest race – a ten lap handicap to round off proceedings – was won by a matter of yards with Morris Goodall's Aston Martin just beating D Jackson's Riley.

VSCC members of the time often enjoyed a charmed life on their encounters with the law. A problem with the location of the circuit was its distance from the relatively expensive hotels of Derby and Nottingham. However, Donington Hall had been used as a hotel and Peter Wike (later to become a prominent member of the Club's Northern Section) in exploring the building had found what seemed to be a dormitory, set out with a dozen beds. Enquiries of the fierce housekeeper, Miss Marshall, revealed it was used by visiting groups of boy scouts, and of pilgrims to the Hall's chapel. A fee for bed and breakfast was agreed upon and the promise of good behaviour given. Wike continues the story:

> "After meetings a bar was opened in the Hall, but this had to be shut at 6pm as there was a service in the chapel at this time on Saturdays. On one occasion the closing hour became somewhat extended and as nobody took any notice of an infuriated Miss Marshall, she sent for the police. They arrived in full panoply, and the barmen hurriedly began to clear up, when a northern voice was suddenly heard to shout "Don't take any

notice of those fellows, they're only in fancy dress!" At once the barmen went into reverse and Ollifer's – Derby's best beer – flowed once more … and nobody was arrested."

The final speed event of the year took place in a very different setting. With the introduction of driving tests in the mid-thirties Croydon's Autodrome Driving School had been built to provide a safe environment in which learners could practice their driving skills untroubled by everyday traffic. From the various concrete surfaced roads that made up the autodrome the Club chose a course that included sharp right and left uphill bends from the start, a 150 yard straight leading to a roundabout (laid out across a slope and with difficult cambers) and a finishing straight running back from same, the line itself being marked with a Belisha beacon. *Motor Sport* was rather disparaging about the whole event, regretting its "circus-like nature" but there is no doubt that the course was challenging and that the competitors thoroughly enjoyed their day, while the onlookers are reported as "just loving it". There was a good entry (variously reported as being of fifty eight and eighty) boosted by Aston Martins from the jointly organising club, and boasting a wide variety of cars.

Lt Col Clutton's Fafnir took 65 secs, his son Sam in the Itala 41.4 secs, while John Bolster (entered in what was then described as his Bolster Special) made best time of the day in 32.2 secs, despite a lurid slide on one of his runs. The ubiquitous Midge Wilby won the ladies class, taking 37.8 secs in her Frazer Nash. One of the slowest runs was made by a tiny 570cc Topolino Fiat saloon driven with great gusto by John Eason-Gibson, but then he did have five (!) passengers, two of them apparently in the front seat. Croydon was not to be used again, being one of the various sprint venues that the Club has briefly used, either once only or but a few times over the ensuing years.

When the scores were totted up at the end of the competition season the winner of the Lycett Trophy was found to be Clive Windsor-Richards in his Vauxhall 30-98.

Although the centre of gravity (or perhaps more accurately "levity") of the Club was in the home counties, there were a few members elsewhere. Kenneth Neve, who had been born in Kent, while a young man had raced motorcycles at Brooklands, worked for Turner & Newall and was to spend much of his career based with them in Lancashire. After a posting to South Wales – from where he had managed to make trips to the Phoenix and had got to know many of the key club members who gathered there – and before returning to his work in the north had asked Tim Carson if there were any members living in that vicinity. Carson suggested he contacted Peter Wike (so called despite his initials of W G S) and accordingly they arranged to meet in the beer tent at Southport sand races one summer's day. And from that meeting the Northern Section of the Club was to emerge.

Back in 1934, and recognising that England was then very much a country of two halves, the founding fathers of the Club had initially proposed a Northern Section, but it came to naught. However, the right people were now in the right place to carry the idea forward, particularly so in the shape of Ned Lewis who had been obliged to stand down from the post of Club Secretary when his job had taken him to Manchester a little over a year before. In September 1937 a group of enthusiasts met where he lived in the suburb of Didsbury and by the end of the evening the 'Northern Section of the VSCC' had come into being. E T Lewis became Chairman, K Neve the Secretary and W G S Wike the Treasurer. Other members of the Committee were to be P (Porky) Lees as Activities Secretary and G W (Geoff) Snelling as Press Secretary.

Seriously fond of their beer and recognising the crucial role that the Phoenix had played in the south, they knew they too needed a "headquarters". With a widely scattered northern membership early attempts to hold monthly meetings at a variety of country pubs proved unsuitable, for in a world well before the advent of mobile phones and emails, contact was largely maintained by post card and the job of letting members know which was to be "hostelry of the month" became too much for the Secretary. Eventually they settled down, with the Waggon and Horses, on the Manchester side of Congleton, becoming their base.

A convention of the Northern Section was that on arrival at their watering hole each should put half a crown (ie 2/6d … eight to the £1) into the kitty. This invariably ran at a surplus and, with appropriate foresight, the balance was banked just before the forthcoming war.

In July 1974 a letter arrived at the Club office.

> "Dear Sir, the other day my Bank told me that I had a small savings account open with them but it had not been used for many years …. On further enquiries it is found to be the balance of the Drinkers Kitty of the Northern Branch, plus interest accrued since 1939. So I enclose a cheque for £10.05p herewith."

The money (thirty five years late) was then put to its intended use, paying for drinks at a pre-war members' dinner held that October.

No doubt in October 1937 many of the Northern Section members had made their way to Donington and then returned home awestruck if not chastened at the sight of the totally dominant Mercedes and Auto Union teams taking the first five places in the Grand Prix, with the best British entry, Earl Howe in ERA R8B, three laps behind and unclassified, a demonstration of force that was to take on a more sinister form in March 1938 with the Nazi annexation of Austria.

1938 and the First Prescott

There were about two hundred and eighty members at the start of that troubled year. At the Annual General Meeting in January Forrest Lycett had unanimously been elected President, as Sammy Davis due to work pressures had stepped down to become a Vice President. With Carson well ensconced as Secretary and with Harry Bowler still as the Competitions Secretary, the Club got on with its business.

The trials season took what had become its traditional form, starting in the Chilterns in March, with Heal's 30-98 and Denyer's Lea Francis taking the top awards. Continuing with the Surrey Trial, run in conjunction with the Mid Surrey Club and won by Kirkham's 12/50 Alvis it concluded with the Gloucester Trial in late November. An unusual entry for this event was the T37A Grand Prix Bugatti of Gordon Lind Walker who managed to win a third class award. However, in the team competition the Bugattis were to finish behind the winning VSCC entrants, the Harrow and also the City & Guilds Car Clubs.

As early as January the Northern Section had put on its first event. Their Northern Trial started at Matlock in Derbyshire and attracted a field of nine. This included the stalwarts Kenneth Neve and Anthony Heal in Vauxhall 30-98s, Leslie Winder in a Silver Eagle Alvis and Dennis Clapham in a 12/50, who won the under two litre award. F King's Lancia Lambda was to win the over two litres class. The approach to such trials was *laissez-faire* to say the least; competitors and marshals travelling around in a queue and on this occasion (as on others) being joined by a number of private motorists who tagged along for the fun. This time the queue was to contain twenty eight cars by the end of the afternoon. Using public tracks and unsurfaced lanes the days of an approved route, police notification, route liaison officers and sections on private land were still a long way away.

The Northern Section was a confident and energetic group and had set its heart on self-determination, feeling perhaps that members down south were simply too far away. At first it was merely a matter of broadly keeping Tim Carson in the picture and his forbearance lasted to such time as an applicant to join the Section was black-balled on unspecified grounds. He grumbled to the main Club Secretary who, together with Forrest Lycett, agreed that the north-south relationship really needed sorting out. A meeting was agreed and held in the "no-mans land" of the Welbeck Hotel in Nottingham. Kenneth Neve, Ned Lewis, Peter Wike and Porky Lees drove south, while Forrest Lycett, Tim Carson, Anthony Heal and Sam Clutton drove north. It was an amicable gathering and Neve and Carson were left to sort out the details with the latter becoming an *ex-officio* member of a now officially recognised and integrated, Northern Committee. To show there were no hard feelings Forrest Lycett, who was always generous in his dealings with the Club, then presented the Lycett Northern Trophy to be awarded to the highest placed competitor in the Lycett Memorial Trophy competition living north of Leek, Staffordshire.

The northerners were to round off their year with what was described as a Speed Judging Contest, which in modern parlance would be called a regularity run. Starting from Scarisbrick, near Ormskirk in Lancashire, it involved travelling over a 43½ mile circuit while keeping as closely as possible to the set average speeds, which were measured at seven secret checkpoints. The winner, in a supercharged Aston Martin, was 23 minutes out, while the 18/80 MG in second place lost 53 minutes. Rally timing has certainly come some considerable way in the ensuing years!

The Club's speed season had got under way in April with the first of two Donington meetings held by the Club that year. Some unusual cars were present. Anthony Heal entered his recently purchased 5-litre straight-eight Ballot which proved a handful on the straights and difficult to steer, but despite this he won both the Open and the Vintage classes in the all-comers race for cars of over 3 litres. Another car of approximately the same age was Peter Hampton's 1½-litre supercharged Targa Florio Mercedes. This won the vintage section in three of the short three lapper races held. Others were won by G Burness driving a Strasbourg Sunbeam, T S Grimshaw in a T35C Bugatti and R H Whitworth in a 30-98 Vauxhall.

Infancy

Within a month the Club was back. At the second meeting on the circuit notable winners included Fee Carson, this time in a borrowed 1½-litre Alfa Romeo rather than the usual Bentley, Craig in a supercharged 4.9-litre Bugatti and Mathew in the Alfa he had earlier lent to Mrs Carson. Among the non-vintage runners was F R (Bob) Gerard, later to find fame in a variety of ERAs, who won the last and fastest race of the day in his 1½-litre Riley.

Finding suitable courses for speed trials had become an on-going problem for the Club, but with Littlestone now gone it next made use of that at Lewes, tucked in behind the South Downs. Here, a gently curved and hard surfaced private road of 733 yards, leading up to the horse racing course, had been a venue for speed events since the mid 1920s. Overall fastest time of the day was made by Whitfield Semmence

Lewes Speed Trials in 1938. R G J (Dick) Nash, who had held the course record in his Union Special between 1932 and 1936, leaves the line in the 15-litre 1912 Lorraine Dietrich as built for the French Grand Prix of that year.

driving his 2-litre AC powered Semmence special, while the vintage cars were headed by Guy Griffiths in a supercharged Anzani Nash – widely known as "The Spook". Anthony Heal had meanwhile acquired another ex Brooklands veteran in the shape of a 1910 10-litre Tipo 561 Fiat. This was to prove the fastest veteran of the day.

Although it was to use the Lewes course again in 1939 the Club still was continuing to cast around for its long sought after hill climb venue, and Tom Rolt was instrumental in finding it. His family had been long time friends with the Royds who lived at Prescott House and he always enjoyed any pretext to visit them as he could then rush up the twisty drive in his GN, particularly enjoying sliding around the loose surfaced Pardon hairpin. In the spring of 1937 he was to learn that the house stood empty and that the new owners of the estate, the Gloucestershire Dairy Company, had bought it intending to sell off its standing timber. Sensing the chance of a purchase Rolt persuaded Forrest Lycett, Tim Carson and Sam Clutton to visit the site with him, following the Shelsley Walsh meeting in May. They realised both its potential, and that their relatively small club could not possibly afford to both purchase the estate and to surface the unsealed drive. Clutton was to provide the answer, for he suggested that they approach the far richer Bugatti Owners Club, seeking an agreement that if they purchased it they would allow the VSCC to hold a meeting there each year. The Bugatti Owners Club had come into being in 1929, was well run and relatively wealthy. It had organised speed events and Donington meetings, some in association with the VSCC, so links between the Clubs were well established. Also, they had been set to purchase their own hill climb course at Dancers End near Tring but had run into difficulties over local objections as to the noise that their meetings would cause. Prescott would appear to solve a number of problems for both clubs, so in 1937 the Bugatti club bought the estate for £2,500 and then asked their members to contribute to the £4,500 that would be needed to surface and improve the hill. £5 debentures at 4½% were issued and the deal went ahead.

The course was opened in April and the first full meeting was held on 15th May 1938. At this there were 53 entries and approximately 2,500 spectators. Among those competing were Clutton, who won the Veterans class in his Itala, Heal on his recently purchased 1910 Fiat and Rolt in the Alvis 12/50 that he was to use throughout the rest of his life.

On Saturday 27th August the first VSCC meeting took place. As there were no RAC timekeepers no official records could be set. Overall fastest time of the day was put up

Infancy

L T C (Tom) Rolt, driving his Phoenix Special tackles the Prescott esses in 1938. Based on the remains of a GN road car, that had been crashed, he had often driven it up the drive of Prescott House in its original form to visit family friends, in doing so recognising the sporting potential of the hill.

by Joe Fry in his Freikaiserwagen, taking 47.62 secs to climb the hill in his rear engined special, while the fastest vintage time was made by T S Grimshaw in a Bugatti T35C, the combination taking 50.74 secs. At 56.22 secs Midge Wilby was quickest the ladies in her Frazer Nash. She had entered three cars for the meeting. The Nash and Atalanta were driven by the owner, while her Lancia was in the hands of Miss Brotchie who must have had real problems on her first run. This took 108.06 secs which she reduced to 65.05 secs on her second.

The day was not without its moments. During practice Fry went straight on at Orchard when his brakes failed, seemingly doing no real damage to car nor driver as his later winning climbs went to show. Derek Mathew, on his second run in a beautiful 1750 Alfa Romeo, also visited the woods at speed, hitting a tree sufficiently hard to bend the car's frame. The veteran class of six entries was reduced by two, Clutton's Itala non-starting for unspecified reasons, while business pressures prevented Forrest Lycett from bringing his Hispano along. Of the four survivors A J Clarke-Kennedy's rarely seen SAVA was driven with such gusto that a beaded tyre, unrestrained by security bolts pulled off, the inner tube ballooning out before it went bang. So then there were three. Of these Anthony Heal in the Fiat was fastest in an impressive 55.91 secs while slowest was the Fafnir (a youthful thirty years old or so at the time) which took Lt Col Clutton up in 102.53 secs, Forrest Lycett going along as passenger on one of the runs. The car had used only a little oil and a gallon of petrol per 23 miles over the 250 miles it covered getting to and from the meeting.

The close knit nature of the Club was evident from the front page of the programme. The Secretary of the Meeting was Miss M Choate, whose address was given as the Phoenix Hotel, Hartley Row, Hants (and who soon afterwards was to become Tim Carson's second wife), the Scrutineer was her father Cecil Choate (who had officiated at the first Donington meeting), the Timekeeper was H P Bowler and the Medical Officer Dr Ewen, who was to become closely associated with the Clutton Itala. Inside the front cover was a note about the Club that could only have been written by Clutton.

> "The Vintage Sports-Car Club, founded 3 years ago, caters for the owners of cars manufactured prior to 1931. The years up to 1930 are considered by the Club to have produce real motor cars in fairly large quantities. There were of course some inferior cars made during those years, but by now these have nearly all fallen to pieces …

> The Club holds 3 Speed Trials and 3 Reliability Trials during each season in addition to map reading contests and other social events.
>
> Full driving membership costs only 12/6d per year with an entrance fee of 5/ – …
>
> There is also a class of Associate Membership for those with the right ideas but (a) no motors, or (b) the wrong motors. This entitles the Associate Member to compete in the majority of events, but not for the Annual Awards or Special Vintage events. An application form for membership is included in this programme."

With the Club membership approaching three hundred, and a well established Committee in place, such apparent stability was soon to become disturbed both from without and within. Hitler's territorial ambitions had long been clear, although for a short time the Munich Agreement of late September 1938 appeared to reduce the risk of war when the three major European powers of Britain, France and Italy effectively gave in to Nazi Germany's demand for the Sudetenland of Czechoslovakia; but the respite was to be only temporary. The Donington Grand Prix, at one stage at risk of cancellation, was moved from its original date of October 8th to the 22nd when it went ahead to be won in a display of dazzling virtuosity by Nuvolari in an Auto Union. While some sort of normality might have appeared to be restored the coming storm had only been delayed.

As Tom Rolt was to write in *Landscape with Machines*, the first volume of his autobiography, the ambience at the Phoenix had become "strangely disturbing": The A30 that ran past the hotel and garage was packed at the weekends with cars "like lemmings rushing to the sea." Their many accidents may have helped the breakdown business, but added to the unsettling atmosphere. Inside the Phoenix the crowded smoke filled bars were noisy with laughter, the clink of glasses, recordings of Duke Ellington and Louis Armstrong being loudly played – while outside the noise of revving engines and the smell of Castrol R added to the air of agitated excitement. Practical jokes galore, as recorded by Marcus Chambers, included the use of devices that when attached to the coil of a car would emit an ear piercing scream when the ignition was turned on, and produce clouds of smoke when the bonnet was raised to investigate. Cigarette papers between ignition points, crossed plug leads and potatoes wedged up exhausts were to delay many in setting out for home, while others – still mobile – might attempt to beat the record from the Phoenix to Olympia. It could be done in thirty minutes on a good night. As Rolt was well aware

> "All this added up to something feverish and fretful, it had an ominous quality which used to fill me with foreboding. Such a hectic party must surely be followed by some dreadful morning after."

The Phoenix Green Garage business that he ran with Passini had been struggling and needed more capital, which he could not provide, and so in December 1938 he was to leave Hartley Wintney. His own personal life was changing, as was that of Tim Carson; he also left the Phoenix shortly afterwards to take over the Sarum Hill Garage in Basingstoke and an era had come to an end.

1939 and the first 'Welsh weekend'

The 1939 Annual General Meeting of the Club technically took place a day too early, being held on 31st December 1938. Forrest Lycett began this third year as President, Kent Karslake joined him as Vice President, Harry Bowler continued as Competitions Secretary while Sam Clutton was back in his role as *Bulletin* Editor. For the second year running Clive Windsor-Richards had won the Lycett Trophy.

The trials season commenced on a bright dry morning in February when the "Northern" competitors set out from Buxton. It must have had one of the smallest ever fields for a VSCC event, just nine in all. Among these were four Alvis 12/50s, one Bentley, which driven by J B Ashton, was to win, and one retirement in the shape of J D Ackernley's BMV. This incredible special was based on a "B for Bugatti" chassis, "M for Morris" axles and a "V for Vauxhall" engine. With its Bugatti and Morris gearboxes both *in situ* it boasted seventeen forward and eight reverse gears. Not unsurprisingly it had broken by lunchtime, but until then had climbed every hill.

Five weeks later the Northern Trial was to be followed by a very different event. Johnny Swainson accompanied by Tom Rolt, shortly before he was to withdraw from club activities to spend several years involved with canals and waterways, set out for the Welsh Marches. Here the two based themselves on the Radnor Arms in Presteigne and devised the Sunday component of what is now generally known as the Welsh weekend. The Welsh Rally, as it was then called, was open to both wings of the Club, the veterans and post war vintage cars.

On the Saturday morning competitors left home aiming to drive to Presteigne by 9.00pm by a self chosen route of 200 miles. At each significant turning point they were to send a telegram to the organisers at the Radnor Arms and on arrival their total mileages were calculated by using string to measure their straight line distances from point to point. The VSCC continues to use string to this day. On March 25th 1939 sixty-six such telegrams were to arrive and be processed by the startled town post office and then delivered to the Radnor Arms. Clive Windsor-Richards, driving a 1924 Vauxhall, must have followed a tortuous route for he sent no less than ten of these. On nearing Presteigne Swainson had asked a Welshman for directions who had helpfully advised "Follow me boyo, and I'll be right behind you". It was a chilly early spring day with snow showers throughout. This was to make life difficult for all, and particularly so for those in the relatively unprotected Edwardians. There were other challenges to be met on the way. John Seth-Smith drove a 1908 single cylinder Sizaire-Naudin over 180 miles from Chelmsford. Its hand operated throttle presented no problem, but with the clutch pedal on the right and the brake pedal on the left he thought it safer to drive cross-legged. On getting to Presteigne be could barely stand up. His drive home was no easier and was to become an epic in the annals of the Club. Peter Hull takes up the story:

> "First of all the handbrake stripped a thread, then the steering arm came unput. Next the clutch refused to disengage, the lamps declined to ignite, the magneto fell off and the petrol tank continued to leak in an increasingly big way. A much saddened man eventually reached Chelmsford in the early hours of the Monday morning and then proceeded to go to bed for several days."

Deservedly he was to be presented a special award for the Most Meritorious Performance. Lt Col Clutton covered 227 miles on his drive to Presteigne gaining full marks for the journey in the 1910 Fafnir, while J Bradshaw in a 1906 Daimler also scored the maximum points available with a drive of 216 miles. Other pre-war cars on maximum points for the "rally" element were the 1910 Mercedes of A Timmis and the Martini of W Worthington. By no means all of the sixteen vintage entrants scored likewise.

On the Sunday morning the pre-war class was judged in a concours, listed in the results as an "appearance competition", in which a high proportion of the marks were to go for originality. Bradshaw's Daimler was the clear winner. Then, with a fine disregard for any legislation relating to holding speed events on public roads, the veterans all went off for a timed hill climb of about half a mile at nearby Stapleton. The slope varying between 1 in 6 and 1 in 10 kept most cars in first gear all the way up – so, perhaps it would fairly claim not to be a speed event. Anthony Heal in his 1907 Renault was fastest (1 min 26 secs) with the Daimler (1 min 29 secs) close behind.

Meanwhile the vintage competitors embarked on their "reliability trial", the observed sections including "Smatcher" which in one form or another has featured in the majority of "Welsh trials" ever since. It was a dry day and the sections proved easier than anticipated so the results were very close, with Clive Windsor-Richards (who for the third time was to win the Lycett Trophy that year) narrowly beating P Lees' Bentley. Perhaps the most sporting entry for the trial was D Fitzpatrick's 1926 Rolls-Royce which, although quite a squeeze on some of the narrow tracks, climbed remarkably well.

On the previous Saturday night the High Street of Presteigne had, for the first time, enjoyed the sight of parked pre-war and vintage machinery along its length, a sight to which the town has since grown used. As *The Bulletin* of the time was to observe: "A number of people said it was the best motoring weekend for a very long time, indeed, and even those who didn't comment themselves so forcibly enjoyed it a lot, so that this is obviously a thing to become an annual fixture." And so it has proved.

With the international situation continuing to deteriorate limited conscription had been introduced in April, but against this unsettled background such events as the Crystal Palace meeting that month helped to distract. Four events involved the VSCC. The inter-club Stanley Cup was convincingly won by the Frazer Nash and BMC Car Club, with the VSCC seventh of the ten clubs competing, while interest in the 3 lap veterans handicap was high.

Despite the 15-litres at its disposal the R G J Nash Lorraine Dietrich was slow away, beaten by Heal's 10-litre Fiat. Clutton was soon out in front with *Motor Sport* observing… "the Itala cornered by sheer brute strength, rear tyres smoking, a wheel first locked under the brake and then revolved backwards on the dry … The crowd just loved it". Clutton was to win with Heal 3.7 secs behind him. The two VSCC members' handicaps over four laps were won by W H Willis's Lea Francis and L C Mackenzie's Bentley, while Harry Bowler, despite excellent driving, had too much of a handicap to overcome.

The Club was to be seen again at the London Circuit in July when the handicap vintage race was inexplicably short at two laps only. This time Hampton in a Bugatti was to win with Clutton's Itala in second place. Nash, who again had been slow off the start, came third. The *Motor Sport* report explained why such cars could not be seen at Brooklands:

> "Incidentally we would dearly love to see these old cars in action over the Brooklands Outer Circuit but … in view of the Ten Year age limit a fatal accident might result in an unsympathetic press."

So rather than thundering round wide banked curves at high speed the next outing was on the narrow uphill slope of the South Downs at Lewes where Clive Windsor-Richards, Delage mounted and who was having an excellent season, was the fastest vintage entrant on 23.25 secs. Heal's veteran Fiat took scarcely 0.25 secs longer while Windsor-Richards, who had also borrowed the Itala for the day, took much longer at 27.52 secs. Meanwhile the country had given assurances to Poland that it would intervene should it be invaded and something approaching normality was to continue for little over two more months.

During August the Club's last pre-war meetings were to take place. A programme of short races over the inner circuit of Donington was planned including the then typical mix of short and long handicaps, a relay race and scratch races for both sports and racing cars. Half a dozen invited clubs were to be involved and the excellent entry included Reg Parnell, from nearby Derby, in the BHW – a single seater special using Alvis front suspension and a supercharged 4.9-litre T54 Bugatti engine. Needless to say he was to win all of his three races. Anthony Heal had acquired another car, a 5-litre Indianapolis Ballot dating from 1919, while in a far younger car – a 1½-litre 6CM Maserati – was another club member and recently elected member of the Committee, Sir John Bowen. A little while before, when appearing in a magistrates court on a driving charge, he had given his address as the Phoenix in Hartley Wintney where no doubt he had absorbed something of the over-heated enthusiasm that could be found there. In the fourth race, going very fast, he lost control on the straight leading to Coppice Corner, crashed through the wooden fence and came to rest in a virtually empty spectators enclosure. He was killed instantly. The first fatality in a club event, he was only in his early twenties. The meeting was continued but with a number of races abandoned and others shortened.

It seemed appropriate that the final meeting of the year took place at Prescott on a wet and gloomy day. Following on the success of the Welsh Rally, part of its format was repeated for the older cars on the preceding Friday. The veterans could choose their own starting points, sending telegrams to the Chief Marshal at the hill to log their journey, from which he could then calculate their mileages as the crow is alleged to fly. Marks were awarded for the distances covered and on arrival cars were additionally judged on the basis of their age and originality. The veterans each then made a timed ascent of the hill on the Saturday before the meeting proper got under way. It did so in a heavy drizzle that was to last all day and which made the start line particularly slippery. C Vaughan, in his special the Becke Powerplus, made some stirring climbs and narrowly won the All Comers class from Sidney Allard in one of his own modern creations. Heal was very impressive in the 1910 Fiat, again beating Clutton in the veteran Itala, while Midge Wilby was beaten in the Ladies class by Mrs Sheila Darbyshire in a Bugatti, despite having two cars at her disposal. Her Frazer Nash came second and her Atalanta – only just behind – in third. The report of the meeting was published in *The Light Car* on September 1st, the day on which the Nazis invaded Poland. Two days

Donington in August 1939; the line up believed to be for one of the many handicap races held that day. On the left is the BHW (Bugatti-Hassan-Wilkins), a special built on a one-off chassis, fitted with independent front suspension from an Alvis and powered by a 4.9-litre supercharged Bugatti engine. Driven by Reg Parnell it won three races on the day. Alongside are two Bugattis, a T35B and a T35, together with a Riley TT Sprite.

later at 11.15 on the morning of September 3rd, Neville Chamberlain was to announce to the nation that it was at war with Germany.

Shortly afterwards members received a six-page duplicated newsletter that contained the Donington and Prescott results which were preceded by an editorial.

This Tedious War

"The Club will be put to bed with its bank balance for the duration. Current subscriptions will continue to be current, until the next event after the outbreak of peace. Otherwise, apart from bringing all outstanding awards up to date it is most unlikely that there will be any further competitive activities for the time being.

If any of us are (a) alive, and/or (b) solvent at the end of it all we must then decide how best to pick up the threads of civilization (ie, motoring) again, and anyone who changes his address during the Nonsense should notify Tim Carson at the Sarum Hill Garage, Basingstoke, Hants."

Renaissance
1945–1955

On 8th May 1945 the German forces surrendered on the European mainland, ending the European war. Although the Japanese surrender was not to follow until August that year the war was effectively over. In June the Committee of the VSCC wasted no time and sat down to consider the future, the Minutes reading:

> "After a general expression of opinion it was agreed that the Club's activities should be revived. H P Bowler was asked to notify the Competitions Department of the RAC that the Club was again active. It was further agreed that a General Meeting combined with a social event should be held on the 8th or 15th September and the 'Wheatsheaf' at Virginia Water and the 'Talbot' at Ripley were suggested as possible venues."

In the event the gathering was held at Bagshot where, as part of the General Meeting, an issue that was to shape the character of the Club in the years ahead was to form the key item on the agenda, for in June the Committee meeting had considered:

> "… the advisability of raising the existing qualifications for membership in view of the decreasing number of pre-1931 vintage sports cars that would probably be available as years passed. Communications on this subject were read from T W Carson (Hon Secretary) … still abroad on service with the RAF in North Africa at the time … and K Neve (Northern

> Section). After a thorough discussion … it was stressed that the Club should continue to organise special events for Edwardians (pre 1915) and Vintage (pre 1931) but that full membership should be available to owners of certain other types of cars. Quality rather than Age should be the necessary qualification for membership."

A key sentence of the proposal – which Windsor-Richards proposed and Clutton seconded – identified how the matter of quality rather than age should be effected.

> "Full membership of the Club is to be open to any person owning a car (of whatever make or year of manufacture) that is found acceptable to the Committee."

And so the Club aimed to move from an acceptance for eligibility based simply on the "built by December 31st 1930" *principle*, to an extension of eligibility based on *practice*, to be determined by the committee. A very English solution had emerged with pragmatism underpinning the approach, and decisions taken building up into a body of case law. Despite the inherent anomalies involved, the approach has served the Club remarkably well.

The commitment to Edwardian and pre-World War I cars that was very evident in the early days of the Club was reiterated. With an insouciant disregard for the actual birthdays of monarchs (Edward VII was king from 1901 to 1910) the original date for Edwardian membership had started from 1905, up to which year the Veteran Car Club originally accepted membership. The VCC then extended its dates to be inclusive of cars of over thirty years old, which in 1945 was to take it up to 1915 and thus coincidental with the VSCC Edwardians. However, the approach of the two clubs has been sufficiently different to allow the Veteran Club, which is more concerned with the preservation of historically important machines, and the Vintage Club which is essentially competitive and holds Edwardian events within its programme, to co-exist peacefully.

Although quick off the mark the VSCC was not the first to run post-war competitive motoring events, for on 18th August 1945 the Bristol Motor Cycle and Light Car Club held its Naish Hill Climb just south of Bristol. The M5, just south of Gordano Services, now crosses the line of the climb, which rose 200 feet in 880 yards via three hairpins connected by a grassy track. Fastest time of the day was made by Dick Watkins in his Watkins-Nash, beating Bob Gerard on his first outing in an ERA, R4A. Such was the pent up desire for motor sport that Gerard, in those pre-motorway days, had travelled over 140 miles from Leicester to reach the venue and enjoy a few seconds of competition, and was to make much the same journey again on a cold wet day in late October when he competed in a sprint on Filton airfield on the other side of Bristol, this time having the satisfaction of making Fastest Time of the Day.

The first VSCC outing of the post-war years, although of enormous significance, was rather more sedate. Held on 15th September at the Pantiles, Bagshot, *The Bulletin* of the time did not record how many attended, but sufficient vintage cars arrived to fill the available parking totally. The oldest car to arrive under its own power was Bunny Tubbs's 1913 Baby Peugeot (but like the Clutton Fafnir the year of its appearance on the scene is in some doubt for a picture alongside the report dated it as being of 1914).

The best kept car, as determined by the judges, was Dr Ewen's Delage while among those who had come a long way to be there was Bill Boddy, accompanied by his wife, who had driven all the way down from Yorkshire in a Scott engined Morgan. The short report of the General Meeting ran as follows:

> "After a grand foregathering with everyone meeting someone he had not seen for years the General Meeting was held. The Committee was re-elected en-bloc, the Club's timing apparatus was fortunately but surprisingly discovered to be in the possession of a member, and the Competition Secretary explained and bemoaned the shortage of available courses."

The Minutes of the Committee meeting of June had reported that after the Club's Prescott meeting of 1939 the timing apparatus had been left in charge of an associate member, Bruce Nicholson … A letter addressed to Nicholson had been returned marked "gone away". While the Committee members must have been relieved that the equipment had eventually been found it is rather sad as well as surprising that none of them recognised this one time custodian of the timing gear as being one of the same two Nicholsons whose letter to *The Light Car* had been instrumental in the founding of the Club.

> "The only point over which there was any serious dissension was the proposed alteration of the rules to admit driving membership to owners of quality sports cars regardless of age, subject to the approval of a majority

of the Committee. After some discussion, however, this was passed by an overwhelming majority."

In 1945 virtually all sports cars eligible for consideration would have been built prior to the war anyway, so the requirement for cars to be pre-1940 did not need to be specified until later.

"The close of the meeting was followed by a tea which by these peacetime standards was really quite something."

Anthony Heal, who had organised the day, had obviously excelled himself, for food rationing was still very much in place, as it would be for some years to come. The Club at this time had approximately three hundred and fifty members and those of them who went home from Bagshot were able to do so relatively well fed, pleased with the progress being made and each with a small plaque bearing the legend that they had attended the first post war rally of the Vintage Sports-Car Club. A fair proportion of them, but a few months later, were then able to attend the Annual General Meeting of 1946. One hundred and thirty members turned out for this and the Committee for the first full year of peace was elected. Forrest Lycett continued as President, the Vice Presidents were to be Sammy Davis and Laurence Pomeroy, while Clive Windsor-Richards became Club Captain. The Honorary Secretary was confirmed as Tim Carson (who was granted a £60 honorarium for the year ahead as a token acknowledgement of all the work that he did in running the Club), Harry Bowler continued as Competition Secretary and Anthony Heal as Press Secretary. Sam Clutton, with A Phelps to look after production matters, were to edit *The Bulletin* while N McCaw, the Treasurer, reported a bank balance of £200. Members of the Committee without portfolio were Cecil Choate, F H Dixon, A F Rivers Fletcher, who was to be a significant member of the Club for many of the years ahead, and Dr A G Ewen.

'The Right Kinds of Cars'

The following ten years were to prove momentous in the Club's history, during which it moved from being a small specialist and relatively insignificant group to becoming one of the larger and more important clubs in the motoring firmament, promoting a wide range of varied events. By 1955, when it reached twenty-one years old, it had grown into an effective organisation that bore all the signs of confident maturity. But back in 1946 the background to its activities remained difficult. The country struggled with the legacy of the recent war, its finances propped up by large loans from the United States, while the very poor grain harvest, consequent upon a particularly wet summer, meant that wheat yields were so badly down that bread rationing had to be re-introduced. Food parcels from the sister Vintage Sports-Car Club of Australia were received with much appreciation, and provided for several of the prizes at club events, while as late as 1948 similar parcels from that great American enthusiast Briggs Cunningham – whose cars were to become so prominent but without quite winning Le Mans – were raffled at the first Thursday night gatherings that once again were taking place at the Phoenix. Next door, at the Phoenix Green Garage, Alan Southon was likewise now catering for the "right kinds of cars".

Decisions as to what exactly are the "right kinds of cars" are fundamental to the nature of the Club. In a very real sense everything flows from its eligibility rules as these determine what sorts of vehicles members own, what they compete in, and what they will see in action when attending club meetings. As history has shown – and indeed continues to show – eligibility is an ever moving target. Over the years the rules have been regularly revised and updated; such revisions reflecting changing circumstances, changing needs, changing tastes and – it has to be admitted – changing prejudices. But wisely, albeit now guided and advised by its Eligibility Sub-Committee, the full Committee continues to guard the door and is the final arbiter of what is, or what is not, to be found acceptable.

Having opened the door to at least some post-vintage cars the Committee decided to consult the membership, writing to all Driving Members (ie those owning vintage cars) as follows:

Driving membership

"As you are no doubt aware, your Committee has been given the power to elect owners of certain post-Vintage cars as driving members.

Whilst the eligibility of the cars has been left to the Committee's discretion, they (the Committee) would like to ascertain the opinion of all driving members on the types that they feel would be admitted.

Below is a list of sundry cars that have been mentioned from time to time. Please make a tick against those you consider should entitle their owners to full driving membership, and a cross against those you feel

Renaissance

should be associate only. When the form is completed, please return to the Hon. Secretary.

	Tick	Cross		Tick	Cross
Aston Martin, 1938			Lancia Aprilia		
AC Competition 2-str., 1937			Morris Cowley 2-str., 1930		
Austin Le Mans 1936			MG Magnette K.3, 1933		
Alvis Speed 25, 1939			MG Monthlery, 1931		
Alfa Romeo 2.3 Pescara, 1936			MG M Type, 1931		
Alta 1½-litre Racing, 1937			Mercedes 16-h.p., 1932		
BMW Type 328			Mercedes 8-cyl. Type 540, 1938		
Bugatti Type 57S			Morgan 4/4		
Bugatti Type 40, 1933			Railton, 1934		
Bentley 4½-litre, 1938			Rolls-Royce Phantom II		
Bentley 3½-litre, 1934			Riley 9 Gamecock, 1934 (sic)		
Delahaye Le Mans, 1937			Riley 9 Imp, 1936		
HRG 1,100 c.c., 1946			Squire 1½-litre, 1935		
Lagonda 4½-litre, 1937			SS 100, 1937		
Lagonda Rapier, 1935			Wolseley Hornet Special, 1933		

Do you also think that **any** pre-1930 car, whether sports, saloon or tourer, should merit full driving membership?"

Members were asked to put a tick or cross against those cars they felt should be admitted or rejected – and not surprisingly there was little agreement among the two hundred or so responses received. Two general messages were however clear. The post-vintage cars selected should certainly be of a sporting nature and they should certainly be pre-war. Thus the date for eligibility remained in the 1930s and the one post-war vehicle being considered (the 1946 HRG) was to remain outside the pale.

Five years later the Committee was to re-visit the matter, the then President Kent Karslake writing to all members in a letter with appendices that was to lay out some fundamental eligibility principles that broadly continue to guide the Club to this day.

Letter from the President to all Members
25th August 1951.

"The Committee feel that the time is appropriate to seek the guidance of members on a matter of substantial importance to the present and future welfare of the Club, namely,

(a) to suggest that all cars constructed in 1931 and subsequently which now bring a member into the driving membership class should in future be called Thoroughbred Post-Vintage cars.

(b) that the makes and types of cars falling into this category should be more clearly defined than they have been in the past.

As a next step, which was taken in 1936, the Club began to cater for cars built in the decade 1905–1915, which were aptly if inaccurately dubbed "Edwardians". At that time no other club concerned itself with the cars of this epoch, although, apart from their performance, they already possessed historic interest. It is perhaps instructive to remark that the youngest of them then was almost exactly as old as the youngest vintage car is now.

The vintage car has in fact now reached the stage where it is beginning to add an historic interest to its other good qualities. For some time, therefore, your Committee has been willing to admit members who own vintage cars which are in no sense sports cars, and recently this policy has been carried a stage further by the formation of the Vintage Light Car Section.

Working on the same lines, and remembering that "those whom the gods love die young", your Committee came to the conclusion that a racing car had already become historic by the time it was fifteen years old. During the last two years, therefore, we have organised the Seaman Trophy Race for "historic" racing cars.

Your Committee have, however, never allowed themselves to forget that the cult of the vintage car arose, and has been fostered by the Club, not because these cars were *old* but because they were *good*. When activities were resumed after the war, therefore, and we found that most of our vintage cars were half as old again as when we last saw them, it was realised that we were in danger of relapsing into a merely sentimental nostalgia for the past, instead of fulfilling the Club's true function, which is to foster the good car. Accordingly it was decided to admit a limited number of members owning cars built since 1930, provided that these cars were good enough. We have called these members "driving members", but we have never coined a generic term for their cars, with the result that in the last Silverstone regulations, for example, we had to state that Event 6 was for "Driving members (cars which have been accepted by the Committee as eligible for Driving membership)". In order to avoid this sort of jargon (and doubtful syntax!) it has been decided that in future cars of this class shall be referred to as Thoroughbred Post-Vintage cars. (In this we have the support of the Oxford Dictionary which says that a "first-rate motor-car, bicycle, etc.," has been known as a thoroughbred since 1894).

You will therefore see that we now have five classes of membership, each meeting a real and well-defined need for owners of –

1. Edwardian – any car built between 1905 and 1916.
2. Vintage – any car built between 1917 and 1930
3. Thoroughbred – non-vintage cars built between 1931 and 1941
4. Historic racing cars, more than 15 years old.
5. Associate, for people without eligible cars, but who can show themselves to be genuinely interested in the vintage movement.

In order to avoid the danger of any fundamental change in the character of the Club, your Committee have been careful to see that "driving members" and associate members together did not exceed 40 percent of the total membership of the Club, so that the owners of vintage cars should at all times retain control of its fortunes. There is no present intention of making any change in this policy.

In deciding what cars should entitle their owners to "driving membership", your Committee were assisted in 1946 by a Referendum and it is proposed on the present occasion again to resort to this democratic device in order to aid your Committee in choosing those models which in future will be classified as Thoroughbred Post-Vintage cars. The attached schedule therefore consists of:

(a) Cars which your Committee are satisfied should be included in this class.

(b) Cars which your Committee are inclined to include, but on which they would like the guidance of members.

(c) Cars on which your Committee have an open mind and with reference to which they would also like the guidance of members.

Please therefore mark with an X those cars in Lists (b) and (c), which you consider *unsuitable* for the Thoroughbred Post-Vintage class, and return the form as soon as possible to the Secretary, "Mellaha", Pack Lane, Kempshott, Basingstoke, Hants.

In selecting our Thoroughbred Post-Vintage cars, we should, I think, be guided by the principle that:

This Club is interested in all cars, regardless of quality, provided that they are old enough, and in all cars, regardless of age, provided that they are good enough.

For the present, however, owing to the difficulty of assessing the quality of relatively untried cars, your Committee proposed not to include as Thoroughbred Post-Vintage cars any cars which are less than ten years of age.

It is the intention of your Committee to restrict future Club events (with the exception of the Pomeroy Trophy competition) to the classes of cars mentioned in this letter, *viz.*, Edwardian, Vintage, Historic and Thoroughbred Post-Vintage.

E K H Karslake."

Along with the letter – reproduced in full as it establishes the Club's position on a number of major issues – were the three lists. The sixty-five names in List A (ie cars which met with Committee approval) were unsurprising, likewise the fourteen names in List B (ie the Committee inclined to approve these) were uncontentious, but the forty in List C (on which the Committee had an open mind) contained a few surprises. The jaundiced view that many Committee members then had of MG is shown by no less than seven listed models of this make were excluded (admittedly a similar number *had* been included in List A) while the inclusion of front wheel drive Citroëns, certainly not built according to vintage principles, perhaps reflected the enthusiasm of a Committee member who just happened to own one of these cars.

Less than six years previously, at the Bagshot General Meeting of 1945, the Club had agreed to the principle of admitting cars built after the vintage date of December 1930. It had since moved on rapidly to embrace a selection of non-vintage cars built up to December 1940 and even decided upon a label for them. The name of such Thoroughbred Post-Vintage cars was soon to be mildly re-ordered as Post-Vintage Thoroughbreds – ie the PVTs we know today.

Racing cars more than 15 years old (it was soon to come down to 12) were being admitted as Historic Racing Cars, thus embracing the majority of ERAs, while at the other end of the performance spectrum was the establishment of the Light Car Section. The architecture of the Club was thus determined.

Trialling Returns

While such far reaching ideas were being debated and refined, motor sport, the *raison d'être* of the Club, had at last got under way after the enforced six and a half year lay-off. The first post-war event organised by the VSCC, largely thanks to the efforts of Harry Bowler, was the Marlow Trial. The 3rd of February 1946 was a very wet day, the trial therefore being referred to as the Marlow Mudlark. Of the forty entrants nine non-started, no doubt some put off by the incessant rain. The three observed sections proved extremely difficult, only one being cleared by anyone at all – with just three competitors struggling to the top of Windmere. The tests, however, livened up the day. The "see-saw" test did not suit Grosscurth's Nash, which broke a chain; the "pitstop" test (change a wheel, extract a plug; put it on the ground and then re-fit) was completed by Dr Ewen's Delage crew in just 53 seconds (by far the best time of the day) while Mrs Rivers Fletcher's adroit tossing of a 12/50 Alvis sparkplug from hand to hand showed how very hot these can become. Giron's Bugatti, meanwhile, fell off its jack.

The Northern Section had to wait until the following year for its first competitive event but opened the batting in March with a gathering of over a hundred members at the Dixon Arms in Chelford, Cheshire. Twenty five came in vintage cars, and the concours for these was won by a very smart black 3-litre Bentley dating from 1925; the prize for the oldest car arriving under its own power going to an 1889 De Dion Bouton.

1945–1955

The Elstree Speed Trials – Easter 1946

While the October 1945 Sprint held at Filton had shown the potential of airfields for speed events it had been a quiet and private affair – for just competitors and officials were allowed on site – but things were to be very different at Elstree in April 1946. The combination of a dry Bank Holiday Monday, proximity to London and a pent up desire to enjoy some motor sport meant that a huge crowd descended on the then still operational Hertfordshire airfield, there to enjoy the first large scale speed event to be held in England after the war. Marshalling the huge, although well behaved, crowds (estimated as being between twelve and fifteen thousand) presented a major challenge for inexperienced marshals, while problems with the loudspeaker system and then the timing gear made the task of the organisers even harder. The meeting eventually got underway an hour late and hand timing had to be used, yet overall the event was judged to have been "a riotous success". Committee member Alec Rivers Fletcher had been the initiator of the meeting and it was he who had persuaded the relevant authorities to allow the use of the venue. Poetic justice meant that he was to win the 750-1100cc racing car class in a borrowed single seater K3 MG. The overall entry was huge and covered thirty five classes, with additional classes for motorbikes. Class winners received a small teak tobacco jar fitted with an engraved plate. Over the quarter of a mile of slightly uphill runway almost everyone who was anyone in the sprinting world had their runs, with Peter Monkhouse (2263cc supercharged Bugatti) making Fastest Time of the Day in 15.2 secs and John Bolster (1962cc un-supercharged "Bloody Mary") the fastest Vintage runner on 16.0 secs. Unusually the *Motor Sport* report was to identify one of its own staff as a competitor. *"Boddy's Alfonso Hispano-Suiza, having towed its broken down tow car to the meeting, misbehaved halfway up the course".* £1000 (a considerable sum in 1946) was donated to Watford Hospital from the gate money proceeds. For a club with a total membership of approximately six hundred at the time,

J V (John) Bolster pictured by his well known special Bloody Mary (and, for reasons unknown, apparently about to eat a boiled egg.) He was to win the Lycett Trophy, the annual aggregate award for the Club's most successful vintage car driver, in both 1946 and 1948.

53

the meeting was a significant achievement and put the initials VSCC firmly on the motor sporting map. Even *The Times* newspaper carried a picture of the event.

Bolster was certainly having a good year, being fastest of the vintage entries at Prescott and going on to win the Lycett Trophy for 1946.

A Variety of Rallies

In the summer of 1946 the name of Bisley entered the list of venues to be used by the Club – the norm being twice a year. Two closely linked locations were involved; the base for refreshments and the social side of things being the Pavilion of the National Rifle Association – while alongside the Ministry of Defence tank training ground was used for the competitive elements of those Bisley days. Rolling sandy terrain, pock marked with tank traps among the silver birches, and criss-crossed with a veritable maze of tracks provided multiple opportunities for getting lost; it is said that the three challenges were getting there in the first place, next completing the tests, and finally getting back to the Pavilion while avoiding the trickery designed for tanks.

The events themselves were usually defined as "rallies" – but "driving tests" quite often crept into their titles – in much the same way as many of the early club trials put as much emphasis on their special tests as on the observed sections, yet rarely called themselves rallies.

Such semantic uncertainties did not seem to worry the competitors who, despite some dire weather over the years, and the shifting marker lines drawn in the sand, were happy to enjoy the combination of socialising and competing. The first Bisley in July started in the afternoon but by November a lunch had been incorporated into the proceedings. The Supplementary Regulations – far briefer and less formal than those issued to would-be competitors today – set out the general scheme of things. Tim Carson, very much "hands on" in his role as Club Secretary, was both Clerk of the Course and Secretary of the Meeting, with Forrest Lycett and P H Dixon as the Stewards:-

> General:
> "This event is organised as a Rally to enable members of the Club to get to know each other and to provide a day's amusement. The Rally will commence at the NRA Pavilion at Bisley near Bagshot at 12 noon and lunch has been arranged at 12.30pm. After lunch there will be two or three good

driving tests. High tea will be provided at 4.30pm. It is hoped to arrange a small film show to fill the gap between tea and "opening time" at 7pm."

Driving Tests:
"The driving tests will be held under the general competition rules of the RAC. These rules will govern protests and all other matters. The entry fee for the driving tests will be 2/ – (two shillings) per car. Awards will be given as follows for the lowest aggregate time for the tests:

(a)   for cars up to 1500cc

(b)   for cars over 1500cc

These tests are open only to members of the VSCC."

The Bisley Rally, December 1951, with the Jowett's driver looking over his shoulder as if to reverse into an invisible garage. This was to be the penultimate meeting for the Club on this site where it held events from 1946 until early 1952. Nomenclature was something of a puzzle at the time, with the "rally" largely consisting of driving tests, on surfaces better suited to trials.

As a combined lunch and tea cost 8/ – (eight shillings) the day, inclusive of tests, could be enjoyed in exchange for a 10/ – (ten shilling) note … while presumably one had to take one's own ration book along as well.

Yet again the weather dealt unkindly with a Club event as Clutton, in the next *Bulletin*, was to point out:

> "The weather on the Bagshot Run was if anything exceeded by the weather at Bisley the following Sunday, and if weather like that, and the rest of this year of disgrace, can't succeed in dampening the enthusiasm of motorists, it seems most unlikely that the politicians will manage to do it, so they might as well give up trying and let us get on with the job. So for that matter, might the weather."

Yet despite the damp and chill of the late November day some two hundred and fifty members turned out, a lot more than had applied for lunch tickets, but somehow all were fed. The range and interest of their cars was considerable. Bentleys, Alvises, and Sunbeams galore were joined by a 1910 Rolls-Royce Silver Ghost saloon (which had not just come to watch, but to compete) a 1914 TT Sunbeam, an 18/80 MG (approved of by Clutton as one of the best MGs ever produced) a range of vintage Alfas and Marcus Chambers – by then involved with racing for the team – in a streamlined HRG.

The two tests were simple; the first a matter of acceleration forward to a line, back to another and then forward again to the first, while the second involved reversing in and out of three bays arranged alongside one another. In the days before supermarkets, and more in tune with the lifestyle of the majority of members, this became known as the pub car park test. These completed, and well and truly soaked, all then repaired to the National Rifle Association's pavilion for tea, after which Harry Bowler's wife presented the prizes …. in keeping with the straightened times these being food parcels from Australia. Clark in an HRG and Richardson in a Bentley were the class winners on this occasion.

The bi-annual gatherings at Bisley continued until 1952, when inexplicably the Ministry of Defence decided that the damage done by sundry vintage cars was making the tracks too difficult for the tanks. Whatever the real reason behind the decision the last

Bisley took place that February, to be replaced by driving test meetings on a variety of sites scattered across the southern counties.

A different sort of rally took place in the spring following the first Bisley. The Eastbourne Rally was modelled on such pre-war events as the Bournemouth, Southport, Brighton and Blackpool rallies, which in turn reflected their origins in the Monte Carlo event. On a March Saturday in 1947 competitors completed their road sections from varied starting points (some had come from Carlisle) to reach the first control just outside Lewes. Here they undertook an acceleration test over 300 yards. One of the last to arrive was a 1911 Model 60 Stanley steam car, driven by L Taylor, who was to make a very impressive if cloudy run. The route then continued over a steep observed section, which stopped several cars, until the second control, on the sea front at Eastbourne, was reached and where competitors were welcomed by local dignitaries, pleased that the rally might raise the profile of their resort. Saturday evening was given over to dinner and dancing at various hotels or the cleaning and polishing of cars in anticipation of the Concours d'Elegance to be held on the sea front next morning. Participation in this did not require that one had also to complete the road sections, though one could enter both. Following the Concours (the Edwardian Section was won by S E Sears' 1912 Rolls-Royce and the Vintage Section by W Stout's 1927 Bentley) the rally competitors then made their way to the Slow-Fast Test on a short hill nearby. Having covered 100 yards as slowly as possible and then accelerating to cover a similar distance in as short a time as possible, marks were scored on the basis of the difference between the times. (The slow-fast test was next to be used at the first of the Madresfield meetings that was to take place later in that same year and where it has become enshrined as an almost compulsory element of the Worcestershire gatherings. Its first appearance seems to have been at the Bisley meeting in the summer of 1946). The Mayor then entertained the VSCC Committee members and their wives to lunch while the final results for the combined Rally and Concours were calculated. These showed a 1911 Rolls-Royce driven by M Alderson to have won the Edwardian Section (the Stanley steamer came third) and C Slater's 1930 Alvis to have been the best vintage entry.

Despite all those involved – the hosts in Eastbourne and the visiting motorists from afar – confirming their enjoyment of the event and expressing hopes for a repeat of the same in future years, this never came to be. Perhaps the format of the long road sections, assembly at some seaside resort and driving tests to provide the main competitive element had simply run its course. The Motor Cycling Club was to find the same when its series of similar but more energetic rallies became unviable in the mid 1950s.

After the exceptionally harsh winter of 1946/47 the trials season stuttered into life. The first event, held close to Bisley in March, was run through melting snow and floods with J Dyer's Riley heading the small field. A later trial held in April in Surrey fared rather better, though Gibbons, competing in a Speed 20 Alvis, would probably have preferred to forget the day. On a hillside section, well provided with trees, he became so entangled with one of these that it had to be cut down before he could be released. Further north conditions remained harsher and for longer. On the due date of the Buxton Trial (9th March) the whole area was under such deep snow that the RAF had to be called in to drop food supplies to cut-off villages, but the re-scheduled date of 13th April proved to be a delightful spring day. However, there were only three entrants. Undeterred they set out with Ashton on a 3-litre Bentley beating a 1929 Riley 9. The third entrant, in a supercharged Lea Francis, had fuel feed problems and could not be classified.

All was to be different on 22nd June – when the first of the long and still ongoing series of Madresfield Rallies (so named in 1947) took place. Before the war the mile long and ruler straight undulating drive leading up to Madresfield Court had been used by a variety of clubs for sprints. A few miles south west of Worcester, in a delightful pastoral setting and framed by the outline of the Malvern Hills beyond, the VSCC Committee had high hopes for the venue. In the summer of 1946 Anthony Heal and Harry Bowler were despatched to Worcestershire to inspect the drive, returning to report that while no longer suitable for speed events it would however make a good place to finish a rally – conditional upon the approval of the Earl of Beauchamp.

From the start this has been an event organised by local members with John Rowley, who was to become the first Secretary of the Midlands Section and later the Club President, overseeing that first day at Madresfield. There were thirty-two entrants, the field dominated by Frazer Nash with a dozen such cars, boasting a variety of engines. The largest and oldest vehicle taking part was the 1908 Itala driven by Dr Gerald Ewen with 12000cc at his disposal, while the smallest was the 747cc Austin of D L Dixon. The morning was given over to the Concours d'Elegance; Lady Beauchamp judged the coachwork, while mechanical aspects were appraised by Messrs Badgery and Goodall. Marks up to 10 could be awarded, the highest score going to P R John's Frazer Nash, while the lowest score at just a single mark was awarded to Finnemore's Nash. If perhaps Finnemore spent a shame-faced lunch time tidying his car he must have been cheered in the afternoon when he narrowly beat John on the driving tests.

Madresfield traditions were established early on. The two tests in that initial year comprising an acceleration blast over 200 yards and a Slow-Fast test of 200 yards at the slowest possible speed and then 75 yards at the fastest. Over the years increasing concerns with safety, articulated by various RAC and Motor Sports Association regulations, have clipped the wings of the acceleration test but the slow-fast test remains virtually unscathed, as do the lunch time picnics, which nowadays are unrestrained by the rationing considerations that were in force in 1947.

Although the oldest car taking part, and indeed the only Edwardian, the Itala was the clear and outright winner. The Vintage class was won by Sprague in a 1925 Daimler with the (then so named) Modern class by Miller in a 1938 Alvis.

Gransden Lodge – July 1947

In the immediate post war years there was much enthusiasm, rather less petrol and an even greater paucity of venues for speed events. February 1946 saw *Motor Sport* carry its obituary for Brooklands, Bill Boddy writing, "one of the saddest announcements we have ever made is that Brooklands is no more". The decision had been taken to turn it into an industrial development area. It took until 1953 before circuit racing returned to Crystal Palace while Donington, which had been used as a military vehicle park during the war, despite the Herculean efforts of Tom Wheatcroft, was not to re-open for racing until 1977. Boddy's pessimism, expressed in the April edition of *Motor Sport*, made no mention of circuit racing. "Certainly there is plenty to discuss in respect of 1946, even if in the end nothing much happens …. personally we shall not be surprised to see only one Shelsley and Prescott occur with of course lesser sprints at Bristol, Dancers End and possibly Bo'ness..."

However, he had not reckoned on the vision and confidence of the Cambridge University Automobile Club (CUAC) who were to run the first post-war race meeting in England on 15th June 1946, with some support from the VSCC, which was one of the invited clubs. On a circuit of just over 2 miles this was held on the runways and perimeter track of Gransden, an Air Ministry airfield in Cambridgeshire. The eleven race meeting of short scratch races took place in what seemed to be the usual summer conditions of the time; it poured with rain. The "paddock" was located in an empty aircraft hanger where it was at least dry, if incredibly noisy and filled with fumes. Despite a few hiccups the meeting was well organised and, despite the weather, fairly well attended.

The auguries for more racing in 1947 looked no better, but in March that year a party of VSCC members had motored up to Cambridge to show their motor cars to some of the keener members of the CUAC. These included such gems as Heal's 3-litre Sunbeam, Rodney Clarke's type 57s Bugatti – with Clutton's type 49 to keep it company – and Bob Ewen in the Itala. Chattering away the CUAC contingent, led by its undergraduate spokesman David Hodkin, expressed the hope that they might be able to obtain the use of Gransden for another year, so it did not take long for the VSCC to agree that to try and organise a joint meeting would make good sense for all involved. The arrangement settled on was that the university group would be responsible for the physical work in setting out the course, while the VSCC would take on the administration and paperwork. In the event it drew the shorter straw.

During March the two organising groups had met, finalised their arrangements and applied to the RAC for a permit. The RAC required confirmation that the Air Ministry (which was responsible for the airfield) had agreed, but this permission took rather a long time to obtain. Meanwhile the Regulations were printed and entries – oversubscribed by 100% – flowed in. Then on 1st July, with less than a fortnight to go until the event, the bomb was dropped by a group opposing the meeting. Clutton referred to them as the "Works and Bricks" people, who seemed to be an amalgam of several organisations opposed to motor sport generally and particularly so on Sundays and whom had been taken somewhat off-guard by the 1946 meeting. This group pointed out that, although under Air Ministry control, the airfield was in fact owned by six separate landowners from whom the site had been requisitioned. Without their formal written approval "Works and Bricks" would sue. The addresses of these landowners, scattered across the country, having been obtained from the Air Ministry, Hodkin and Clutton set out to contact them all. On Thursday 3rd July and against incredible odds they actually succeeded. The Clutton Bugatti did nearly 300 miles in the day, inclusive of chasing a Fordson tractor across the landscape to obtain a signature from a startled farmer, while having achieved its tasks for the day shortly afterwards it broke a half-shaft, no doubt to gain its breath. The youthful Hodkin delivered the signatures to the Air Ministry at 6.30pm and the next morning the Competitions Department of the RAC received its written consent that the meeting could indeed go ahead. But the "Works and Bricks" people had not quite had their say. In the week leading up to the event both the CUAC and VSCC teams were busy at Gransden, preparing for the meeting, when a letter reached the Clerk of Works in charge. This pointed out that although permission to hold the event had been given this did not include permission to use the water and power on site. These were both turned off on the Wednesday. Fortunately the joint clubs had some friends in high places so that a letter of approval from no less a personage than the Secretary of State for Air was received shortly afterwards, and after a nail-biting ten days, it was at last certain that the meeting could go ahead. David Hodkin, strongly supported by Sam Clutton and the Carsons at the VSCC office (where a huge volume of "on-off" publicity material and correspondence had needed to be prepared) had between them saved the day.

The August edition of *Motor Sport* carried a glowing report, its opening paragraph summing up the day:

> "The thanks of all enthusiasts who gathered at Gransden Lodge airfield on July 13th are due to the CUAC and VSCC for the splendid circuit racing witnessed here. In general the organisation was excellent while what more could one want than the ten races on the programme which comprised a 20 lap "Formula Libre" scratch race for the *Motor* £100 prize and the Gransden Trophy, a 10 laps scratch race for vintage racing cars, scratch races for vintage cars and unblown sports cars, two short handicaps, an Edwardian handicap, handicaps for Bentley and Bugatti cars and the first race for the 500cc Club cars. The rain kept off, the scores of voluntary helpers worked hard and effectively and no accidents marred the racing. Certainly David Hodkin and Cecil Clutton deserve the warmest congratulations and their respective clubs deserve to prosper. Some 15,000 people attended. Would that we in England could have this kind of racing every Bank Holiday, instead of once a year."

Three of the races directly involved VSCC entrants, with the 5 lap Edwardian handicap the first of these. The handicapper had done an excellent job for the limit man – C Abbot in a 1904 ex Brooklands Mercedes – only just held off the scratch man – Peter Clark in a 1914 Mercedes – with Ewen in the Itala close behind. The 5 lap scratch race for vintage sports cars attracted a good field, inclusive of three Vauxhalls, three Frazer Nash and a pair of Bentleys. Alan May's 1924 30-98 Vauxhall led the way from Mackie's 1930 Talbot with Forrest Lycett third in his 1930 4½-litre Bentley. The vintage racing cars then enjoyed a 10 lapper for the 1908 GP Itala Cup. This had recently been presented to the Club by R Wil-de-Gose who had raced the car successfully when they had both been in their youth. Despite strong opposition Habershon's 1927/37 GP Delage, a car which used parts from the Seaman car and a chassis frame built for the Princes Bira and Chula, although only fifth away from the start was soon in front to stay there, beating Jack Fairman's Bugatti and Marechal's Bentley. Habershon was enjoying a good season in this car, for at the Prescott meeting held soon afterwards, he again was the winner – in both the Open and Vintage classes. The main race of the day at Gransden was to be won by R D Poore in his 3.8-litre 8C-35 Alfa-Romeo closely chased throughout by George Abecassis in a T59 GP Bugatti, while the ERAs of Harrison and Heath languished much further down the field. Salvadori, troubled by locking brakes, was third in a Tipo B 2.9-litre Alfa-Romeo.

In the background, but crucial to this notable day, were the Air Ministry and Bomber Command who gave enormous assistance throughout, lending moral support as well as equipment and providing a fire tender and medical personnel. All went home happy after the only mainland race meeting of the year while the Flood Victims Relief Fund – the charity that Bomber Command had chosen to benefit from the meeting – was sent a cheque for five hundred guineas from the proceeds.

Vintage Prescott was to follow at the end of August, with the Habershon Delage to the fore, but close behind it in the up to 2 racing car class came Bruce Spollon (later to become President of the Club) in the 1925 Triangle Special. The winner of the racing car class of over 2-litres was Peter J Stubberfield in his Type 35B Bugatti, who was later to make such a huge impact at Vintage Prescotts with an unbeaten record of wins – except at the single meeting of 1951 – in every year from 1949 to 1957. At this stage the car was a two-seater, which not long afterwards was converted to its well known "monoposto" form.

Contemporary magazine reports of these meetings make no mention of the background against which they had taken place. 1947 had been a drab, dull and difficult year with the country struggling to recover from the physical and financial consequences of the war. Shortages of virtually every kind held back recovery while it had even become necessary to ration potatoes as, in the incredibly harsh winter, a high proportion of those in store had rotted in the cold. At least the basic petrol ration had allowed for some pleasure motoring to take place and Gransden and Prescott had lifted some of the gloom; that is until November when even that had to be withdrawn.

There is a natural resilience about the Vintage Sports-Car Club which was shown at the Annual General Meeting held at Heal's restaurant in early December. Determined to look forward to happier and more expansive times it voted to become a Limited Liability Company. This required that it had a Company Secretary, which allowed Tim Carson to be appointed at a salary that more closely matched the considerable amount of work that he already undertook on behalf of the Club. Forrest Lycett, after ten years of hard work and generous support, stood down as President and Laurence Pomeroy, motoring journalist of repute, took over in his place. Due to a technicality the registration of the Club as a Limited Liability Company was delayed for a couple of months and it required an extra meeting in February 1948 to re-visit the agenda and re-pass all the various motions involved. Those who attended were rewarded for their commitment by some excellent ham sandwiches, the ham kindly provided, in those austere times, by the Sports-Car Club of America. There were nearly 900 members at this time, of whom two thirds were Driving (ie Vintage) members.

Luton Hoo – March 1948

If the VSCC is resilient it can also be obstinate and despite the lack of petrol for any form of recreational motoring a determination to run a speed event early in 1948 emerged. The horse racing fraternity – which remarkably and in the face of considerable opposition, had continued to run race meetings throughout the war – realised that while one could not obtain petrol to allow one to attend a recreational gathering at a race course it was still possible to obtain a business petrol allowance to attend a nearby horse sale. A car auction was accordingly arranged in the confines of Luton Hoo, where, on Sir Harold Wernher's estate near Luton, the drive had been used for speed events on and off since 1908.

The course chosen was unusual and potentially very fast; just under one and a half miles long on a "there and nearly back" basis. Downhill from the start it crossed what was to be the finish line on the return, curved round right to go uphill to a turning point, where competitors went clockwise around a large yellow painted oil drum in the middle of the road, then back down the hill again to reach the finish. The majority of entrants for the speed event arrived on the Sunday afternoon, following the car auction that had taken place at noon that day. *Motor Sport* reported a 1920 23/60 Vauxhall selling for £35, but that most cars offered failed to reach their reserves. The meeting had been organised for competition cars running on methanol ("dope") and thus not subject to the petrol restrictions. While no doubt a few used such fuel to reach the venue others came by train. The local motoring firm of Dunham & Haines, run by ex Brooklands driver C G Dunham, devised a special offer which included collecting competing cars from the railway station, towing them to and from the course – and housing them overnight if necessary. Others arrived behind a variety of tow cars, the police taking an assiduous interest in these, as well as in spectators' cars, looking for any evidence of fuel use transgressions. As Bill Boddy was to comment:

> "Every Trade Plate in the land must surely have been at Luton Hoo, so some people were privileged to spectate unmolested."

The Club had received 130 entries for the meeting but limited itself to just half of these. It is estimated that 12,000 spectators turned out to watch on that Bank Holiday Monday, those not able to come by car arriving by train and coach in the town, and then by special service buses to the course. Although there were no specifically Edwardian or Vintage classes (it was an open meeting promoted by the Club in aid of the National Institute for the Blind) many of its familiar driver-car combinations took part, with Bolster – as so often was the case – putting up the best vintage time. Bob Gerard, by then emerging as one of the most polished and rapid British drivers, put up fastest time of the day in his ERA.

In three successive years, especially so by its organisation of the 1946 Elstree speed trials, the 1947 Gransden Lodge race meeting and the 1948 Luton Hoo sprint, all against the odds, the Vintage Sports-Car Club had shown that it was one of the brightest stars in the motor sporting firmament. The close knit hierarchy and determined and audacious personalities that made up the Committee had carried it forward in a manner that few outside the Club would have believed to have been even remotely possible.

Growth and Development

With membership approaching a thousand the Club had continued to grow and recognising the need for a market place the following notice was circulated to members late in 1947:

> Vintage Sports Car Exchange
> "The Club has decided to open an exchange for its members. It is hoped that this will enable those with the vintage sports car at heart either to find a good home for a trusty steed that they wish to sell, or to satisfy

their craving for vintage ironmongery if they wish to buy. Cars for sale and wanted would be registered and prospective buyers and sellers put in touch. Any cars not sold, or wants unsatisfied, would be advertised in a circular to all members at frequent intervals.

The plot is as follows:-

1. Cars to be registered when available. Fee 7/6d (seven shillings and six pence) giving type, body, engine capacity and HP, year, history and price asked

2. Prospective buyers would be supplied with a list of cars available (fee 7/6d) (seven shillings and six pence) of the types required. If none available, their want would be registered until further notice.

3. VSCC members would be supplied with a duplicated list, to be sent out at frequent intervals, of cars available and wanted. Insertions in this list would not involve any further charge.

The charge is made to cover costs only and will be subject to revision when the response to the scheme is known.

The above is only a starting point, as it is hoped shortly to enlarge the scheme to include spares.

All communications about the above scheme should be addressed to:

J M Hill,
28, St. Philip's Avenue,
Wolverhampton,
Staffs

Who has kindly offered to handle it."

Max Hill was a stalwart of the Club, owning and competing in a wide range of cars over the years; this family tradition still continued by his son Keith Hill and granddaughter Susan. A keen photographer, his stills and cine films provide an informed insight into Club events of the 1950s and 60s.

Renaissance

A few extracts from the December 1947 Exchange List give an idea of the market place at that time.

> Riley Special. Redwing chassis. 2 seater aluminium body. Alvis 12/50 engine. 2 SUs Nash clutch. Riley 4 speed gearbox. £160
>
> Vulcan 1912 2 seater. Good condition. Believed genuine mileage 5000. Good tyres £100
>
> 38/250 Mercedes Benz 55 blown 2 seater. 1930 7.1-litres. Mileage 45,800. 5 new tyres. 2 spares. New hood. hc pistons. First class mechanical condition. Over 100 mph. Any trial. £850
>
> Frazer Nash TT replica. 2 seater. 1½-litre. 11.9 hp. 1933. Offers only £450

The Riley was offered for sale by Tim Carson, who continued to trade from his home near Basingstoke. Tyres often featured in his advertisements, new, re-treaded and second hand, while for a short time, he offered model cars in kit form for sale. The Sports Car Exchange lasted rather better than the model cars, going on for many years until eventually it was absorbed into the Club's *Newsletter*.

The loss of the basic petrol allowance made it difficult for members to continue to meet for what *The Bulletin* had once named "Pint and Prattle Parties", and in particular for the first Thursday of each month gatherings at the Phoenix. Ever resolute the Club responded by making arrangements for a coach to carry members from London to what was defined as the *alma mater* of the Club. Even the then President, known for his fine tastes in everything inclusive of cars, food and wine, was persuaded to join the coach party one evening. As Clutton reported;

> "I see" said President Pomeroy on entering one of these conveyances for the first time in his life "that the Lower Orders travel in very good style," whereupon grasping his Fortnum & Mason hamper on one hand a bottle of Claret in the other, he sank contentedly among the luxurious seats of the conveyance. "But if only we could have one without the wireless."

Further away from the then heartland of the Club the Sections continued to organise their own social gatherings; Northern, Midlands and Border Sections being in existence at this time. A huge sigh of relief was to go up from all of them when in June 1948 the basic petrol ration was restored – although greatly reduced from its former level.

The First Silverstones

By the late 1940s some of what were to become the staple elements in the Club's calendar had begun to emerge. With Prescott and Madresfield now established Silverstone was next to join them as a fixture. The RAC operated the ex-bomber airfield for the first three years of its life as a racing venue, and after the inaugural British Grand Prix of 1948, the VSCC became the first club to use it for competitive events, organising a straight line sprint on a central runway on April 23rd 1949. The first two thirds of the kilometre were gently uphill, the cars running in pairs. Forrest Lycett, now retired from the Presidency, opened the course in his 8-litre Bentley, blowing away the dust that had settled on the car over nine years of largely enforced rest. His time of 29.69 secs and his finishing speed of 115 mph were barely exceeded by a handful of competitors. Peter Stubberfield's T35B Bugatti – that was to enjoy a long and distinguished run as a hill climb car – took 28.80 secs to cover the kilometre, beaten only by J B Norris in a 2-litre Alta on 28.43 secs, while Leslie Johnson, a respected racing driver of the era who drove the Lycett Bentley on the competitive runs, was fractionally slower than the owner's course opening time, taking 29.73 secs. Not unsurprisingly for an April day at Silverstone it was rather cold, but despite being generally deemed a success it was to be the only such Silverstone Sprint held by the Club, for in the following year it was replaced by one of two Club race meetings then held on the circuit. But before this, back in early July 1949, the Club's first Silverstone race meeting had taken place. The circuit ran along the centre runway from Stowe to Copse, then along the perimeter track back to Stowe. The large entry of 170 cars between them had to tackle practice, ten races, and a one hour "high speed trial"; and somehow all these activities were squeezed into a single day. The one hour "high speed trial" was Rivers Fletcher's brain child and required that competitors had to complete a target number of laps within the hour, inclusive of two stops – one to make a wheel change and the other to change a plug. J C Dancer in a very well prepared vintage Morris Minor was unlucky to not quite make his targeted 20 laps within the hour, while in the unlimited capacity class W A L Cook, in a Bentley, had over three minutes in hand, for by fifty-eight minutes he had completed his two pit stops and the required 25 laps of the 2¼ mile circuit.

The races themselves were, with one exception, over four laps. These saw some stirring battles down the fields while, in the scratch race for unsupercharged sports cars, the real contest was for the lead. Symondson's T37S Bugatti scrapped with Newton's Bristol powered new High Speed Model Frazer Nash throughout – the older car narrowly winning. The eight lapper "main event" was for the "1908 GP Itala" Trophy, unfortunately marred by nine non-starters and two retirements from the nineteen entrants. J Habershon who, by a big margin, had earlier won the race for vintage supersports and racing cars in his GP Delage, likewise dominated the seven remaining survivors in the "Itala" race, during which he also made the fastest lap of the day.

He was not to do quite as well at the Prescott meeting that August which was won by Peter Stubberfield's Bugatti. John Bolster, who normally would have been expected to have been well in the running for fastest time of the day in "Mary" could not be present as he was still recovering from his horrific accident at that year's British Grand Prix. But a welcome return to Club activities was made by Tom Rolt, resplendent in a Panama hat, who had come to compete on the hill in one of his two Alvises.

While the 1948 speed event at Luton Hoo had proved such a notable success in overcoming the lack of a basic fuel allowance it had also allowed the Club to enjoy by far the best sprint course it had yet been able to use. It was wide, well surfaced and smooth and, but for the oil-drum "hairpin" turnabout, provided a series of fast open curves over its one and a half mile length. The day of the 1949 sprint started wet but improved, as did the times. Notable runs included that by Duncan Hamilton, always a forceful driver, who left the course in his Maserati, dodged behind several trees and in re-gaining the road cut down all the telephone lines carefully put in place by the organisers. Tony Rolt was a little less exciting in a supercharged Alfa Romeo, its engine half of the legendary Bimotore, while Dennis Poore, later to make such a big impression on the national hill climb scene, was likewise Alfa Romeo mounted and fastest of all in the unofficial run-offs that concluded the meeting. However, the competition proper was won by Peter Walker in an ERA, while Stubberfield's was the fastest vintage car.

A sad accident had occurred in practice when the very popular Ken Jarvis, who competed in a supercharged single seater 750cc Austin, hit a tree at speed and was killed instantly. Despite the excellence of the course in terms of width and road surface, Luton Hoo was a strong reminder that motor racing is indeed dangerous, the very fast course lined with substantial trees and metal railings being particularly hazardous. But attitudes to such safety considerations were somewhat different in 1949 and fatalities often greeted with a shrug of shoulders but little more. The familiarity with sudden death remained a legacy of the war and did not perhaps have the impact that it has today. Dangers apart, this was to be the last Luton Hoo meeting. Spectator numbers had been down on the previous year and, with permission no longer forthcoming to use the course in the future, it joined the growing list of VSCC speed event venues that had been used for just a year or two before sinking into oblivion.

Mainly Madresfield

Earlier in the year had come a rather gentler event which has certainly not disappeared from sight – the annual Madresfield Rally as it was then described, settling down to its place in the Club's year. "The best of our semi-social occasions" according to *The Bulletin*, it attracted "just the right number of entrants – thirty five – including Edwardians, Vintage and Post Vintage." The Brooklands slogan of "the right crowd and no crowding" was living on. The standards in the Concours, won by Edgar's immaculate green 1932 Alvis, were very high that year – the judges working hard to determine the right

Madresfield 1951. With a great mechanical future obviously ahead of her, a little girl gives her considered advice to those repairing the front spring on J V H Lumsden's 1910 Rolls-Royce.

balance they should reward between original condition and perfect restoration. The number of tests had gone up to four. The first was the familiar slow-fast, the outstanding performance being that of Skinner's Rolls-Royce which averaged just 1.2 mph on the slow section, which was slightly downhill at that. As *The Bulletin* observed:

> "one or two people thought they would be clever and protract their slow-running time by tacking, which was not at all the point of the exercise, and it really will be tiresome if we have to start tightening up regulations for informal events of this kind to outwit pot-hunting efforts by crafty customers."

They have of course needed to be tightened up considerably over the passing years. *"O tempora! O mores!"*

A reversing test, parking by a kerb against the clock and the final blast of 200 yards acceleration made up the quartet of tests. Combined with the Concours competitors then had to chose which four of the five should count towards their final score.

Milner, in a big Benz:

> "had very firmly got hold of the notion that the thing which counted was *speed*. Thus while his efforts did not collect him many marks they were very enjoyable to watch, and he was obviously enjoying himself too, so everyone was perfectly happy. Milner was first away in the acceleration test which he accomplished in the remarkable time of 12.2 secs. He then continued accelerating briskly over the next hill – and over the next hill – and out of sight for good – and we never saw him again. Presumably he must have slowed before reaching the Park Gates and main road as there was no evidence of terrain having suffered any unusual violence."

At the end of the June day, when the marks were totted up, A W Showell in a Sunbeam was found to have won the Edwardian Class, J Jane in a Lancia the Vintage Class and Dr D P Harris (the brake and gear levers of his Frazer Nash drilled for lightness) the Post Vintage Class.

The competition year concluded up in Yorkshire with the Nidderdale Trial, starting at Pateley Bridge. This was at a time when interest in trialling was at a relatively low ebb within the Club with only thirteen of the fifteen entries turning out for this "follow my leader" trial. Jane, whose 1923/25 Lancia Lambda had done so well at Madresfield, was again on good form losing no marks at all, despite boiling on the long steep climb of Lofthouse Bank. He had also been quick on the test immediately before lunch, held in the main street of Pateley Bridge. Times have indeed changed. Deservedly Jane was to win the Lycett Trophy for 1949.

Racing in the Early Fifties

The next five years were times of immense change and of rapid growth for the Club, seeing significant development on virtually every front. These took place against, and partly because of, a background of sustained economic growth within the country and the western world, both picking up speed after the not so distant world war. Petrol rationing had come to an end in May 1950, while the 1951 Festival of Britain had been designed to create an atmosphere of optimism and new beginnings after years of privation. The climbing of Everest and the Coronation of Queen Elizabeth II in 1953 chimed in with the feelings of a new age, while the abolition of the last of rationing in 1954 confirmed that the recent past could at last be put behind. The time to

Renaissance

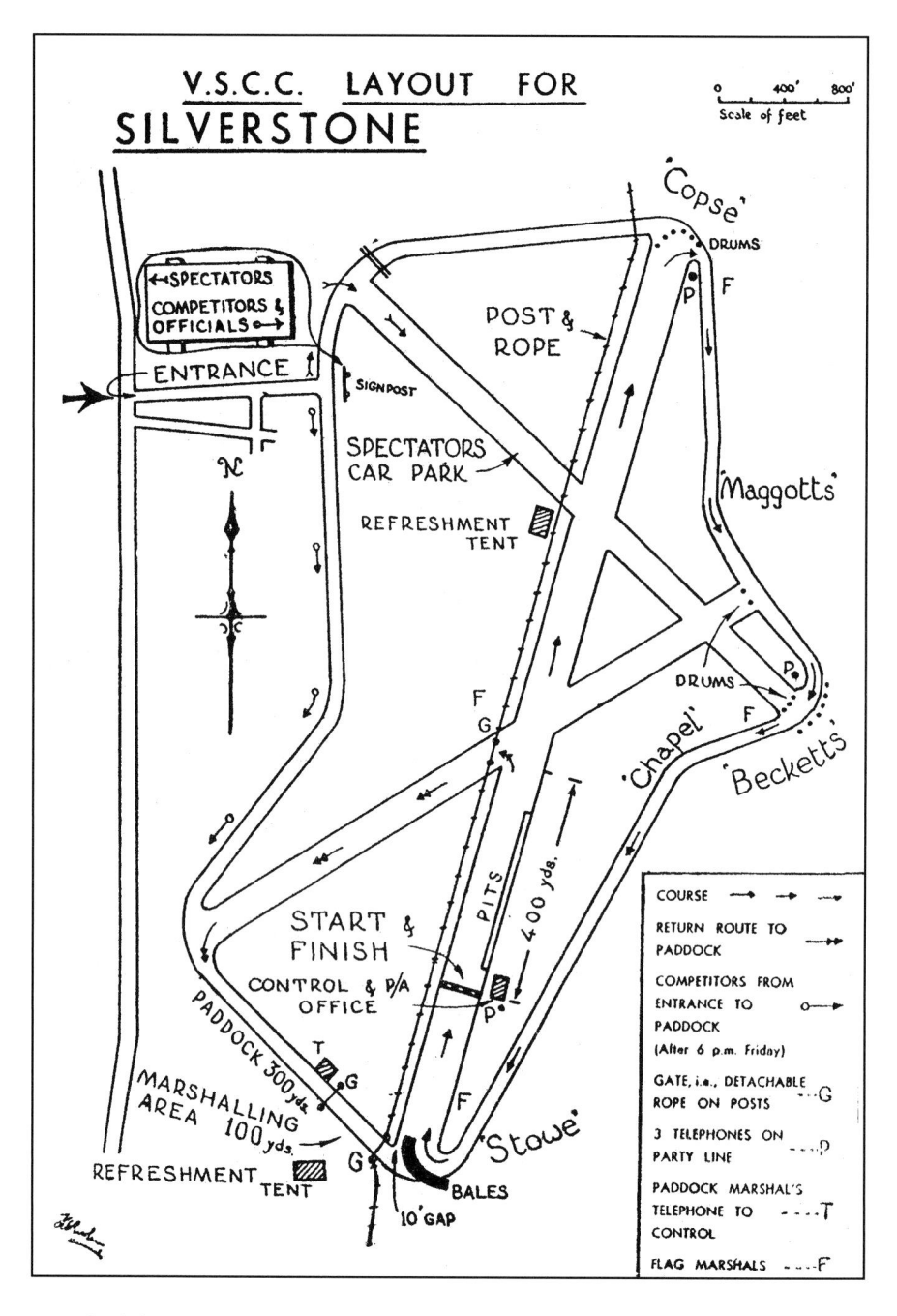

The original Club circuit at Silverstone as used in 1950. Woodcote, un-named on the plan, then provided the way into a circuit, on which drums and straw bales marked the outsides of corners. Three telephones on a party line linked the flag marshals stations, while the "gate" onto the main straight from the spectators area was simply a "detachable rope on posts". In 1952 the Club circuit was to be significantly revised, turning right at Becketts onto the old runway down to Woodcote, with the pits re-located along the straight to Copse.

move forward was at hand and the Club was ready for innovation and expansion. With Pomeroy in the third year of his Presidency, Carson well established as Secretary, Clutton still editing *The Bulletin* and with some 1250 members on the books in the spring of 1950 it was well positioned to do so.

For the first few years of the 1950s VSCC motor racing simply meant Silverstone, where two meetings were held each year; with Prescott as the only non-circuit speed event. A remarkably high proportion of the membership went racing at this time, about 300 doing so in 1950 from a total membership of 1255 as reported at the AGM that year – ie nearly 20%. Motor racing was so much more accessible in those optimistic days, no crash hats nor flameproof overalls required, with scrutineering requirements similarly relaxed. Given a reasonable sports car in reasonable condition one needed little more than enthusiasm and an entry fee to be able to compete.

A new trophy had been presented to the Club that April, which Dick Seaman had won by coming third in the 1938 Donington Grand Prix. It was to be competed for by those in the new class of historic racing cars now admitted to the Club's events, thus ERAs and their contemporaries could now come to the grid once they were fifteen years old, but they had to wait until July before they could do so.

In April the first of the two Silverstones was held, with practice on the Friday evening and Saturday morning before the event proper. The weather was awful but a programme of short scratch races and handicaps went ahead inclusive of the popular one hour High Speed Trial. The meeting even incorporated a half-mile sprint with Stubberfield's Bugatti and Clutton's 12 cylindered 10688cc Delage (jointly owned with Forrest Lycett and in beautiful condition) winning their classes while Heyward, in his 1½-litre Norris Special, was quickest of them all. In July the weather was far better, albeit Clutton's Delage and Ewen's Itala were off form, so of the vintage racing cars Rowley's 1927 GP Delage was able to win the Itala Trophy, with Byrom's 1930 T35B Bugatti behind.

The first of the series of Seaman Trophy races was held over 100 kms and turned out to be an excellent race, with George Hartwell's 1½-litre ERA R2A beating Rowland Dutt's 2.6-litre Maserati by a small margin, with the latter making fastest lap. The vintage class was won by Pitt's 4½-litre Bentley. The other named race of the day, the Itala Trophy, was at first led by Byrom's T35B Bugatti until magneto trouble started to slow him, enabling John Rowley on his GP Delage to get by. The remainder of the

Silverstone. May 1954. The Le Mans type start of the one hour High Speed trial has got underway. A T Pugh (1928 1496cc Frazer Nash) scrambles aboard No 17, while alongside Flt/Lt J L Rees (1927 1645cc Alvis) reaches for the starter. In the background L J (Lou) Wickham (1929 Alvis 1496cc) is setting off in No 15. He was to campaign this car in all types of Club events for some forty years.

programme was made up of the usual mixture of short scratch and handicap races, inclusive of one for the Edwardians. This was won by a 1913 Lanchester, exhibiting huge body roll on the corners. The Itala, cornering more as racing cars should do, was over-handicapped and out of the running.

The following year, 1951, saw the sun shine on both the Silverstone meetings with challenging targets set for the May meeting's High Speed Trial. Only 18 out of 45 starters qualified, some having been delayed by the Le Mans start, at which not all of those without starter motors managed to turn their starting handles fast enough to make quick get-aways. In June there was disappointment at the low level of entries of older cars, and especially so in the Edwardian class. Even the Itala Trophy had a poor

And a few laps later. A T Pugh is back in the pits for his compulsory tyre change; the spare wheel is still on the counter, while one of his two mechanics prepares to slide the jack under the car.

entry, the historic section being won by R D Poore's Alfa Romeo 8C 35, while Clutton in the Land Speed Record Delage was best of the vintage entries. The last race of the day provided much entertainment for competitors and spectators alike – being a 12 lap relay race. Each team was made up of three cars, each of which was required to do four laps, the handicaps for the team being based on the anticipated performance of its fastest car. At the pit stops the team's sash had to be passed from one car to the other and Plowman having dropped his sash went back to collect it. Others having mislaid sashes substituted pocket handkerchiefs, but no one seemed to mind.

1952 saw the introduction of a new Club circuit at Silverstone – which was to be used with little alteration into the 1970s – and was marked by the high level of involvement in hands-on motor racing as shown by Committee members, for Bowler, Clutton, Ewen, Neve and Rowley all competed. And for the first time all of them had to wear crash helmets, for these had become compulsory at the start of the season. However, such protection was combined with a variety of clothing; sports jackets, ties, pullovers and even macintoshes being worn on the grid that damp day. Four abreast on the grids, that for the Itala Trophy comprised Jack Williamson (4½-litre Bentley) Jim Byrom (T35B Bugatti) Sam Clutton (LSR Delage) and Jack Sears (1914 TT Sunbeam). Byrom was very much on form, leading off the start and winning by the big margin of 44 secs over the 10 laps, with Clutton in second place.

Come July, Silverstone again played host to the VSCC with the Seaman Trophy being run over 100 km. Dennis Poore in his potent Alfa started favourite, but was given a very good run for his money by Graham Whitehead in ERA R8B, who briefly got ahead at one stage. Another ERA (R1B) was to finish 3rd in the hands of C J Hamilton who had climbed up the field profiting from various retirements ahead of him.

What the well dressed racing driver should wear. Sam Clutton prepares to race the 1923 V12 10½ litre Delage in the second of the two Silverstone meetings held in 1952, the year in which crash helmets became compulsory. Clutton was to come second in the Itala Trophy that day, but later sustained burns when making his escape from the blazing car during the last race on the programme.

Race 9 was a 10 lap mixed handicap, running normally until Clutton was seen rushing down to Woodcote with long flames pouring out of the Delage's bonnet and licking around the cockpit. He had no hope of remaining in the cockpit and of braking the car, so he climbed out of his seat and clambered onto the tail, steering with an outstretched arm in an attempt to stop the Delage running amok. The car finally ploughed into an earth bank just before Woodcote, tossing its somewhat burnt and shaken driver off the tail but with relatively little damage to itself. The flames were extinguished, Clutton was taken to hospital (and later, and with no success, told to give up motor racing by his business colleagues) while almost un-noticed Graham Whitehead had caught up the field to win the handicap. A cylinder had come adrift on the Delage, it having sheared all its studs.

To cheer everyone up the last race of the day was just what was required, being another 12 lap team relay race. *The Bulletin* reported that:

"Those who watched this event from the control area were simultaneously thrilled, terrified and paralysed with mirth. The number of phenomenal avoidances was legion and it was a race in the truest sense, the Frazer Nash team driving with demonic fury to snatch the lead from the Bugatti team, to do which they had to wipe off a 36 second handicap. The 'Nash team used a bright golfing umbrella as pit signal and John Charnwood in …. the Delage wore his sash like a blue moustache. John Vessey's tyres shrieked with delight, the Arnold-Forster Nash recovered its form and was displaying unexpected understeer, and the spectators jumped up and down and clapped their hands and rolled on the ground with the ecstasy of it all."

The meetings in 1953 and 1954 were not quite as exciting. Byrom was to win the Itala Trophy in '53 but had to wait until 1955 before doing so again – albeit the intervening year saw another Bugatti victory, that of A F Eminson's type 37A winning. The Seaman Trophy of 1953 was well supported, the entries including the 4.9-litre Bugatti engined BHW that had done so well at Donington in the hands of Reg Parnell in 1939 – but gearbox troubles put an end to any such aspirations. For the second year running Poore's Alfa Romeo was just able to hold off the Graham Whitehead ERA, with J Williamson next up in R10B. Williamson was to win in 1954, followed to the line by Keith Schellenberg who, among other sporting activities in an adventurous life, had captained the British bobsleigh team at the Olympics. In 1953 Schellenberg had come second in the vintage category driving an 1100cc Riley but for 1954 he had moved steeply up the capacity scale by racing the 8-litre Bentley "Whale".

Renaissance

> *Headline in the business pages of the* Observer *from June 1954 as then reported in the* Newsletter.
>
> "The Dunlop Rubber Company. A year of solid achievement."

Away from the hurly-burly of Silverstone life was somewhat calmer; with hill-climbing providing a less hectic arena within which technique and specialist experience could support long runs of success. Between 1949 and 1957 Peter Stubberfield, in his 2.3-litre supercharged Bugatti, was virtually unbeatable at Prescott with, but one exception, making Fastest Time of the Day in the Vintage class at every single meeting. The exception was in 1951 when two meetings were held and at the second of these in September the fastest time was to go to Dr W A (Doc) Taylor in his Caesar Special. Stubberfield had however been fastest in both the Open and Vintage classes at the August meeting and thus could claim nine FTDs across nine years of competition on the Gloucestershire hill.

Some twelve years later Ron Footitt, in his 2-litre Cognac Special was to achieve an equally impressive run of success. Having been the fastest of the Vintage competition at the 1973, 1975 and 1977 Prescott meetings he then settled down to produce an unbroken run of Vintage FTDs from 1979–1986 inclusive.

A Growing Club

The first half of the 1950s was to see an unprecedented growth in Club activities and in membership numbers. Quite how Tim Carson and his wife Margery coped with the corresponding increase in their workload, working from their cottage on the outskirts of Newbury at this time, must remain a matter for conjecture and admiration, especially so as they combined this with a move from their earlier home near Basingstoke. There were 1140 members at the start of 1950. This had nearly doubled to 2000 during 1952 and was to nudge 2500 by the beginning of 1955. Alongside these increases were similar increases in the number of events being organised, many of which have since become icons in the Club calendar.

The 1949 calendar had comprised the two Silverstone meetings, the annual gathering at Prescott and the Luton Hoo sprint. Two Bisley rallies were also held, as was Madresfield, while further north the Nidderdale Trial was based on Pateley Bridge.

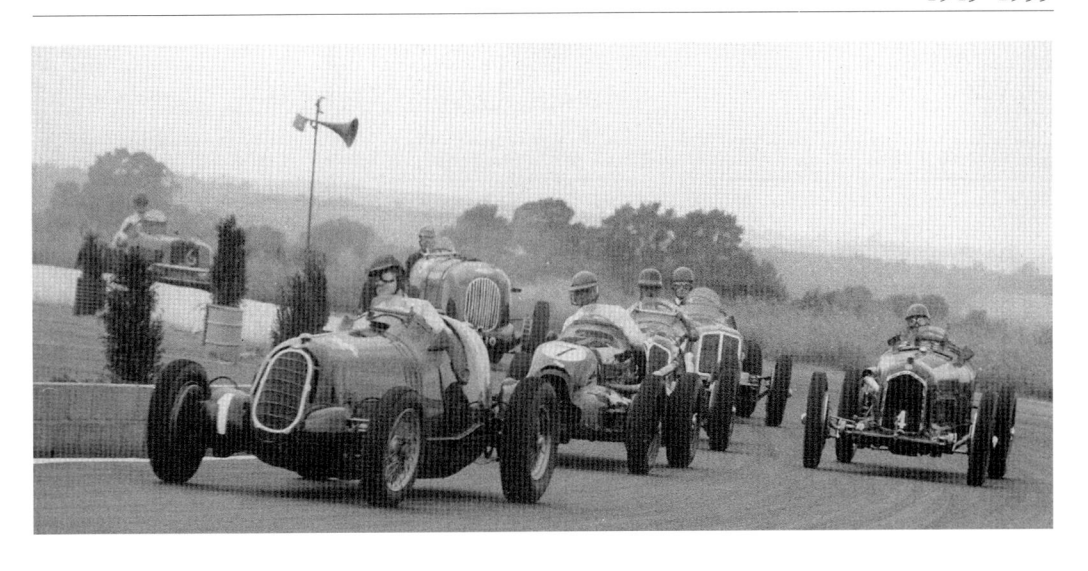

Quintessential Silverstone in the mid 1950s. Dennis Poore (3.8 litre Alfa Romeo) leads a group in the Historic Seaman Trophy. He is closely followed by Brian Shawe-Taylor (ERA R8C) and an unidentified Alfa Romeo P3, with the Bentley Barnato Hassan ("The Whale") pressing close behind. The race, won by H C Spero in a Maserati 8CM, was run on 6th August 1955 during the Club's second meeting of the year at the Northamptonshire circuit.

For 1955 the planned calendar was far more extensive:

January	Measham Rally
February	Slough Rally and Driving tests
March	Pomeroy Memorial Trophy
April	Northern Road Trial (Derbyshire)
April	Silverstone Race Meeting
June	Oulton Park Race Meeting
August	Silverstone Race Meeting
August	Edwardian and Light Car Rally
August	Prescott Hill Climb
September	Madresfield Rally
September	Concours d'Elegance (Goodwood)
October	Welsh Rally
November	Eastern Rally
November	Northern Trial
December	Southern Rally

And all of this for a subscription of just 25 shillings.

The Measham arrives. The 'Welsh' returns

Earliest of the new arrivals to join the 1950s calendars was that of the Measham Rally, first held on Sunday January 8th 1950, initially involving a fairly gentle format. Very much a Midland Section affair seven local motoring clubs had been invited to take part, among them the Hagley and District, which has a long standing relationship with the VSCC, inclusive of the Loton Park hill climb connection. Members from the invited clubs could still use modern cars on VSCC events at this time.

The first event comprised two parts; short regularity sections of 20 miles starting from one or other of points to the north and south of Measham (one of which was Reg Parnell's garage) followed by four driving tests on a hard surface. Vintage and Edwardian entrants were eligible for a bonus of one mark per year of age before 1930 while, as was the norm at the time, 3 wheelers were not eligible. The rally converged on the grounds of the Measham Motor Sales organisation, close to Burton-on-Trent, for the tests and where Dr D P Harris, a keen Frazer Nash exponent, had persuaded a supportive Mr G A Hill of the car sales organisation to allow competitors to use a large area of tarmac for the tests. One of these involved a two lap blind around the main sales building and quickly became known as the Measham Grand Prix. After completing the first lap a stop had to be made, driver and passenger had to leave the car and run around it, leap back in and complete the second lap. Overall the best performances at this inaugural Measham were made by P B Reece in a Riley and J L Snow in an MG, both taking home silver cups.

Perhaps the 20 mile road sections had been too short and too easy, but 1951 was to make up for this. Starting from Hawkstone Park near Shrewsbury, at 11.00pm on a foggy January night, the sixty entries (selected from over a hundred who had applied) faced a route of 183 miles, which was identified by six figure map references. These took competitors through a number of time controls and via a stop and re-start test on a particularly slippery hill, with the intention of getting them all to breakfast at Measham from 8.00am onwards. They were still trickling in two hours later.

No-one had achieved a clean sheet on what had been anticipated would be a relatively straight forward journey to the test site, where again four test were to be held. Thus its reputation as one of the more challenging events in the Club calendar had been quickly established. The route for 1952 went up to 200 miles and required six Ordnance Survey maps to cover it all while in 1954 it went up even more. Without really intending to do so John Rowley, the first Clerk of the Course, and Dr Harris, who had negotiated the site for the driving tests, had quickly established a Club classic.

Next of the "new" arrivals on the calendar – although more accurately it was a "revival" – came the Welsh Rally, returning to Presteigne after an absence of nearly twelve years in October 1950; and where, with scarcely a hiccup since, it happily continues to this day. The Supplementary Regulations for the revived event would have presented few surprises to those who had taken part in 1939. It was limited to four wheeled cars "manufactured before December 31st 1930" – thus PVT cars were excluded – as indeed they have been on the Reliability Trial element of all subsequent Welsh Trials. At the time authority certainly required more unquestioning acquiescence than it could expect to get away with today. Entries were limited to 50 and "the promoters" reserved the right "to refuse entries *without assigning a reason*" … a fairly common phrase in many such regulations of the time.

The event was run in four sections:

Section A	Rally	Vintage and Edwardian cars
Section B	Appearance Competition	Edwardian cars only
Section C	Hill Climbing Test	Edwardian cars only
Section D	Reliability Trial	Vintage cars only

The Rally again allotted marks on the basis of the mileages covered between 10am and 6pm on the Saturday to finish at the Radnor Arms in Presteign (such were the spellings in 1950), telegrams having to be sent to the Chief Marshal at the hotel to validate their routes. Bonus marks were allocated on the basis of age. On the Sunday morning the Edwardians were inspected for condition and originality, marks being given accordingly, and then off they went to the nearby Stapleton Hill to be timed over an unspecified distance on a gradient of one in six and allocated marks according to a handicap devised by Clutton. Meanwhile the Vintage contingent had time to either have a lie-in or to go to church on the Sunday morning, for their Reliability Trial did not start until "about 12 noon after the conclusion of the Hill Climbing Contest". They then had a course of about 35 miles to cover, during which they were required to ascend five observed sections, with the promise that "no chassis breaking sections will be included" and "in the opinion of the organisers the course is ideally suited to Vintage cars". At the start bonnet seals were attached and a penalty of 20 marks was to be exacted if these were broken. In comparison failure on an observed section only carried

Two aspects of the Welsh weekend in 1955. W L T (Leslie) Winder climbs Forest Hill in his 1924/28 1057cc Humber on the Reliability Trial as held for the Vintage entrants on the Sunday morning.

10 penalties, so no doubt those who liked to check oil levels or search for the causes of strange noises during an event were relieved when this requirement was dropped in subsequent years.

On the day several of the Edwardians struggled on Stapleton Hill but Pomeroy's Prince Henry Vauxhall romped up, with S J Skinner second fastest on an elegant 1910 Silver Ghost. They were eventually to go off with the top awards in the Edwardian class. Next the Vintage contingent had its turn on the hill where, despite some fast climbs by Bentleys and others, not many could beat Pomeroy's time. A crucial element seemed to have been the suitability of gear ratios for the short climb, for resultant speed was by no means matched to engine capacity in a number of cases. The rest of the Vintage route included a steep timed test at Discoed, a special test involving much to-ing and fro-ing across lines, and of course Smatcher. Despite the promises of the organisers the upper and steeper part of the hill proved very rough, a contemporary report recording

> "Aldridge made a fearless approach at almost reckless speed leaving the grand 30-98 to streak up the 1 in 2½ and leap from gulley to gulley in a series of frightening crashes."

While on the same morning, C J Bendall in his 1911 Rolls Royce Silver Ghost, makes a stately ascent of the timed Hill Climbing Test at Stapleton, as then held for Edwardian and the non-trialling Vintage entrants.

Renaissance

He was to win the Premier award. Then last of all came Stafford in an Invicta who:

> "got into an almost inextricable predicament. Having made an excellent start he ran out of petrol on the steeper part (autovac failure) and slid backwards and sideways, so that he ended up broadside with not an inch between his back and the bank; and his front and a precipice. A rope was tied to the tail and pulled by many spectators to prevent the car sliding forward and down the precipice, while others kicked and shoved the front bodily sideways till it was again pointing down the hill."

So trials have not changed that much over the years and yet the competitors still come back for more. After this particular Welsh (at that stage called the Presteign Rally by *The Bulletin*) competitors had plenty of time to return to the Radnor Arms for tea before setting out on their long journeys home. The format for the revived event had proved its worth and with only minor changes was to continue in this vein for many years.

Driving Tests, Rallies and Trials

While members' interest in trialling in Southern England appeared to be ebbing away the hardy members of the Northern Section pressed on to make their Nidderdale and Blubberhouses trials established features of their calendars. Driving tests were also organised at Bawtry; in April 1952 these were combined over one weekend, the tests being held on the Saturday and the Blubberhouses Trial on the Sunday. Entries were not high for either event but twenty were to set off in the trial, another of the familiar "follow my leader" type, and which was won by G C Bishop in a Riley who proved a master of the "slow trickle" technique to get him up the hills.

Once the certainty of Bisley had been lost, driving test venues tended to come and go during the fifties, with Witley and Slough in the south and Rochdale and Southport in the north making appearances in the calendar. The 1953 Slough event, held in March, was very much intended as a Bisley replacement and the Trading Estate where it was to be located did not sound a particularly attractive option to rolling heathland; but despite this there was a good turnout of both competitors and spectators, among the former being Ron Denne who drove the Clutton 1910 Fafnir on its first competitive outing for some time and who came away with a 1st Class award in the over 1500cc Class. Many of the driving tests of the time would today need to be covered by

Gymkhana regulations, for they certainly would not have qualified as Auto Tests. Test Three at Slough involved blindfolded drivers driving around a circuit of cones against the clock, navigated by a vocal passenger, while the final test involved an out-and-back journey with the requirement to change a wheel on the way. No wonder that spectators turned out in good numbers.

The next event was held in December when it was chilly and misty, but at least not wet. Blindfold driving was no longer required, but this had been replaced by another "high spectator value" test involving a Le Mans start, while another involved a "pit stop" and the removal and replacement of a wheel. Finally came the "bag snatching" test. This involved starting from Line A, rushing to Line B, the driver getting out and running to a nearby drum to snatch the bag resting on same, getting back into the car and returning to Line A together with the bag. Similar tests featured at many of the contemporary driving test meetings (still usually called rallies) while width judging and kerb parking tests were frequently encountered, along with the ever popular slow-fast test.

In December 1952, a few days before Christmas, the 21 year old Hamish Moffatt arrived at Lympne to fly, with his 1923 11.9 Lagonda, to Le Touquet, and hence to Africa. Inspired by a journey that a friend of his had made across East Africa in a 1921 Calcott during the previous year, he intended to cross Africa himself in his 1420cc four seater – a far from sophisticated car and with a cruising speed of barely 40 mph. The 12,500 mile journey proved to be an epic, taking him to the southern end of the continent via the Sahara, the Congo and the Victoria falls in just six weeks of actual motoring.

A self taught but talented mechanic, along the way he was obliged to fabricate a big end bearing, change another, replace broken springs with blocks of wood, bind up the chassis when it broke with a splint of wood, and cope with over sixty punctures. For much of the time he travelled alone, and perhaps regretted giving a lift to a young European whom he allowed to drive and who managed to deposit the car into a largely dry river bed to the detriment of its already damaged springs. One night, motoring alone, he lost a wheel which bounced down the road to be inspected by the single lion he saw on the trip. Fortunately the lion was interested in neither the wheel nor in Moffatt who, after a worried night huddled in the car, was able to continue unharmed to eventually arrive in South Africa and to check in at the Automobile Association's offices in Cape Town.

While the non-racing membership in the South seemed largely content with one site events, and in particular with driving tests, their compatriots in the Northern and Eastern Sections were more inclined to get out and about, so that the early fifties saw a number of road rallies appearing on the scene. The organisers of the Eastern Rally, held in October 1952, must have been very disappointed by the small entry of only eleven that set out on their route of some forty miles identified by verbal route directions ("straight on at crossroads, left at T junction" etc) and via a number of time controls on the way; but increased numbers returned with renewed enthusiasm and to a more sophisticated event in 1953. Leaving from the Ferry Boat Inn at Holywell near Huntingdon, where a regular social gathering was held each month, the route to be covered involved 6 time controls and 4 driving tests, the whole to be covered at 26 mph. Teams of three cars were entered by the Southern, Midland, Eastern and Northern Sections and to resolve ties there was a map reading exercise against the clock – most navigators relieved that this was held in private. F E Day's navigator has not been identified, but their Bentley was to win. The Eastern was again held in 1954, thirty two starters tackling a 50 mile route via nine time controls and four driving tests, all at an inclusive average of 26 mph. No wonder it needed a quick car to win – in this case Doc Harris's Frazer Nash – while Tim Carson was seen selling that year's Club Christmas cards in the bar back at the Ferry Boat Inn finish. The Eastern Rally was to settle down and become a regular feature of the Club calendar for some time.

The Nidderdale Trial had struggled to attract good entries each November so in 1953 it was decided to organise a Ribblesdale Road Rally, demonstrating Lancashire/Yorkshire fraternity by starting in the Ribble Valley in the first of these counties and finishing in the Dales at Wharfedale in the second of them. As was usual, tests were incorporated into the road mileage, one of these involving coasting down a steep hill then up to stop astride an out of sight finishing line. An Alfa Romeo is said to have achieved a terminal velocity of 70 mph on the test, while a Riley Nine overdid things and turned over. However, life was a little more gentle after the lunch stop (held at Hellifield Railway Station – well known to Settle & Carlisle enthusiasts) inclusive of a dash of 10.4 miles over the moors, involving a gated road and a target time of 31 minutes. Two were early, two got completely lost, while a 12/50 Alvis, through no fault of its own, took over an hour to cover the section.

The 1954 event was to attract an entry of twenty seven, including a 1912 Sunbeam as the only Edwardian, and involved five timed road sections (all at 20 mph) and a similar number of tests (for which no time allowances were given) with two well known

By 1956 the February Driving Tests had migrated to the perimeter track of Heston airfield. Stan Waine (1926 7372cc Isotta Fraschini) waits impatiently while his pit crew, John Rowley (who was later to become a President of the Club), jacks up the front N/S wheel to spin it before he may then lower it and release the car to go on its way.

and successful competitors of the time – Peter Binns in an OM and Harry Spence in his well known Lea Francis, coming away with 1st Class Awards.

The Light Car Section is Formed

No doubt the Nicholson cousins, who in 1934 had set out to establish a club for impecunious enthusiasts owning relatively low-powered cars, would have smiled wryly had they passed the Folly Inn at Adstock, about five miles from Buckingham, on 14th April 1951. There was gathered not quite a dozen of unassuming motor cars; three Lagondas dating from 1914 to 1924, plus one each from AC (1925), Clyno (1926), Humber (1930), Peugeot (1922), Riley (1923), Stellite (1916), Talbot (1923) and Woodrow (1914) – in part reflecting their earlier vision and from which the Light Car Section of the Vintage Sports-Car Club was to emerge. Among the drivers who had guided the vehicles there were two in particular who jointly could claim to have been the founders of the Section and were to become the first Chairman and first Secretary – viz Bill Boddy and Arthur Jeddere-Fisher. A remark in the correspondence column of *The Bulletin* in late 1964 generated the following response from Boddy in the winter of that year.

"I note, too, that Arthur Jeddere-Fisher is quoted as having started the Light Car Section and I readily admit that he did all the hard work of organisation and formulated some rather complex rules to ensure that Very Powerful Cars could not creep in by the back door. But I think the thing was really forced on the Committee by my persistent articles on the subject in *Motor Sport* and *The Bulletin*. At the time it was a mighty unpopular idea, frowned on by Cecil Clutton and others, but as Nigel Arnold-Foster has observed it has weathered those days quite effectively. For my sins I find I own two heavy light cars in the guise of a 1924 12/20 Calthorpe and 1925 Cluley and three light cars, namely a 1922 8hp Talbot-Darracq, a 1927 Family Morgan and an Austin Seven which turns out to be not quite vintage. The only one which runs is the Cluley – shame on me!"

For years Boddy had pointed out the charm and significance of these last survivors of really cheap motoring, praising their worth, that of Clynos among them, in one of which he had driven to Adstock. For whatever reason Clutton could not abide the make, while Clyno owner and aficionado David Filsell tells of a conversation he had with him during which he was asked what sort of car he was then driving. "A Clyno" replied Filsell. "Dreadful cars" snapped Clutton. "Have you ever driven one?" asked Filsell. "Of course not" came the unapologetic reply.

It was a link to the Lagonda Club that had been responsible for the gathering at Adstock, and among those present were two 11.1s, Jeddere-Fisher's and Barkers together with Hamish Moffatt's 11.9 Tourer, in which he was later to make his epic journey across Africa. However, it was the Humbers and Talbots who were to comprise the bulk of Light Car membership in the fifties, to be followed by the arrival of large numbers of the ubiquitous Austin Seven thereafter.

The rules that Jeddere-Fisher developed have proved very effective in excluding the Very Powerful Cars of Boddy's letter, and in confining membership of the Section to non-sporting vintage cars developing not more than 30 bhp. Thus an ambivalent Club Committee, came to welcome such apparently unlikely cars with Steady Barker (then Editor of *The Bulletin*) pointing out that "The VSCC, defender of lost causes and champion of all ages, is conscious of their duties." (It should be pointed out that he himself had motored to the Adstock gathering in a 1914 Lagonda 11.1). With many two wheel braked cars among those in the Section, with low power outputs and not always the best of handling characteristics, it takes skill to drive a light car effectively – so rather surprisingly Laurence Pomeroy, as champion of a rather different sort of vintage car, came out in their support by declaring that "the fundamental definition of a sports car is a car that needs a sportsman to drive it."

The Section settled down quickly with a second event in 1951 held at Sun Rising near Banbury, inclusive of a timed climb up Tysoe Hill, while in subsequent years rallies (in the sense of gatherings) were to follow in Central England and in particular around Cheltenham on the Saturdays preceding Prescott meetings. The calendar has steadily developed with the now very well established Light Car weekend, held in the Llandrindod Wells area each spring, starting off the year, being first organised by Keith and Jane Hill in 1970. Initially this involved a road run to get to the base for the weekend, followed by driving tests, but these were soon replaced by relatively gentle trials hills on the Sunday following the Section's now famous dinners on the Saturday night. Seymour Price has organised the trials element every year since 1986, with the only insuperable problem being that the event almost always coincides with the weekend when the clocks go forward, so that the combination of a late night after a good dinner followed by an early start the next morning taxes the resilience of most participants.

A summer gathering, inclusive of a navigation cum regularity event on the Sunday, now takes place each June, while the season concludes with driving tests in late September.

Edwardians, who had often been catered for by a separate class within Light Car events, became formal members of the Section in 1975 and in this form the Section now flourishes. There were 15 members in 1951; this had risen to 250 by 1976 and to 500 by 2003. It is now well over 700. At times concerns have been voiced that the Section had grown too big but somehow it has managed to retain its easy going atmosphere, with enjoyment being seen as far more important than competitiveness, and in this it harks back to an earlier age within the Club.

The Committee prides itself in holding probably the shortest committee meetings within the motor sporting world, and it is very much the case of the Light Car and Edwardian Section being run with the very lightest of touches.

The Pomeroy Memorial Trophy

As well as a new Section a new event was also added to the Club calendar in the early fifties. In June 1946 *The Bulletin* had carried a short article announcing that a new trophy had been presented to the Club by Messrs Pomeroy and Badgery in honour of the former's famous father – Laurence Pomeroy Senior. The trophy was a model by Rex Hayes of the then technically advanced 1914 Vauxhall Grand Prix car and had been presented to celebrate the type of car in which Mr Pomeroy had been particularly interested – namely luxurious high-speed tourers. Initial suggestions were that an event be run for cars of over 2¼-litres and that it should comprise a road section, a series of special tests to measure speed, acceleration and flexibility, together with a sprint hill climb. Fuel consumption was also to be judged on a ton/mpg basis while the Clutton-devised "Edwardian formula", which took into account age and weight and expected bhp/litre related to year of manufacture, would be applied. Certainly the approach lent itself to the extensive use of slide rules in working out the results, this very much in keeping with the mindset of Laurence Pomeroy Junior. *The Bulletin* concluded by suggesting that

> "this extremely interesting and novel event should certainly be a star turn in our annual calendar and it is very much hoped that it can be put into action at an early date. In the meantime this preview of the regulations can provide intending aspirants with food for thought. After all it is about the only sort of food that is still unrationed."

The "intending aspirants" had to wait until 1952 before the Pomeroy Trophy could be competed for, but a little while longer before all their food was to come off ration during 1954.

The earliest events comprised six components, open to four wheeled cars of over 2000cc competing in either the Edwardian Class, the Vintage Class or a General Class with no restrictions as to the year of build. Starting at Silverstone at a lunchtime in March the tests at the first "Pom" comprised a standing start ¼ mile leading straight on to a flying start ¼ mile. Then a one hour high speed reliability run around the Club circuit was undertaken. Target speeds took into account engine capacity, year of manufacture, braking provision, with an adjustment made for the number of seats. Thus for two wheeled braked cars their target speed was 22 multiplied by the sixth root of CY and for four wheeled braked cars 24, again multiplied by this sixth root where C = the engine capacity in cc, increased by 5% for every seat less than four (dickey seats counted), and Y for the year of manufacture less 1900. Other tests had similarly complex marking systems so to dare make a protest would call for at least a set of logarithmic tables in addition to the protest fee.

Fourteen competed in the first "Pom" (more properly known as the Pomeroy Memorial Trophy Competition), rising to twenty in the second year, compared to the seventy plus who compete today. After their time at Silverstone had been completed with a "steering test", which involved completing a large figure of eight against the clock, it was off on the road sections. The first of these involved the journey from the circuit to the Royal Hotel in Cheltenham where the night was spent, followed by a circular route, complete with a number of secret time checks, from the spa town on the Sunday morning. The average speeds for these were high; in 1952 28mph for cars with four wheeled brakes was required and 24 mph for those with only two. The sixth and final component of the competition related to fuel consumption over the whole event. The regulations read:

> "... cars must arrive at Silverstone with full tanks. Competitors should fill up near to Silverstone and bring sufficient quantity in a can to ensure a full tank. At the end of the competition cars will be re-filled under supervision and competitors will be required to sign a declaration of the amount of fuel added during the competition."

Changing times indeed.

Kent Karslake, President at the time, accompanied Pomeroy in his Prince Henry Vauxhall on the first event, who worried throughout that he might win his "own" trophy, which would have looked bad … or not win it using a Vauxhall which would look equally bad. Karslake appeared to have enjoyed the experience while Pomeroy must have been much relieved that the Trophy eventually went to a 1924 Vauxhall 30-98 driven by Peter Binns while his own 1914 model won a second class award. The best non-vintage award went to a 1932 Alvis Speed 20, despite being up against such moderns as a Jaguar XK 120. As Karslake observed "so the formula was worked out right after all".

As with so many aspects of the Vintage Sports-Car Club, steady evolution to accommodate the lessons of experience and changing circumstances has seen the "Pom" regularly updated to continue to provide succeeding generations of competitors enjoyable and challenging competition, and to present them with the conundrum of deciding if an Edwardian, a vintage or a modern car is likely to prove the most appropriate mount, for this the only Club event that still allows contemporary motor cars to take part.

In an attempt to make the event more "large car friendly" and to reflect its aim of identifying outstanding and comfortable high speed tourers, a leg room requirement was introduced in 1956; a horizontal measurement from the pedal pad to the centre line of the rear axle being taken. In the case of rear or mid-engined vehicles the measurement is taken from the pedals to the engine bulkhead. In the early sixties it was recognised that high speed touring required that the occupants of the car should actually be able to take some luggage along with them – and so came the requirement that two fairly substantial suitcases (60cm x 40cm x 20cm) should be carried separately from the passengers, albeit luggage racks are allowed. The fuel consumption element was dropped in 1959 when the overnight stay moved to Banbury rather than Cheltenham, but a road section was still held on the Sunday morning, this not being abandoned until 1966. Eligible minimum engine sizes have been reduced slightly from the original 2¼-litres (as originally deemed sufficient to provide for relaxed cruising) to over at least 1950cc and to 1495cc for cars with superchargers.

Likewise at Silverstone changes to the circuit have imposed changes to the tests, in particular the original ½ mile sprints, as the new corners of Brooklands and Luffield reduced the effective length of the Club straight. But despite, or perhaps because of such constant evolution, the Pomeroy remains an event that cannot be won other than by a very skilful driver in a very effective high speed touring car of its era.

Of the fifty-nine events held between 1952 and 2014 two have been won by an Edwardian (in both cases by Jack Sears in his 4-litre 1914 TT Sunbeam) twenty three by vintage cars (with Frazer Nash dominant) seventeen by various cars classified as Post Vintage Thoroughbreds and seventeen by "moderns" ranging from Ferrari GTO, via Ginetta G4 to both a Ford Cortina and a Ford Escort. One doubts if all would quite meet Pomeroy's perception of a luxurious sports tourer, while somewhat ironically there has only been one victory by a Vauxhall – and that in the first ever year of the competition. But certainly the ongoing changes made to the regulations have kept the event open and unpredictable. Only one hat-trick has been achieved over the years, that by Patrick Blakeney-Edwards driving a 1929 Frazer Nash in 2007, 2008 and

2009. Anthony Blight had come close to one in the sixties, with wins in his 1935 Talbot 105 in 1966 and 1967, then missing a year before his third win in 1969.

The Anglo-American Rallies

While the "Pomeroy" has become a permanent and prominent feature of the Club's calendar two linked and specialist events were to make strictly one-off appearances in the 1950s – the Anglo-American Vintage Tours. These were promoted and largely paid for by the British Travel and Holidays Association as part of its "Come to Britain" campaign at a time when the need to earn dollars was paramount. The tours involved teams of ten (comprising five each from the Edwardian and Vintage eras) from both the Veteran Motor Car Club of America and the Vintage Sports-Car Club. Significant road mileages were to be undertaken in each other's countries, interspersed with a number of special tests.

The VSCC team for the first of the tours comprised a 1906 Wolseley Siddeley, a 1908 TT Hutton, a 1910 Rolls-Royce, a 1913 Sunbeam 12-16, a 1913 Lanchester, a 1920 Vauxhall, a 1925 12/50 Alvis, a 1926 Sunbeam, a 1928 Frazer Nash and a 1928 Bentley 4½-litre. Other notable vehicles used, carrying officials, were Clutton's 1908 GP Itala, Karslake's 1919 Hispano Suiza, the Pomeroy Prince Henry Vauxhall, the Lycett 8-litre Bentley and Jeddere-Fisher's 1913 Lancia Theta. Looking down the "dramatis personae" of competitors and officials it can be seen to have been very much a gathering of the great and good – and as *The Bulletin* acknowledged prior to the British event, scheduled to take place in the late summer of 1954, "although the most part of the tour will not benefit the members it nevertheless cannot fail to be of benefit to the Club as it will be accompanied by a great deal of publicity on both sides of the Atlantic".

The tour started in Edinburgh, complete with a bagpipe send-off, and worked its way south over a week covering 768 miles in all. Every day saw a couple of time checks, while there was a slow-fast test at Newmarket, a timed climb at Prescott, a stop and re-start at South Harting in Hampshire, and so to the eventual finish at Chichester. The Itala proved troublesome on the trip, twice running bearings, but the most dramatic journey was made by the American 1906 Stanley Steamer which among other adventures had to fill its water tank via hose pipe from the public lavatories in Moffat, caught fire near Harrogate and experienced mutiny (later amiably resolved) with passenger and driver refusing to communicate with one another at one stage. Eventually the Steamer was forced to retire, its place being taken by the team reserve – a 1916 Stutz Bearcat.

On the Saturday the competitors, along with representatives of many other car and motor cycle clubs, gathered at Goodwood, where a number of driving tests were held on the circuit, followed by a grand parade of just over three hundred cars. Tom Rolt, who had been the organiser and Clerk of the Course for the whole affair, had carefully placed the slowest vehicles at the rear of the long procession that stretched out over the circuit, back to the Soame Steam Cart at its rear. From the front he gently led the way. "As we moved off" as he was to write in his biography,

> "I became acutely aware of the powerful machinery breathing down the back of my neck … but as I crawled along in bottom gear hoping that I could prevent the procession from eating its tail … those behind me failed to appreciate the reason for this slow motion exercise. With a snarl a Bugatti tore past me, closely followed by a Mercedes emitting a scream from its blower, hotly pursued by three thunderous Bentleys. The floodgates had been unloosed and there was nothing I could do about it. The surprised and startled owner of the Steam Cart had not even opened his regulator before he saw a melée of fast cars bearing down on him. Chaos ensued … Providentially there was no accident and somehow the anxious marshals managed to slow the cars down and shepherd them off the circuit."

John Clarke's 12/50 Alvis made the best individual performance on the Rally, while the British team emerged the winners, and Tom Rolt was made an Honorary Member of the Club for all his considerable efforts in organising the event.

In 1957 the return match took place in the United States – four of the original VSCC team being joined by six others chosen from over a hundred and twenty applicants who had wished to take part. The American team was very strong and dominated the event, the route of which involved 800 miles of motoring in 8 days. This was inclusive of a 54 mile section of Pennsylvania turnpike that had to be covered at a 50 mph average, and a two and a half mile speed hill climb which, but for the fastest time being made by the English E type 30-98 Vauxhall, was dominated by the Americans. Alistair Pugh's Frazer Nash was to do well on a "wiggle woggle" test and also on braking and emerged as overall winner of the event – but the team prize conclusively went to the American hosts.

Maturity

A year after the Anglo-American tour had gathered at Goodwood, the Club was to meet again at the circuit on 10th September 1955 to formally celebrate its coming of age.

The social runs, scavenge hunts, treasure hunts and timed main road runs, envisaged in the original membership booklet as being central elements of the Club calendar, had been replaced by the varied and extensive sporting programme that had commenced in January 1955 with the sixth running of the Measham Rally. The Longmynd Hotel near Church Stretton provided the start for the event that was located in its by then established homeland of the Welsh Marches. There was snow on the ground as competitors climbed up to the hotel, fifty eight of them from invited clubs so that Morgans, Jaguars and, especially TR2s (there were eleven of them) were in abundance, by far outnumbering the Club's own entrants. Navigators had forty minutes in which to plot one hundred and twenty map references before setting off into the snowy hills, the "moderns", which were expected to be the quicker of the entrants, leading the way. A stop and re-start near Newtown caused few problems, but by Builth Wells the wider tyres of the "moderns" were proving less effective at cutting through the snow and were causing some delays. There was a compulsory rest-stop of 20 minutes near Presteigne, hot coffee served around the heat of a brazier, then eastwards to Cannock and eventually Measham. Here the traditional tests, inclusive of the two lap "Measham Grand Prix", took place – after the first laps cars having to stop to symbolically top up their radiators from the empty jug provided. The competing Volkswagen Beetle had to pretend to have a radiator, opening its front luggage boot to provide imaginary access. This, the hardest of all the Meashams to date, was won by Air Commodore N R Buckle in his 1928/29 Lancia Lambda, with a 1950 Riley the best of the "moderns".

The second event of the twenty first year was the Slough Rally, an industrial estate replacing the wastes of Bisley for the tests. Bleary eyed marshals – for it had been their annual dinner on the night before – oversaw the usual mix of tests popular at the time, inclusive of "wiggle-woggles", backing in and out of garages and the almost compulsory Le Mans type start sprint. Gwynne, Riley, Lancia and Frazer Nash emerged as class winners.

More tests and a road section were again involved in March, with the "Pomeroy" starting at Silverstone on a day of wind and rain. Pomeroy himself competed in a modified

Ford Zephyr and although barely in the spirit of being a luxurious high speed tourer he must have been grateful for the roof. The road section, still involving measurements of fuel consumption, as well as a stop and re-start, took place in a revised locale, finishing at Brackley.

The following month the first of the, by then traditional, two Silverstone meetings took place, including the usual one-hour high speed trial. The Itala Trophy for vintage racing cars was won by J C Byrom in his Bugatti T35B. (He had finished in the first three in 1950, 1951 and 1952, while he won in 1953 – but not in 1954, so must have been pleased to be back at the front). A 10 lap All-Comers race saw a mighty ERA versus Bugatti battle but perhaps the pair of 3 lap handicaps provided the most charm. The Edwardian race was just won by the limit man in a Humber, with Neve's TT Humber and Jack Williamson on the Itala having a memorable scrap behind. The Light Car handicap drew 22 entries, Arnold-Forster's Trojan being timed at 38 mph on the main straight, down which Williamson's Bentley had touched 102 mph in an earlier race. The Light Car winner was B W Johnson in a 1922 Morris Cowley.

Further north that April a two day Buxton Rally had been held. On the Saturday, following a concours, the road section (based on regularity timed at two secret checks and the recording of information collected en route to establish that the right roads had been followed) took place. Three well known and experienced competitors emerged at the head of the field – Harry Spence in his 1930 Lea-Francis, Peter Binns in a 1927 OM and Dr D P Harris in his widely campaigned 1934 Frazer Nash. Sunday was rather more relaxing, with driving tests held in the Pavilion Gardens grounds where a kerb parking test, a slow-fast and a blindfold test amused the drivers and the numerous local spectators. The Light Car Section was also out in April with twenty competitors

> *May 1955* **Newsletter:-**
>
> *Skinner had explained at the AGM earlier in the year how complicated it was to run the Rolls-Royce Section when members would not pay their subs. He must then have had some success for the inaugural meeting of the Rolls-Royce Section was held on 1st May at the Red Lion Hotel, Henley when 28 Rolls-Royce were in attendance. They ranged from a 1910 limousine that had been driven down from Staffordshire to a 1936 Phantom III. Among their numbers was a 1914 Barker bodied tourer, still with German sniper bullet marks in its radiator that it had acquired while on active service in France.*

gathering in South Oxfordshire at the foot of the Chiltern Hills. Hill climbing, noise, braking and mpg were all measured (along with the inclusion of a slow-fast test that seems to have become almost *de rigueur* in such events during the fifties) with Frank Lockhart's 1923 Rover the clear winner, largely by dint of notably low fuel consumption. The Rolls-Royce Section followed suit by gathering at the Red Lion Hotel Henley on May Day, theirs being a more decorous affair, for the twenty-eight cars were judged for a concours in the morning, while their drivers sat down for lunch shortly afterwards.

June 18th saw a new race meeting introduced to the Club Calendar. Oulton Park had been opened two years previously and this attractive driver's circuit seemed ideally suited to vintage and post vintage historic racing, as the Northern Section had been quick to realise. The usual mix of short handicap races filled most of the programme, the 10 lapper All-Comers event, which saw a monumental battle for first place between Broad's ERA R5B and Vessey in a Tipo B monoposto Alfa Romeo – and an equally hard fought race for third place between Byrom's T35B Bugatti and Gordon McDonald's very effective 4½-litre Bentley showed the potential of the circuit. The next year the Seaman Historic and Vintage Trophy races were to be moved to Oulton Park from Silverstone, where they were to remain for several decades. John Broad took

Grass roots Club racing. The Oulton Park paddock in June 1955, with competitors assembling for Race 4, a 5 lap handicap. From left to right: B W Johnson 1922 Morris Cowley, D Firkins 1927 Austin Seven, W L T Winder 1923 Humber. The race was to be won by M J Harris in a 1929 Austin Seven, which also made the fastest lap.

his motor racing preparation seriously and in anticipation of the first meeting drove his transporter around the circuit to get to know its characteristics. One of them was the Bailey Bridge just before the start area, which unfortunately was rather lower than the transporter, which thereby lost its roof. Undeterred, Broad continued his reconnaissance on a pedal cycle – anticipating the bicycle races the Club was to hold at some of its later meetings at Oulton.

The second Silverstone meeting was held in good weather, and saw the last of the run of Seaman Memorial Trophy races to be held there. Broad, unusually, overdid things but only incurred minor injuries. As often proved the case the last race was the All-Comers with Terry Carson's ERA (Tim's son) and Keith Schellenberg's Bentley "Whale" finishing half a second apart, while the Relay that concluded the meeting was, as ever, excellent entertainment.

The day before the Prescott meeting in August, 10 Edwardians and 12 Light Cars had made their way to the hill taking part in an average speed run, to conclude with brake and parking tests on arrival. In the days before the camping field opposite the hill had come to be part of the meeting, the paddock itself was used as a dormitory; tents, vans and caravans being very evident that year. Paradoxically the tranquil setting of the Prescott paddock does not always promote the best of behaviour and *The Bulletin* report of the meeting noted that ".. the paddock had a fair number of modern tinware present (Jaguars, twin exhaust Anglias etc) who were all blasting away on their objectionable wind-tone horns and apparently continuing to do so into Cheltenham" … and similar problems have alas re-surfaced at Prescott over the years. The meeting itself was a great success, Broad on top form made the fastest climb of the day in 45.83 secs, his opposition including five other ERAs. Not unexpectedly, Stubberfield was the fastest vintage car, his Bugatti ascending the hill in 45.95 seconds, while the Edwardian class was won by Jack Sears in the 1914 Sunbeam.

Madresfield, now being held in September, was its usual and traditional self, while another autumn tradition took place in October with the Welsh weekend. Among the telegrams sent to the organisers monitoring progress to Presteigne on the Saturday were those in Latin from Barry Clarke, while Howard in a Lancia sent his in what seemed to be Welsh, as at least some of the staff in the Post Office would have been able to tell. John Roberts, who was driving an Austin Seven, deserved some sort of prize for devotion to motoring for he had been married the day before so that he could set out on the rally early next morning. It is not recorded if his brand-new wife then came along to bounce for him. Outstanding performances on the event were made by S J Skinner's 1910 Rolls-Royce, Captain A J Ayers' 1927 Jowett and Harry Spence's hard working Lea Francis, which regularly distinguished itself in such a way during the fifties.

Three more events concluded the Club's year. The Eastern Rally, run on a miserably damp day, was won by the accomplished rallyist Peter Binns in his OM, while the Northern Trial (originally known as the Nidderdale, but re-named when it was moved to Wharfedale) was won by Leslie Winder, a very experienced triallist, as ever in a Humber. Another seasoned campaigner, Dr D P Harris in his Frazer Nash, was also to win an award – but not so Harry Spence, as on this occasion he was organising the event.

The year was to finish with the December driving tests, this time on Odiham airfield – yet another different site for this constantly re-located event – and where the established mix of Le Mans starts, "wiggle woggle" tests and a blindfolded trip around a tangle of oil drums took place. Barry Clarke managed to stall his 1913 Austin mid-way round the latter, so blindfold still in place he got out of the car, eventually found the starting handle, but alas failed to persuade the car to start.

The Twenty-first Birthday Party

So, after just twenty one years of life, six of which had been interrupted by war, the Club had grown to over two and a half thousand members and offered a wide range of competitive events spread across the major motor sport disciplines. Among them were numbered half a dozen which have since become hardy annuals and which remain icons within the Club calendar:- racing at Silverstone, hill climbing at Prescott, the Measham for rallying, the driving tests and concours at Madresfield, the complexities and variety found within the Pomeroy and, for triallists in particular, the unique Welsh weekend. Without these events the Club would indeed be very different.

The birthday was celebrated at Goodwood on a bright and breezy day in early September, where what must have been one of the finest ever collections of vintage and Edwardian motor cars gathered. The proceedings began with a series of driving tests between thirteen teams; two Edwardians and eleven others. Each team comprised a pair of cars – the Edwardians being two TT Sunbeams (Jack Sears and Sir Francis Samuelson) and the other pair the Itala (Jack Williamson) and the 1914 Prince Henry Vauxhall (Laurence Pomeroy).

Renaissance

The teams from Alfa Romeo, Alvis, Bentley, Frazer Nash, Hispano Suiza, Invicta, Lagonda, Rolls-Royce, Sunbeam and Vauxhall included similar gems: a 1923 Targa Florio Alfa Romeo, two very rare Bentleys, the Bugatti "Black Bess" as made in 1913, John Ahern's 3-litre Invicta (owned from new by this distinguished railway modeller), a 1905 TT Replica Rolls-Royce, rare Sunbeams and so on down the alphabet to a 1920 E type 30-98 Vauxhall.

The tests were familiar in format, but unfamiliar in that the cars ran simultaneously against their team partners. J V Skirrow (1930 Frazer Nash) was fastest on both the bending ("wiggle-woggle") and garaging tests, in both cases beating Jack Sears in his 1914 Sunbeam. The acceleration test (over 200 yards) was won by the two Bentleys coming first and second (Mountfort and Armstrong). These two also made up the winning team, Frazer Nash coming second and Bugatti third.

After a demonstration of Edwardian and vintage motor cycles came a pause for lunch, then Forrest Lycett re-opened the course with two quick laps in his well known Bentley. Next came a grand parade of Edwardians, 55 in all, headed by the 1910 Fafnir that had

Goodwood, September 1955. The Club's 21st birthday party with a clutch of OMs and Rolls-Royces about to set off around the circuit as part of the demonstration that was to celebrate the wide range of fine cars found within the Club.

opened the course at Aston Clinton in 1935 – the Club's first ever speed event. Then came the vintage parade of over 170 cars, with *The Bulletin* report very fairly pointing out that it "was to some extent a parade of the Best Vintage Cars, and was in no sense typical of a crowded road in, say 1928. There were no Clynos, no Trojans, no Rover twins, and not a Bean to be seen." There were however a couple of baby Austins, one of which had been a concours finalist and judged to be one of the best finished vehicles in the whole parade. "But it was a parade typical of the Club and all it stands for."

And to round it all off came a quartet of Presidents: Clutton in the Itala, Lycett in his Bentley, Karslake in a yellow Hispano and Pomeroy in his cream and silver Prince Henry Vauxhall in line abreast, leading the concours finalists around the circuit. All rather elitist and in some ways unrepresentative of many of the cars used regularly in competition by many of the members, but indisputably it was all rather magnificent. In an elegant and memorable manner the Club had celebrated its coming of age.

Five Founding Fathers

Among the hundreds of members present at the notable Goodwood gathering five in particular can be singled out as having played a crucial part in the development of the Club. Paradoxically of the group of four which had met to make up the Club's first ever meeting in October 1934 – the Nicholson cousins and Mr & Mrs E T Lewis – none were to become particularly prominent. Ned Lewis (who had the distinction of being the first paid-up member by virtue of his handing over his subscription at that meeting) would surely have become so, had his work not taken him away to Manchester; but at least he had been able to serve briefly as the first Competitions Secretary and then Secretary before moving away, later to become a founding and core member of the Northern Section. By Christmas of that first year the membership list significantly contained the two names that were to dominate the Club into the 1960s.

Tim Carson, Clerk of the Course and Secretary of the Goodwood meeting was still a young man when landlord of the Phoenix, and already one of the most prominent and influential Club members. His competition background and extensive knowledge of vintage cars (it has been calculated that he owned representatives of over forty different makes at some time or another) underpinned his credibility, while his self-effacing efficiency made him an excellent organiser. He was the natural successor to Lewis as Secretary in 1937 and when, shortly afterwards, he married Margery Choate a partnership was established that provided the bedrock on which the Club was to be built.

Moving away from the Phoenix they established their new base at the Sarum Hill Garage, Basingstoke, before war intervened and took Carson away to the Western Desert as a Flight Lieutenant (MT) in the RAF. On his return Tim and Margery built themselves a bungalow in Park Lane, Basingstoke – named "Mellaha" after the former Tripoli Grand Prix circuit – running the Club from there; Tim at first in receipt of an honorarium and Margery of a small salary, but soon regularised as salaries for both. Margery seems to have been indulged by *The Bulletin* editors, for in the early days they published a number of essentially domestic articles written by her – the earliest described the building of the bungalow and, later on, a series of continental holiday reports. (April 1947: "Moved to Mellaha. Tim says most urgent job is to build a garage… Plans for plasterboard garage submitted to Town & Country Planning Committee. Letter from Planning people who state not unreasonably, that they cannot pass plans as area of garage would be larger than that of bungalow and this is a Residential Area". May 1953: "Middleburg, Holland … Find pleasant quiet hotel here. Totter off thankfully to large bedroom, beautifully clean with two washbasins … Enormous breakfast consisting of boiled eggs, beef, ham, salami and four kinds of bread.")

Such articles served to emphasise what a family atmosphere then pervaded the still small Club; members pleased to learn of Secretarial doings. In turn, until 1968 when proper office premises became essential, if any member should turn up at the Carson home-cum-office the kettle would always be put on to greet the guests.

It was entirely appropriate that the Club President at the time of the 21st birthday celebrations should have been Cecil (Sam) Clutton, who along with Carson had become a member during the first year of its existence.

An outstanding character, his personality and convictions illumined much of its early life. Clear in his vision, boundlessly energetic and totally committed; as Editor of *The Bulletin* he gave the Club a distinctive voice from its very beginnings. His enthusiasm for the vintage ideal – if at times overstated – never wavered. His long association with the Itala and a host of other highly desirable motor cars that he also owned across the years, and his deep involvement in the running of the Club, did not minimise his achievements in other fields. Within the family firm of Cluttons he (in his own words) rose from being an "impecunious surveyor" to a senior partner. An expert witness in planning actions, he was also directly involved in the management of Crown and Church estates and was duly appointed a CBE. His love of fine mechanical objects also manifested itself in two other ways. Classical pipe organs (which along with cars involve a multiplicity of tubes and linkages) and a love of Baroque music were taken seriously enough for him to become closely involved in the restoration of a number of instruments, including the organ of St Pauls, and to be elected as an Honorary Fellow of the Royal College of Organists. Also interested in smaller things, he was an enthusiast for mechanical watches. In part it was his support and encouragement that helped George Daniels to emerge from obscurity and become established as a world class watchmaker. Daniels likewise could appreciate the qualities of both the large and the very small, and after racing Bentleys was eventually to become owner of the Itala. In common with many highly talented people, Clutton could be a very difficult man, and not unsurprisingly, remained a bachelor throughout his life. Strong opinions, an unforgiving intolerance of any delay or weakness and a very short fuse would not have made him an easy person to live with, but when he eventually retired to the Isle of Man he did establish a happy relationship with a cat. The feline fancying Carsons (they usually had three cats) would certainly have approved.

The distinctive 8-litre Bentley of Forrest Lycett was much in evidence that September day, opening the course in the afternoon and as one of the quartet heading the grand parade that was to follow. Likewise Lycett himself had been prominent and influential within the Club, from the late thirties until 1947 when he retired from the Presidency after ten years in office. As the rules have since changed to limit Presidencies to three years this record will never be broken. Lycett was a very successful businessman who was both wise and (anonymously) generous in his support of the Club, with a fine sense of judgement that served him well, both behind the wheel as a very fast yet safe road driver, and when dealing with Club matters. He remained young at heart, covering the measured kilometre during Belgian speed trials near Antwerp at 141.131mph in his Bentley at the age of 74. Yet, as Clutton observed, he was constrained by a "profound pessimism lightened by flashes of dry humour". Both behind the wheel and chairing a Committee meeting his judgement was excellent. The Club flourished under the guidance of this polymath; his wide range of cultural interests including a deep knowledge of Gothic architecture and of medieval stained glass.

With a similarly wide range of interests Laurence Pomeroy, President from 1948 to 1950, had likewise been one of the quartet of past Presidents who had led the grand parade. A caricature of the man would no doubt have shown him settling his large frame down to enjoy an epicurean picnic, monocle in eye and slide rule ever ready in his hand, but in truth he was a serious minded and highly numerate man of great technical knowledge who built up an international reputation as a journalist and editor. A

Renaissance

Two past Presidents chat in the paddock at Oulton Park in 1958.

On the left is Forrest Lycett, whose ten year Presidency ran from 1938 until 1947. At the age of seventy four he was to take his highly developed 8 litre Bentley to Belgium, there to be officially timed at over 140 mph on the Jabbeke autoroute. The most important of the Club's annual aggregate trophies, The Lycett Memorial Trophy, is named in his honour.

On the right is Laurence Pomeroy, who followed him into the Presidency in 1948. An internationally respected technical author and editor, it was through his influence that Mercedes Benz were to bring their pre-war racing cars to the circuit for a high speed demonstration in the year of this photograph.

family man, with a love of travel and of cricket, he was always ready to use his influence on behalf of the Club and his clear and analytic mind to address its problems. He also had the reputation of being very kind.

While not quite so publicly visible at Goodwood Tom Rolt, the organising presence behind the meeting, made up the fifth member of the quintet who had done so much to develop the Club in its formative years. He was to spread his talents wide, for having been an early Committee member, and making his mark with his advocacy of Prescott and the organisation of the first Welsh weekend, he was to become seminal in the preservation of the waterways with his classic book *Narrow Boat* and founding membership of the Inland Waterways Association. Also his deep involvement with the Talyllyn narrow gauge railway was central in establishing the world's first preserved steam railway.

The very real talents of these five remarkable men were largely responsible for creating a successful and distinctive Club – but by no means were they alone in work or influence. Included among many others was Kent Karslake – the fourth of the Presidents on the front row leading the parade – who had been in office from 1951 to 1953. His active involvement in the old car movement had started back in the 1920s, when he ran a 1912 Hispano-Suiza while a student at Oxford, and included membership of the Veteran Car Club and participation in several Brighton runs. An enthusiastic automobile historian his knowledge ran deep.

Harry Bowler, Committee member from 1935 to 1973, had a racing record going back to Brooklands and continued to race a Bentley with the Club post-war. When the Goodwood party was fast becoming a memory he was to serve as President from 1957 to 1960.

Finally mention must be made of Anthony Heal, the President who never was; but who surely deserved to be. His membership of the Committee ran from 1937 until 1975, another unbeaten record, while he also served as Secretary of the Club just after the war when the return of Carson from the services was delayed. A member of the family furnishing firm of Heals in Tottenham Court Road he became its Managing Director and for many years the Club's AGMs were hosted in its top floor restaurant. He had wide ranging motoring interests – which extended into traction engines – and a special liking for Sunbeams, racing a GP Sunbeam in the early 1950's. His definitive work *Sunbeam Racing Cars 1910–1930* was published in 1989, while he was also well known for campaigning the 1910 Fiat that he had acquired before the war. He was widely recognised as a very polished driver and Guy Griffiths, the photographer, writing of him after his death, concluded that –

> "Anthony was one of the best road drivers I have ever passengered, an underrated competition driver … and one of the three most important people in the Club's history."

So why was he never to become the President? His *Bulletin* obituary recorded:

"He owned a 5-litre Ballot of distinguished racing provenance and it was the sale of this car to the Americas, subsequent to Anthony's ownership, that upset Sam Clutton so much so that, though Anthony had become Captain of the VSCC, he was never to become President. Anthony probably sold this car for the simple reason that he did not want to have too many motor cars. The fact that Anthony was not responsible for the sale overseas did not affect Sam's judgement."

The Club that Carson built
1956–1972

Tim Carson who, but for the war years, had been continuously in post as Secretary since 1936, together with Margery by his side, was to use the fifteen years that followed the 21st birthday celebrations to develop and consolidate the rapidly expanding Club. Calm and steady in demeanour, his considerable organising abilities were brought into play at virtually every major meeting in the ever lengthening calendar; while alongside him a succession of Presidents provided the overall leadership and guidance required. For the first quarter of a century of its life the management of the Club had been firmly grounded in London and the southern counties, with regional Sections, obliged by distance, to function somewhat separately from the core. It was not until 1958, with the opening of the eight miles of the Preston by-pass, that motorways effectively began to "shrink" the size of the country and a more national perspective began to emerge. In 1960 Kenneth Neve, doyen of the flourishing Northern Section, became the first President from outside the home counties. He was to be followed by John Rowley of the Midlands Section three years later.

While the Club broadened its perspectives it was also becoming much larger. From a thousand members in 1947 this had more than doubled by 1952, the time of the 21st birthday party, and was then to reach three thousand by the late fifties. This rapid growth was to continue for a few more years, so that by the early sixties membership had reached four thousand, but thereafter settled down to a more steady rate of increase.

Over the years, as members are ever wont to do, in addition to fettling and driving their motor cars competitively or otherwise, on specific evenings in specific pubs they tended to gather together to discuss the qualities of various makes of vehicle, mixing prejudice and expertise in equal measure in a cocktail of (usually) contented chatter. The Phoenix had led the way and the meetings there continue on the first Thursday of each month. A *Newsletter* from 1958, listing fifteen such pub meets, gave a good idea of the geographical spread of the Club at the time. The home counties remained the core, with two meets in Hampshire, one in Surrey and two in Kent – plus one in Hampstead. Further west there was a regular pub meet in Gloucestershire, one each in Devon and Somerset and a single Welsh gathering in Glamorgan. North of Birmingham (where there was a monthly meet) there were three others in England – in Cheshire, Nottinghamshire and Yorkshire – and just one (Edinburgh) in Scotland.

Perhaps more knowledgeable than most, "O Fogey" (which hid the identity of Kent Karslake who served as President from 1951–1953) in his *Bulletin* article "Elementary Vintagism" written in the early fifties, gave good advice to new members as to how to handle such situations. From his references to the prejudices and preferences of Carson, Clutton and Heal (Club Captain at the time) it can be concluded that he was a Phoenix habitué.

'First Steps for New Members'

"It is customary, when propping up the bar, to talk about your vintage cars, if you own any vintage cars. If, for any reason you do not find it convenient to own any vintage cars, it is still customary to talk about them. In these circumstances you are requested to stand a little further away from the bar so that other people get a chance to order a drink. It is important when talking about vintage cars to know what to say about them. In particular it is important to know which ones to admire … On the whole it is probably safest to lavish your most extravagant praise on the 30-98. This is a kind of Vauxhall. There has never been any concerted move in the Club to deny the excellence of the 30-98, probably because of a well-founded fear that the Secretary would send those responsible … a second demand for their subscription when they had already paid. All the same if you are naïve enough to ask what 30-98 means no two people will give you the same answer. At one time there was a school of thought which held that the drivers of these cars were permitted to proceed at

98 miles an hour in a built up area. The police, however, never fully subscribed to this view and it is understood that several courts were persuaded to convict… The people who don't really think much of the 30-98 are the Bentley people, but even they keep quiet about it for the reasons mentioned above. The important thing to remember about Bentleys is that instead of having horse-powers they have capacities. These capacities are measured in litres. The capacities of their owners, on the other hand, are measured in pints … The other important thing to remember about Bentleys is that they have labels. These are of various colours and are always mentioned when cars are advertised for sale as buyers are very particular about getting the right colour. It is understood that there is no significance in the various colours.

Bugattis resemble Bentleys in that they do not have horse-powers. In all other respects the two makes are quite easily distinguishable. For example although Bugattis do not have horse-powers, they scarcely have capacities either. Instead they have type numbers. These numbers run from 1 to 57

"It's nice to have a hobby to keep you occupied these winter evenings."

but several of them have got lost and cannot be traced even by the most erudite. It is completely impossible for anyone to learn their significance … therefore it is better to confound people. The easiest way is to ask an expert what is the difference between Type 22 and Type 23. He will give you an answer but you can easily refute him by asking any other expert who will contradict him. There is no difference between Type 22 and Type 23. In fact when the subject of the type numbering is avoided Bugattis are quite good cars for beginners to talk about.

There is a very large number of Sunbeams in the Club. These all belong to its Captain. Before discussing Sunbeams therefore it is as well to enquire if the Captain is present. If he is not it is quite possible to be quite patronising about Sunbeams.

It is well to admire all Edwardian cars. No one will quarrel with you on this score, unless Mr Clutton is present, when he will except the Sizaire-Naudin. This will mean nothing to you and may therefore cause embarrassment. Consequently it will be as well not to discuss Edwardian cars when Mr Clutton is present. Probably it will be as well not to discuss vintage cars either. It would be safer to discuss watches and organs, if you know anything about watches and organs. Since you do not it will be safer not to discuss anything. Personally I expect our discussions to be confined to the subject of libel actions… It is also inadvisable to admire obscure foreign cars like Hispano-Suiza: most of the members have never heard of them. Those who have, on the other hand, think that they know all about them and are correspondingly incapable of carrying on an intelligent conversation on the subject… it is safer to lavish extravagant praise on the 30-98. This is a kind of Vauxhall."

The challenges posed by attendance at a pub meet as identified by "O Fogey" do not seem to have frightened too many members away, as they are at least as popular as ever before. At the start of 2014 the *Newsletter* was to list sixty-eight such social gatherings – well spread out across the United Kingdom, the previous dominance of the home counties membership no longer evident. Only rarely will the conversations focus on 30-98s, Bentley variants or Bugatti types and are more likely to be concerned with less esoteric makes such as Alvis, Austin or Riley, while such meets also serve as a valuable clearing house for concerns, contacts and questions. "The oil pressure takes an age to get up to a reasonable level after starting. Can anyone suggest why this should be?" "My three-brush dynamo has gone on the blink again. What was the name of the firm that fixed yours last time?" "I am looking for a bouncer for the Herefordshire Trial. Would anyone like to come along?" Now, in the internet age, the various Forums on the Club website serve much the same function but without the beer; so it is reasonable to conclude that pub meets will continue to flourish in the years ahead providing amenable and friendly settings in which Club membership can become tangible and real.

The racing programme evolves

When the Club came of age in 1955 it offered just three race meetings per year; the two Silverstones, split by the newly introduced Oulton Park meeting, and a single hill climb at Prescott. Over the next fifteen years (the last phase of the Carsons' stewardship) an additional circuit race meeting was to be added to the annual fixture list, together with two new speed events. The first such addition was the sprint at Curborough near Lichfield, first visited by the Club in May 1964, since when the 900 yard

Thirty years on. In August 1968 three car/driver combinations were to return to Prescott where they had all competed in 1938. Tom Rolt's ducksback 12/50 Alvis (complete with the original style of VSCC badge and rather worn front tyres) heads Ronnie Symondson in his Type 57 S Bugatti and Sam Clutton in the well known Itala.

largely flat yet tricky course has become firmly established in the calendar. The entry, though not particularly large, was of good quality, including Neve's 1927 Bugatti and the Brescia Bugatti of Hamish Moffatt which he managed to blow up. Basil Davenport in his 1923 GN Spider was to win a First Class Award, while Fastest Time of the Day (thus beating the two ERAs present) went to John Horton in his 1951 Connaught – such relatively modern historic racing cars having been admitted to the Club's racing programme in only the previous year.

The following year, in the September of 1965, the Club's racers gathered at the Castle Combe circuit in Wiltshire, as they were to do for three years. In 1968 the fourth race meeting within the Club's calendar was then moved to another ex-airfield circuit, that of Thruxton near Andover, where it was held until 1974 before yet another move took the racers to Donington.

In 1970 Shelsley Walsh, jointly promoted with the Midland Automobile Club, became the second hill climb on the Club's calendar where it has firmly remained ever since; the hill itself a sheet anchor for the motor sporting scene. Inexplicably the VSCC entry was rather disappointing at only forty-four – of which eight non-started – but Sandy Murray in ERA R1A, Jonty Williamson in the 10½-litre Delage and Alan Cotton in his A-type Connaught distinguished themselves in the racing car classes. R1A had experience on the hill dating back to September 1934, the first year of the car's existence, when it had won its class there in the hands of Raymond Mays.

The oldest of the trophies regularly competed for by vintage racing cars within the Club is the 1908 GP Itala Trophy. The cup was presented by R Wil-de-Gose who had raced the Itala at Brooklands in 1910 and 1911. As well as bearing his name it also carries that of Dr G A Ewen, who had both maintained the car and (with Clutton) had raced it for many years before his death in 1953. The first race for the trophy had been held at Silverstone in 1949 and has continued to be a feature of the opening meetings ever since. By 1955 the race had become something of a Bugatti benefit and although a T37A in the hands of A F Eminson was to win in 1956 a Bentley was to do so in 1957. But for a single Amilcar win in 1958, and Sunbeam wins in 1965 and 1966, the trophy was to be shared by Bugattis (6 wins) and Bentleys (4 wins) through until 1970. The Itala itself was to celebrate its own 60th birthday at the 1968 meeting, competing with Clutton at the wheel. The winner that year was Neil Corner, whose Bugatti T35B just beat that of Bernard Kain by a margin of 0.6 seconds, after an extremely hard fought race.

A year after the introduction of the Itala Trophy it was to be joined by another important item of silverware, the Richard Seaman Historic Memorial Trophy, first competed for at Silverstone in 1950. The trophy itself was that won by Seaman when he had finished third, by virtue of an epic drive in a works Mercedes, at the Donington Grand Prix of 1938. A second trophy, also originally won by Seaman for a race at Donington – the 1936 JCC 200 mile – is awarded to the winner of the Vintage category. Initially the two categories were run concurrently but became separate races in 1963, when the Historics covered just over 55 miles of the Oulton Park circuit, while the Vintage race was set at 33 miles.

You never can . . . *Tell !*

For the first six years of its life the contest had been held at Silverstone, with an ERA (George Hartwell R2A) winning the historic section and a Bentley (A G Pitts 4½-litre supercharged) the vintage race, a pattern that was to become familiar in the years ahead. Dennis Poore (Alfa Romeo 8C/35) then achieved a hat-trick before another ERA victory (Jack Williamson R10B) and a rare Maserati victory (H C Spero 8CM) brought the Northampton series of races to a close.

On moving to Oulton Park the Seaman Historic Trophy was to become an ERA benefit, starting with a notable victory by J T Stuart, in the ex Bob Gerard car, R14B. Virtually new to the car, Stuart had told the commentator prior to the race that he wanted to settle in and take things nice and gently. He shot off the line and drove furiously to lead all of the 23 laps. Later in the afternoon there was a 10 lap race for 1½-litre cars. Stuart was second away from the start, overdid the first corner, stalled, leaped out and re-started, by now at a considerable disadvantage. Nine laps later he had overtaken the entire field, having made the fastest lap along the way.

Of the first fifteen Seaman Historics run at Oulton Park ERAs were to win all of them bar one – when in 1964, run under different regulations that allowed post-vintage racers to take part – W E Wilks in a Cooper Bristol headed the field. Their highest numerical turn out was in 1958 when there were nine of them on the grid – a day also made memorable by the appearance of two pre-war Mercedes for a 10 lap demonstration with Peter Collins and Tony Brooks driving the 1938 W154: 2.9-litres of V12 producing 483 bhp and the 1936 W125: 5.6-litres straight eight producing 646 bhp. Streaks of black rubber were left all round the circuit by their spinning back wheels, leaving spectators all but speechless at the spectacle.

Of the ERAs that competed in the Oulton Seaman meetings the ex Prince Bira car R5B (Remus) proved outstanding, winning with Bill Moss at the wheel in 1957 and 1958, before the Hon Patrick Lindsay took over the helm and achieved a hat-trick in 1961, 1962 and 1963. He was also to win in the car in 1965 and to come 3rd in 1970. R11B (Humphrey) also had a distinguished career in the early days at Oulton, Douglas Hull coming 2nd in 1958 to follow this up with a win in 1959; after which the car had to wait a decade before again being driven to victory, now by Martin Morris, in both 1969 and 1970.

But Peter Waller in R9B was to have the most consistent record of them all. Having finished 3rd in 1958, 1960 and 1962, he then went on to come 2nd in 1963, 1964 and 1965. (Had the regulations not allowed the Wilks's Cooper Bristol to compete in 1964 he would no doubt have won that year). His long awaited victory did however at last arrive in 1966 when, in a very wet race, he beat Bill Morris in R12B to the line. In 1967 he drove Lindsay's car R5B to come 2nd, and then returned to R9B to come 2nd yet again in 1969.

In the Vintage Trophy races Bugattis could not quite achieve the dominance of ERAs. Of the Oulton Park Seaman races up to 1970 they were to win nine of the fifteen held, the others going to Bentley and Sunbeam (two each) and to an Amilcar and a Delage (one each). Jim Berry in his T35B was the outstanding Bugatti driver with a hat-trick of wins in 1959, 1960 and 1961, while Neil Corner, who won in a T35B in 1968, was also to achieve one of the two Sunbeam victories, this in 1970. Sandwiched between these two wins was one by a very familiar T35B, the ex Peter Stubberfield hill climb car owned by Frank Wall and driven on this occasion by the ubiquitous Hamish Moffatt.

The line up for the Seaman Memorial Trophy races held at Oulton Park in 1956. On the front row are: J T Stuart, 1937 ERA, No 8 ,who was the clear winner. R D P Wilkinson in ERA No 6. J M Crowther 1932/3 Alfa Romeo No 3. H C Spero 1934 Maserati No 2, who was to finish second.

Alas the 1967 Oulton meeting was a reminder of the dangers inherent in motor racing, though fatal accidents have been mercifully rare at VSCC events. The terrible Le Mans accident of 1955, closely followed by that on the Mille Miglia two years later, had caused the whole racing community to pause and take stock after what amounted to a loss of innocence. Safety precautions were steadily tightened, but not always sufficiently so and not always in time. At the 1956 April Silverstone meeting Dudley Cooke crashed his Lagonda in one of the several handicap races and was to die of his injuries, while in 1962 in a freak accident at the same circuit two marshals (Geoffrey de Nevers and John Hunt – still remembered by an annual marshalling award) were also killed. Contemporary photographs from the fifties and into the sixties show marshals in casual clothing standing or sitting close to the circuit, often with no more protection than the occasional straw bale or marker drum. Meanwhile competing cars, that had lined up five abreast on the grid, rushed by – drivers attired in whatever clothing they found comfortable to wear. Thus when Clutton set out to race his Delage at Silverstone in July 1952, in the race that was for him to end in flames, he was at least wearing a crash hat, as had become compulsory from the start of that year; but otherwise he might well have stepped out of a local surveyor's office, clad as he was in jacket, white shirt, collar and tie. But while fireproof overalls and gloves might have prevented some of the burns he incurred they cannot prevent impact injuries, and so could not save the life of Mike Chippendale (who raced under the pseudonym of Johnson) who fatally crashed his Connaught at Oulton's Old Hall Corner some fifteen years later.

Concerned to extend the range of cars taking part in its race meetings, the Club decided to allow 12 year old historic cars to compete as from 1963, thus admitting front-engined single seaters built up to 1951. Two Connaughts were the first of these to enter the fray, competing in the 10 lap All Comers race at the April Silverstone of that year. J P G Horton's 1950 car was the faster of these and won the race ahead of Lindsay's 1936 ERA, who kept up by inspired driving which compensated for his lower top speed. Horton was less fortunate at the July meeting, his car refusing to start, leaving the race to be won by the ever competitive Pat Lindsay in Remus (ERA R5B). At the other end of the age spectrum only half a dozen Edwardians turned out for their handicap, interest in racing such cars very much on the wane. The limit men were John Bolster on the unusual racing mount of a Rolls-Royce Silver Ghost and Roger Collings on his Züst. Perhaps the race should have been called the Presidential Stakes for the other runners included Clutton (President 1954-56) Neve (President 1950-62) and Rowley (President 1963-65) and Collings who was to become President a few years later (1986-89). The Clutton Itala of 1908 came in first followed by Kenneth Neve in his 1914 TT Humber, with Sir Frances Samuelson in another 1914 TT car – his 3125cc Sunbeam – third.

From the February 1969 Newsletter:-

Chitty-Chitty-Bang-Bang, the only one in the world, 230 bhp @ 1400 rpm. 18,824 Benz engine. Taxed, insured, MOT. Offers considered, preferably over £10,000

Considerably younger racing cars were to grace the Northamptonshire circuit in April 1965, the first time that Post War Historic Racing Cars built before 1951 had been welcomed by the Club. Three of those elegant racing cars of the fifties – Maserati

250Fs – made up the front row of the grid with a collection of Connaughts and Cooper Bristols behind. Pat Lindsay retired Remus during the race which, rather to everyone's surprise, was deservedly won by Cottam's Connaught. By the July meeting a proper trophy had been established for such cars. Presented by Laurence Pomeroy, it is a Rex Hayes model of a 1953 2-litre Grand Prix Ferrari of the type that Mike Hawthorn had used to narrowly beat Fangio's Maserati at the French Grand Prix of that year. The Hon Pat Lindsay was to be the first winner of this Mike Hawthorn Trophy, now driving a Maserati, his 250F, ahead of Spero's similar car and Salvage in a Connaught. Over the next half a dozen years the front contenders for the Trophy, in addition to Lindsay's and Spero's Maseratis, included the fast but fragile front engined Lotus 16s of D E Boorer and W E Wilks, the Tec Mec Maserati of Tony Merrick and, with a beauty to rival that of the 250Fs, the Aston Martin DBR4/250 of Neil Corner. To prove that development as well as design are equally important in making for quick racing cars the Aston, in VSCC hands, was persuaded to become far more competitive than the factory had ever achieved with what was then its own works car. And finally, among these front running cars was Alan Cottam's Type A Connaught, an outstanding performer on the circuits, and particularly so on the hills.

Cottam was one of the earliest competitors to campaign an historic racing car in Club events and was quite amazingly successful in the Open class at Vintage Prescotts. Wilks had been the first historic racer off the mark in his Cooper Bristol, by winning in 1964, and then with but one break from 1965 to 1977 inclusive, Cottam was to win every single one of the rest. The exception was in 1967, when the popular winner was Frank Lockhart in his Rover Special, apparently this being the first outright win for the marque since the 1907 TT. Cottam did not feature in the results of the meeting at all so it seems reasonable to suppose that he did not compete that year. Up until 1970 the outstanding vintage runners on the hill were Peter Stubberfield (who was to win the Club's Hill Climb Trophy from 1953 – when it was first awarded – through until 1957); W A (Doc) Taylor in his very rapid and equally noisy Caesar Special (who won the Trophy in 1958 and then every year from 1962 until 1965) and Bernard Kain in his 1926 35B Bugatti, the Trophy winner in 1966, 1967 and 1969.

Trials resurgent

Away from Prescott and the circuits members continued to enjoy driving more everyday cars, when competing in what were then still known as reliability trials. Back in 1934/35, in the days when a "follow my leader" event could be organised almost wholly without red tape, and (before baseball caps) at the drop of a hat, they had fondly hoped to be able to enjoy a trial a month. It was not to be. In the mid fifties and into the sixties, trialling within the Club was at a very low ebb.

But for the enthusiasm of a group of northern members it could easily have died away; among the notable names of these enthusiasts being those of W L T (Leslie) Winder, Harry Spence and Peter Wike. Later the name of Peter Smith was to join the list of those northerners largely responsible for the survival and recovery of trialling. Leslie Winder, whose sons were also to become keen competitors, had organised the early Nidderdale and Blubberhouses trials which eventually became consolidated into the Northern Trial and which – other than the Welsh – was for many years the only trial appearing on the Club's annual fixture lists.

The Northern, usually held in November and often coinciding with Guy Fawkes, made it clear via *Newsletter* announcements and in its Supplementary Regulations that it was very much a trial and not to be confused with a rally, so that cars with good ground clearance were required. In 1957 the start was at Ilkley and the seventeen entries – of whom thirteen started – were divided into two classes, Sports Cars and Tourers. This small entry included some well known names whose faithful support of trialling did much to keep it alive within the club. Harry Spence, usually to be seen in a Lea Francis, was not competing being that year's organiser – but Leslie Winder in his much trialled 8/18 Humber was there, as was his son Christopher in another Humber, together with Pat Stocken in her widely campaigned Trojan and Doc Harris (instigator of the Measham) in a Frazer Nash. The day included four special tests in addition to the observed sections, not all of which suited the Nashes. Both Harris and Grice (GN-Nash) lost reverses on one of these, while Grice also managed to engage two gears at the same time and bent his back axle. Another back axle gave trouble, for Hawkins broke that on his Riley, while Attock (in an unspecified car) split his fuel tank. The term reliability trial certainly applied to the event.

When the results were worked out Austin 7s (an early foretaste of things to come) were found to have won both the Sports and Touring car classes – the latter by Barry Clarke at the beginning of his long and successful trialling career that has since continued for well over fifty years. His wife Shirley had driven up alone from the south of England in order to pick up Barry from Leeds station on the previous night. Her own journey up was something of a trial in itself, but despite stops for plugs, eventually a plug lead, a loose dynamo drive and sundry investigations of squeaks and rattles the Chummy

Hamish Moffatt, unwilling to be distracted from getting his hard worked Bugatti away from the line on the 1963 Welsh Trial, with rear tyres well let down for maximum grip. He was to win a First Class award, the Presteigne Trophy for the overall winner going to R G Winder in a 1928 Austin Seven.

safely made it to the Crescent Hotel in Ilkley, so that a future President of the VSCC was able to win his first trials award on the following day.

The organisers of rallies and trials being particularly vulnerable to external circumstances can so easily see all their work turned to naught. In 1960 a foot & mouth epidemic caused the event to be cancelled while in 1966 competitors – and especially so those who had motored up from the south – were disappointed to be confronted by a blizzard on the morning of the trial. There had been hopes that a few sections might be arranged on a nearby sloping area of land but, as it became well nigh impossible to reach even that, the year's Northern reluctantly was cancelled.

For 1967 it was decided to hold the trial on a single site – Post Hill – by courtesy of the West Leeds Motor Cycle Club who used it for their events. Harry Spence was again in charge and he arranged the day along the lines of a modern production car trial, each hill, a mixture of mud and slippery grass, being attempted twice. Their characteristics suited those of the Anzani engined Frazer Nashes for those of Christopher Winder and Nigel Arnold-Forster, (which together with a BMW 328 and a 1925 Jowett 7/12) came away with First Class awards, while Barry Clarke, ten years after his first appearance on a Northern, was to win a Third.

Arnold-Forster's record of service and achievement within the Club was outstanding. Editor of *The Bulletin* in 1954-1955 and again from 1966 until 1970, he won the Club's annual aggregate award, the Lycett Trophy, in 1957, 63 and 65 and the Lycett Memorial Trophy (that had replaced it) in 1972, 1973 and 1974. And if this was not enough he was also Club President between 1972 and 1974.

The Lakeland

A year later came the first running of an event that has since become a staple within the VSCC calendar. Dick Smith, with Frank Rushton and Alan Dunn, organised the first Lakeland in 1968 as successor to the Northern Trial, and they continued to do so, aided by friends and family, right through until 2013. Between them Dick Smith, with his three sons Andrew, Simon and Alan, were to be Clerks of the Course of what they built up to be an iconic event in the Club's calendar over more than forty years. To commemorate their achievement each was presented a plaque, made of Honister slate, at the conclusion of the 2013 trial, so a little bit of Drumhouse now resides in their homes. Starting at Buttermere that first year, the smallish entry followed a fixed route which included a long lunch stop at the Kirkstile Inn, where it eventually finished; the *Newsletter* having previously pointed out that "a generous extension of the licensing hours has been applied for." Cars were broadly divided into short or long chassis categories; in 1969 this was refined so that specials, Trojans and Frazer Nashes, plus short wheelbase models, were in one class, with the remainder in the other. Well known entrants on the first Lakeland included Harry Spence, taking a well earned break from organising, Leslie Winder in his Humber, John Rowley in a Vauxhall 30-98, and the eventual winner, Christopher Winder, again taking his Frazer Nash to victory.

The Lakeland Trial 1968. David Bell, in a Wilkinson-bodied replica 1924 SB Alvis 12/50, attacks a hill with gusto, aided by a determined bouncer.

The growth of rallying

During the fifties rallying – in the shape of precise and often challenging navigation, plus accurate time keeping within usually challenging schedules – was growing in popularity within the motor sporting world. However, it was a form of competition that was relatively slow to spread within the VSCC. The Eastern Rally, established back in 1952 with the active support of the Peterborough Motor Club, had settled down to a regular November spot in the calendar and combined navigation with driving tests, while the Northern Section did something similar across in Derbyshire.

The nomenclature problem was then at its height. On a Saturday in April 1956 what was called the Northern Road Trial was held in the Buxton area. The morning's activities involved a road section, sufficiently difficult to cause a certain amount of wrong-slotting, en route to a mini hill climb against the clock, with a "stop astride" the finishing line required. More road mileage took competitors towards the lunch stop in Castleton, en route completing a second driving test before their beer and sandwiches. After lunch a tightly timed road section led to the third test, a lap of a rather deep pond and a reverse into a narrow gateway between substantial gate-posts. And hence back to Buxton after the conclusion of the "trial".

The "rally" was then held next morning in the town's attractive Pavilion Gardens and comprised four driving tests. Kerbside parking, reversing, and width judging was involved, while test 3 required the usual blindfold driving so popular at the time. The last test proved the most challenging, requiring garaging after a Le Mans start. When the flag fell the driver had to run to the car, get in, start it, reverse out of the "garage", turn round, reverse back into the "garage", stop, get out and run back to the starting point.

From the April 1962 **Newsletter:-**

R G Davis, 35 Lea Road, Brockworth, Glos has a complete Auto-Vac petrol lift in good order, which he will give to any member in exchange for an ounce of tobacco.

Later in the same month a Club rally, in the now generally accepted sense, was held in Devon, jointly promoted with the Bentley Drivers Club. Titled a "Night Navigational Trial" navigation and timing were its main elements, the route using many challenging moorland roads, but alas it only attracted a dozen entries, ten of these from the

VSCC. However, the Measham, now in its well established format as a long distance night navigation event, was flourishing. The 1955 event, held on 7th January over a night that saw fog, clear periods, snow and a bitter frost, attracted 78 entries. 33 of these were of vintage cars, 9 were PVT, with the balance made up by modern cars from invited clubs. It was not until 1964 that it was to become a "closed" event, confined to VSCC members in qualifying cars. Except for a single 75 yard acceleration test, held on a 1 in 8 gradient, the night was entirely given over to timed road sections, while the following morning the Measham site provided for both breakfast and a trio of driving tests. Some extracts from *The Bulletin* report, written by an unidentified competitor, give a good picture of the nature of the event.

> "Warm and full of black coffee in the Longmynd Hotel above Church Stretton it was not pleasant to contemplate a night to be spent charging about the sporting mountain roads … the frightful mountain roads of Wales. The car, however, seemed to be in good fettle and we had paid the entry fee so there was no excuse to back out … At the appointed hour we collected a piece of card simply *covered* with six figure references … we made for a relatively secluded spot and started to deface our expensive maps with heavy pencil lines. There was no let-up for about twenty minutes when we had a pause to curse the organisers for making us run on and off three different map sheets in a matter of a mile or two. At last we reached the end of the route card and hurried down to the car.
>
> Off with a flourish we dived down the steep hairpinned road into Church Stretton … then up into the really desolate country above the town … Everyone seemed to be going well until about eight miles from the first control, where there was a sort of tee junction. On the map this spot looked like a tiny farm track off to the left with the proper road going straight ahead – and as there *was* a tee junction a few hundred yards further on where we had to turn left many people thought they must have missed the track and reached the junction. Anyway it *was* the farm track and though the sportier types managed to get though … the longer and heavier cars were unable to get up the muddy track, and for some time unable to go back either because of the queue of cars behind… Then came a long stretch of cross-country roads, by-passing Llandrindod Wells to Newbridge-on-Wye and the only special test on the route … The next control provided the undoing of several people but more by good luck

At the finish of probably the hardest Measham Rally ever - that of 1959 when heavy snow fell during the night and decimated the field. From fifty nine entries fifty one started, of whom only six (including two moderns, as were still allowed at the time) were classified as finishers. The Measham Trophy was won by B C Dunphy in a 1929 Riley, while R V Lorenzato's 1923 Vauxhall seen here was among the many cars outside the time limit.

than good management we found it and hurried on for the next control. We found it in the end, but only after a long struggle with a road that I am sure wasn't on the map. (This is the navigator's favourite phrase – beware of it!) ... We then had a very welcome compulsory halt of an hour's duration at a place on the A5. I never did discover if it was a garage or a barrack hut or a cross between the two. John Rowley was busy trying to make his brakes work but most people were inside surrounding a great pot-bellied stove, drinking coffee and eating sandwiches.

After this warm-up we had a fairly straight forward route to Measham, the chief hazard being the ice which had begun to form in places on the road. The route was straight forward excepting one devilish place north of Cannock. Called Brocton Coppice it was full of little tracks through a piece of rather deserted country that once had been a wood. We wandered about those wretched tracks for ages, leaving fresh wheelmarks in the thin snow that had recently fallen until eventually we found the right one ... However, it was a really fresh sparkling morning by now and the last lap to Measham was really quite fun with the roads just icy enough to make them interesting.

And we never felt cold until we got to Measham."

Due to the Suez crisis of late 1956 and the threat of petrol rationing, along with the Pomeroy, the 1957 Measham had to be cancelled. The weather was also to intervene in 1962 and 1963 when heavy falls of snow prevented the event from being run. By the mid sixties the organisation of road rallies was becoming increasingly difficult, especially so in those hilly areas where roads and lanes encouraged sporting motoring. The Eastern Rally, on the relatively un-rallied side of the country, continued unscathed, the entry for the 1966 event, held in October that year, reaching sixty. Starting from Stilton it provided a straightforward challenge for navigators as they encountered time controls and the then novelty of route boards around the lanes of Northamptonshire.

The Buxton Rally of 1958. Two OMs prepare for a special test, but D W G Smith in the 1925 car does not appear to be watching the starter's flag. Waiting behind him is P J E Binns, in the 1927 model, with which he was to win the event.

The Buxton Rally was not to fare so well. Peak District roads were being over-used by the rallying fraternity, the National Park being too convenient for motoring clubs based in the many towns and cities around its perimeter. The RAC list of "black spots", through which rallies were not permitted to pass, grew steadily longer and increasingly restrictive, so that the Northern Section was forced to move its event into Cheshire for the short lived Broxton Rally. In 1966 it was to be moved again to the Hambleton range of hills in the North Yorkshire moors where the eponymous Hambleton Rally in this less populated area was quick to establish itself in the Club calendar. Starting at Thirsk, it attracted an entry of thirty for the first such event. After a morning coping with tulip diagrams and an afternoon mainly of map references, a Rolls-Royce was to emerge as the winning car.

The Pomeroy evolves

Meanwhile the Pomeroy Memorial Trophy – based on an idea that has been variously attributed to Harry Bowler (President 1957-59) and John Rowley (President 1963-65) – was continuing to produce a varied crop of winner that appropriately represented high speed tourers (albeit some were nearer to being racers) from across the years; for example a modern Aston Martin DB3S won in 1961, a vintage 4½-litre Bentley in 1962 while an Edwardian TT Sunbeam (repeating an earlier victory) was to do so again in 1963.

The event itself continued to evolve. In 1959 the fuel consumption element had been dropped from the competition which still occupied two days, with the navigation-cum-regularity sections on the Sunday starting from Banbury rather than Cheltenham. Also among changes to the regulations made that year was the lowering of the engine capacities required for entry – down to 1950cc for unsupercharged and to 1465cc for supercharged cars. For handicapping purposes supercharging was taken to add a third to an engine's capacity. As ever, scrutineering precedes competition and *The Bulletin* report for that year tells us that

> "A strange but not unpleasant noise heralded the arrival of Hamish Moffatt in his new Brescia Bugatti, which the scrutineers seemed to think failed in some trivial matter to comply with the regulations. As it only lacked number plates, windscreen, doors, mirror, some lamps and other trifling accessories, there were those who murmured that the said scrutineers were taking a somewhat illiberal view of their duties."

The road section, that traditionally had occupied the Sunday mornings following the Silverstone based tests and high speed trials, were next to be dropped in 1968, falling victim to increasingly demanding RAC authorisation requirements; but the White Lion at Banbury continued to provide for the comforts of competitors while the results were being worked out.

The "Pom" formulae used to determine the winners have been very successful in measuring the comparative performances of very different cars from different eras. After a trio of vintage Talbot victories in the sixties – by the redoubtable Anthony Blight in his 105, who also won two first class awards in the decade – these came to an end in 1970. Among the competitors in "moderns" that year was a clutch of competition oriented Ferraris; Neil Corner in a GTO, Frank Wall in a 250 GT Berlinetta and Colin Crabbe in a 1966 GTB, and the opposition they provided proved too much for the older cars. Corner in the 1965 GTO was the winner. But in 1971 the balance was restored when Clutton was victorious in a 1928 Type 43 Bugatti.

As perhaps might have be seen at a Pomeroy Memorial Trophy meeting, where annual attempts are made to differentiate between the merits of pre-war and post-war high speed touring cars. At a chilly Silverstone, held early in the year, there is little doubt that a long coat is the more appropriate wear.

Developments on the 'Welsh'

In its 75 year history the October "Welsh Weekend" has been through many manifestations. It has appeared in fixture lists under a variety of titles to cover the various combinations of trials, regularity tests, navigation rallies, driving tests and concours that the weekends have involved, and it continues to be welcomed to Presteigne by the banner that is hung from the Town Hall, clearly proclaiming the event still to be a rally. It also continues to be, most probably, the best loved event in the Club calendar. And a "rally", in the sense of a gathering together of sporting motorists after a long drive, it continues to be; while Presteigne High Street, crowded with vintage vehicles on the autumnal Saturday night of a "Welsh", looks much as it always has done on such occasions.

The 1956 event was in the established format of the time. Three classes (one Edwardian and two Vintage) catered for a mix made up of four elements, a rally (ie the Saturday's run of 200 miles) an "appearance competition" (ie concours), a regularity test and a reliability trial. All classes had to undertake Saturday's mileage in order to reach Presteigne by 6pm, while on the Sunday the Edwardians were judged for the Concours and undertook their regularity test – that year without a timed ascent of Stapleton Hill. The vintage competitors had the choice of sharing "the Edwardian" concours and the 30 mile regularity run, while the others took part in the trial. That year the trial was to involve an acceleration test on Whitehouse Hill, observed sections at Garth and Knucklas – where there were two – and Llangoch. After lunch it was off to Discoed and the Smatcher.

In the ensuing years the concours dropped from view, while in 1958 a navigation element was introduced to the regularity run and was to feature for a handful of years. At about this time there was a certain amount of debate about the format of the weekend with proposals being made that there might be a shorter road section on the Saturday to allow some trialling on arrival; but this was to take some time to materialise. In 1959 the measurement of petrol consumption was dropped from the competition, while shortly afterwards the navigational element was deleted from the components of the weekend. Driving tests, usually held in the ex GWR station yard, took their place, occasionally combined with a concours.

Despite such changes and "tinkerings" the basic shape and character of the 'Welsh' remained the same, with Sgt Bennett of the local constabulary (in later years he was to become a member of the VSCC) casting a tolerant and kindly eye over the proceedings on his patch. In 1969 *The Bulletin* reported that by the time he had retired to bed and the last customers at the "Barley Mow" had done likewise, the pub had but six pints of mild left in the taps. Further up the road at the "Radnorshire" four hundred pints had been sold. Late on the Sunday night there was "a loud crash in the middle of Presteigne as a certain little man fell off the roof of a hotel into a milk crate while trying to climb into a lady's bedroom. He was to be seen hobbling around some weeks later still cussing himself, the milk crate and slippery Welsh slate tiles."

The next year was to see an almost perfect Welsh weekend. "The Welsh Trial of 1970, based as usual at Presteigne, will go down in the history of the VSCC as one of the best events held by our Club. The entry was first class, the driving forceful, the hills superbly picked, the weather perfect and the countryside looking at its absolute best in autumnal hues ... Sergeant Bennett was heard to complain the following day that we were unusually well behaved."

A variety of Driving Tests

Few of the sites used by the Club for its many driving test meetings in the late fifties and sixties could compare with those of the Welsh Marches in terms of their scenic settings. However, they served their purpose and, importantly, served the needs of the many members living in and around southern England. The Bisley "rallies" had been replaced first by the Witley "Rally" and then later by driving tests held on a car park of the Slough Trading Estate; perhaps not the prettiest of settings, but very suitable both in terms of location and available space and where they attracted good entries and plenty of spectators. Other driving test sites were to include the disused airfield at Heston (from where Chamberlain had flown thrice to have talks with Hitler in the troubled month of September 1938), Odiham airfield in Hampshire, Lasham – now well known to glider pilots – the army campus at Shrivenham and, familiar to Carson from his earlier years, Charterhouse School. Heston was to remain home to the winter driving tests for many years until in 1961 they moved to yet another ex airfield – that of Silverstone. The usual diet of slaloms, Le Mans starts, wheel changing and acceleration tests still dominated, while Madresfield (called a rally well into the sixties) continued to provide suitable challenges generally in a straightish line, and to enjoy the unique backdrop of Madresfield Court and the Malvern hills. It boasted a long list of awards additional for those within the classes. In 1957 there were awards for the best Light Car, closed Vintage Car, Edwardian, Frazer Nash and Rolls-Royce, in addition to the concours.

Further south, in the then driving test heartland, a new event was to join the list; a concours and "rally" based on Beaulieu. In 1957 this started in the New Forest with a short run taking participants to Beaulieu itself, and so to lunch. Digestion under way, the concours was judged in the afternoon. As with so may Club events it was to evolve, its eventual format becoming a concours held at Beaulieu in the morning and

A photographer photographed. Max Hill, whose films and photographs provide an extensive record of Club events in the fifties, is seen here tackling Test 2 ("un-parking") in his 1930/34 Type 49 Bugatti at Madresfield in 1958.

then a short run to the Esso petrol refinery at Fawley, where driving tests took place in the afternoon. Although the event itself is now long gone, its major award, the Montagu Trophy, is still being put to good use, now being awarded to the winner of the self-judging concours, open to competitors at the Madresfield driving tests.

The Frazer Nash Raids

Sections within the Club have a tendency to come and go, survival largely reflecting the levels of commitment and enthusiasm shown by their officers, while one in particular has weathered the years better than most. The summer of 1969 was to see the long lasting Frazer Nash Section on the top of its form.

The Alpine Rallies of 1932, 1933 and 1934 had seen Coupes des Alpes for penalty free runs being won by Frazer Nash on what then was the most challenging event in the rallying calendar. Doc Harris, vintage rallyist and Nash exponent, had suggested that the Section might perhaps arrange a commemorative journey to the Dolomites and 'storm' some of the passes that once had been used in competition. David Thirlby, another real Nash enthusiast and author – and later to be a long serving Editor of *The Bulletin*, took up the idea and carried out a reconnaissance that took him and his Frazer Nash to the South Tyrolean town of Bolzano. With support from Denis Jenkinson and Michael Bowler he was able to arrange that a special class for Frazer Nash could be included in the local Corsa della Mendola hill climb on which 15 hairpins in 9 miles challenged competitors as they raced up to 6,000 feet. He was also able to find a large enough hotel, with an even bigger garage, fit to accommodate travel stained Nashes arriving from England; and so the event was "on". 40 Frazer Nashes were entered for what (apparently due to a mistranslation) became known as the Raid. 36 cars actually started, of which 5 had competed in pre-war 'Alpines'. From Crystal Palace, accompanied by a van lent by Renolds, the chain manufacturers, and laden with spares they set out on the 500 mile journey to the Dolomites to cover the distance in a little over two days. Over the Brenner and Giova passes they stormed to Bolzano, there to be greeted by a large banner (shades of Presteigne on the Welsh) bearing the words "Welcome Frazer Nash raid". In addition to the Nash class on the hill climb there was less serious competition to be had on the square in front of Bolzano's law court building, when a driving test contest between half a dozen nimble small Fiats and Frazer Nash took place one afternoon, in front of an enthusiastic and approving Italian crowd. The remaining days in the Dolomites were spent climbing the classic passes of the area at speed, including the mighty Stelvio via 48 hairpins to 9,000 feet. Then after a week or more of perfect weather it was back to England again, but this time in pouring rain. The Raid had proved such a success that similar trips to the Alps have taken place every ten years since.

In a very different sort of car the Lycett Memorial Trophy for 1969 had been won by J A (Tony) Griffiths driving a 1930 Austin Seven Tourer – a tremendous achievement reflecting great determination, painstaking preparation and skilful driving across the year, a feat which he was to repeat in 1970 and 1971. The Nicholson cousins, by then all but forgotten by the Club, would surely have been absolutely delighted.

Tony Griffiths, very nearly in full flight, at a driving test meeting in 1971 – the third of the three consecutive years in which he was to win the Lycett Memorial Trophy. His Austin Seven Tourer was first registered on 5th October 1930 – the day of the R101 airship disaster – then being used as everyday transport for many years until embarking upon its competition career.

Into the Seventies

During the fifteen years since the Club's twenty-first birthday party the calendar, with some mild expansions, had developed and settled down to a well established pattern. The plans for 1970 comprised:

January	Measham Rally
February	Charterhouse Driving Tests
February	Pomeroy Trophy
March	Light Car Trial, Wales
April	Silverstone Race Meeting
April	Hambleton Rally and Driving Tests
May	Beaulieu Concours and Driving Tests
May	Curborough Speed Trials
June	Light Car Rally, Wiltshire
June	Oulton Park Race Meeting
July	Silverstone Race Meeting
August	Prescott Speed Hill Climb
September	Madresfield Concours and Driving Tests
September	Thruxton Race Meeting
October	Welsh Rally – Presteigne
November	Eastern Rally
November	Northern Rally
December	Silverstone Driving Tests

In addition to eighteen competitive events the calendar also contained a number of film shows. For some years these had been held in Hammersmith, while for 1970 the list included film evenings in Manchester, Birmingham and Bath, in addition to two in London.

In 1963 A P (Tony) Bird had joined the Carsons in the office, followed a year later by Peter Hull who was expected to take over the Secretaryship when the Carsons retired. Both had highly appropriate backgrounds. The bearded Tony Bird – a Riley man who edited the *Riley Register Bulletin* for over twenty years – was quietly calm and efficient, except when the sight or simply the rumour of a dog being present at a racing circuit would seriously upset his equilibrium. Peter Hull was likewise a long time member and, although a 1927 Alvis 12/50 owner, was author of a standard work on Alfa

Sam Clutton, President from 1954 until 1956, in the 12 litre Itala, seen here at Prescott in August 1969 when he was to win his class.

Romeo. His brother, Douglas, was an accomplished racer and a rare winner of both the vintage and historic Seaman Trophies; the former in a Type 37A Bugatti and the latter in ERA R11B. Both were keenly interested in flying and Peter had become an RAF flying instructor early in the war and it so happened that one of his pupils was to be a certain Sam Clutton. The tale is told that when his flying instructor suggested that he should bring a bicycle up to Codsall airfield in Staffordshire Clutton replied that he would bring his Penny Farthing. Hull suggested a less esoteric machine would be more suitable, to which Clutton responded that the Penny Farthing was his only bike. Eventually he did acquire a more usual form of pedal transport but did not follow the convention of painting his name and rank on a mudguard. So instead of "P/O Clutton" the words "Mr Clutton's bicycle" were to adorn his.

As the Carson retirement drew nearer the Hull family moved into 3 Kingsclere House Stables, where the office had long been located, while the Carsons moved to a smaller house nearby. No better way to show what life was like in the office at Kingsclere in the late sixties can be found but to use Margery Carson's own words as they appeared in a *Bulletin* of the time. The "Nigel" concerned was Arnold-Forster, its then Editor.

Kenneth Neve, President from 1960 until 1962 and doyen of the Club's Northern Section, also seen on the Prescott esses in 1969, driving his 3300cc 1914 TT Humber.

"Nigel says that it is time the veil was lifted from what goes on in the Club office, so just in case you pictured us lolling back in armchairs, smoking cigars and drinking champagne, here it is. And if you are bored, or think you could run everything better yourselves, please write to Nigel, not to us!

Although we all try to be able to do any of the work involved, it works out roughly like this:

Tim and Peter run the competitions, organising events and dealing with entries. Tony organises all the marshalling duties at our many events, keeps records of lap times and the markings for the annual trophies. Margery deals with all accounts, subscriptions, banking, petty cash, etc (and raises hell if anyone else touches anything to do with money, since none of the three men can add two and two together correctly). All deal with letters as necessary, except that the really tiresome letters are firmly pushed on to Peter, as he is by far the most patient member of the staff.

This is, of course, a terrific over-simplification, especially as the activities tend to come in bursts.

Each month, there is the upheaval of the Club circular. As soon as Peter joined the staff, this job was firmly given to him, his status as an author being the excuse. All the Hulls have a habit of filing papers on the floor and Peter assembles the circular mainly by playing a sort of patience on his hands and knees. It's quite a relief when it is finally typed and sent to the printers, because we can once more move about the office and even have a window open. After that, some 5,600 envelopes have to be run off on the addressing machine, which can be extremely temperamental. Tim usually does this, and there is a noticeable tendency for Tony and Peter to find jobs elsewhere while this is going on. Margery, having suffered Tim's tantrums for some years now, just ignores them. The envelopes are, thank God, filled by outside help and a special Post Office van is ordered each month to carry the enormous weight.

A 1970 Newsletter *request:-*

"The Revd Robin Newman seeks sponsorship for his planned Lands End to John O'Groats trip in his 1928 Austin 7 in aid of the repair fund for his church, St Dingad's in Dingestow in Monmouthshire". He made it, and later thanked members for their generosity, while the church is standing yet.

Each month, too, there is a Committee meeting at which, among the other business, an average of about 30-40 new members are elected. Putting these through involves about 14 different operations. And those changes of address! The incidence of gypsy blood is very high in this Club – we get about 40-50 of these every month.

We work out the engraving for, order and send out about 400 awards per year (except when we can press them into the oily hands of members at events). Packing these up is one of those jobs when everyone suddenly seems terribly busy, and poor old Margery generally gets let in for this on the theory that "women are so much neater at doing up parcels". She also packs up about 500 car badges per year and over 6,000 Christmas cards, as well as lapel badges, ties, *Bulletin* binders, etc.

Getting the Club calendar out each year is an absolute nightmare. Dates have to be given to the RAC by 30th September the year before, often before the International dates have been fixed, so one is never sure whether either the circuits or the dates will be available. After a great deal of juggling, this is eventually achieved and the timekeepers, scrutineers, ambulances, caterers, police, etc., have to be booked for each event. Routes for rallies now have to be submitted six months ahead and are more than likely to be turned down and have to be altered or sometimes cancelled.

Perhaps the most hectic time in the office is January and February, when subscriptions pour in from the 5,600 members (except from the perennial bad payers), and we get well over 200 letters per day. There are nearly 1,000 members who pay by banker's order. These come in with double-barrelled names printed singly, single-barrelled names printed double, and many are illegible. Sorting these into alphabetical order is no mean feat. We run a sort of production line at this time – Margery entering up the payments and writing the membership cards, Tony addressing envelopes and Tim and Peter sticking on stamps. After this, we start sending rude reminder cards to the 1,200 or so members who have not paid because "we always find those cards of yours so amusing!"

The few weeks before a race meeting are always pretty fraught. We invariably get more entries than we can accept, and try our best to get all competitors one race and possibly a place as a reserve. In the confusion, it is not unusual to find that we have put the same car in a race twice, or a Maserati in the Light Car race. Interesting though this might be from a spectator point of view, it has to be re-arranged and miraculously, all generally seems to come right in the end. While all this is going on, Tony is sorting out his 200 or more marshals, and sending detailed instructions out to them all about the many different jobs they do. And all this happens four times a year.

Every third year, we publish a list of members. Hundreds of hours are spent checking addresses and cars, and typing out the list for the printers (a spare time job for us all for weeks) and, horror of horrors, checking the proofs.

This is all rather routine, I could write pages about the letters we get from all over the world as well as at home. Can we find spares for obscure makes found in barns in darkest Africa? What were the original colours of certain makes? Are we interested in what looks like an old car seen in a field beside the railway line somewhere between Euston and Scotland? (make or date not mentioned, nor does anyone know if the car would be for sale anyway). Is the Club doing a Christmas card this year? (usually received around 20th December, when details of the cards have been given in circulars from September onwards). Why don't we have a race meeting every weekend? (those poor marshals). Does the Club run an insurance scheme? (brokers have been advertising in *The Bulletin* for years).

By the time you read this, we hope to be established in new and larger offices. It will seem strange not to have to send Peter up to his loft every time we want more awkward boxes or *Bulletin* binders, and not to have so much stuff parked on the office floor that reaching the other side is like an obstacle race. And not to have 4,000 Christmas cards under the bed at the Carson home because there is not room for them at Kingsclere!"

The 1952 Directors' report stated that "we have steadfastly set our faces against incurring heavy fixed charges such as a headquarters", instead paying a small rental (then £52 pa) for the use of office space within the Secretary's home. This arrangement was to last for many years until ever growing membership numbers forced a change.

In an increasingly professional age, and with an increasingly crowded office taking over the Hull's home, the need for larger premises was paramount. A first floor office on a new trading estate in Newbury was found and the terms were very good; £350 rental per annum, plus £109 for the rates. The move was made early in 1968.

With the Carson retirement imminent Richard and Rosemary Burke – with a background as the organisers of the Hambleton Rally – were appointed to the staff in August 1971. Very sadly Richard was soon to fall ill and, still only in his mid forties, died in July 1972. His place was taken by Jim Whyman, while Rosemary remained on the staff.

But life at this new address was not to last for long. In 1973 the owners of the property obtained a new valuation, as a result of which the rental level went up to £2,500 pa, with the rates rising alongside to £210. The hunt was on for a permanent home, and suitable premises were eventually found at 121 Russell Road, Newbury; where the Club was to be based for the next quarter of a century. The property then comprised the ground floor of an ex Do-it-Yourself shop and included a building at the rear that could be used as a store. It was purchased for £10,300 and after a lot of hard work by Rosemary Burke and Jim Whyman, aided by some local members in decorating and preparing the premises, the move took place in October 1973. Even the rates were lower than before.

The end of an era. Tim and Margery Carson at the Thruxton meeting of 1971, following their retirement from the Club that they had served so well.

Meanwhile the Carsons had retired, Tim's last meeting in an official capacity being Silverstone in July 1971. Among the five-lap handicaps on an excellent day of racing, spoilt only by some late falling rain, was a particularly well supported race for Edwardians, while there was a pair of races involving ERAs, the Hawthorn Trophy and

The Club that Carson built

an All-Comers race, both to be won by Neil Corner in R4D. The day had attracted the largest ever line-up of ERAs to be seen at a race meeting, thirteen – inclusive of the ERA Delage – a beaming Carson photographed among them. At the Thruxton meeting later that year a presentation was to be made to Tim and Margery, while in the following New Year's Honours Tim was awarded the MBE for his services to the Club. It would be hard to underestimate the contribution that between them the Carsons had made to the VSCC. Tim had been at its core for nearly forty years, with Margery by his side for almost all of them. The Directors' report for 1971 concluded with an appreciation of their work and the words "Thanks to a splendid couple who devoted their lives to the interests of the VSCC". They retired to Sandgate just outside Folkestone, convenient for ferries to France.

Russell Road – The Early Years
1973–1983

It must have long been recognised that the Carsons would be an extraordinarily difficult act to follow, leaving as they did a legacy of fun-filled enthusiastic efficiency, deep knowledge and a real sense of family within the Club. The choice of Peter Hull as successor to the Secretaryship was inspired, for he more than rose to the challenge. Affable, efficient and apparently incapable of being provoked, he is best remembered for his loud, frequent and distinctive laugh. As a man who got on with things, as well as with people, he produced focused and handwritten minutes of the monthly Committee meetings that rarely ran to more than one sheet of A4 paper. He did, however, also use a battered old typewriter on which he bashed out extraordinarily emollient letters and post cards in response to any objections or grumbles that reached the office. A master at defusing difficult situations, no-one could be cross with Peter Hull for very long.

With the retirement of the Carsons and the appointments of Peter Hull, Tony Bird and the Burkes, the Club recognised it had moved into a new era in an increasingly complex and bureaucratic world. Maybe Clutton had likewise found this in his own professional world, for at the start of the seventies he was to retire and move to the Isle of Man, an island he had got to know well in his RAF days. He bought the Old Rectory at Lezayre and became involved in island life – as organist to the local church and as his own cook at the dinner parties he gave, in between discussing horological topics with George Daniels (who had also retired to the island) enjoying his collection of keyboard instruments and exercising his Scott motorcycle, Bugatti type 46 saloon and a disappointingly unreliable Frazer Nash at enormous speeds along the local roads and lanes. He certainly did not abandon his life on the mainland and continued to be deeply involved with the VSCC, to the extent of breaking the Edwardian record at Prescott in the Itala in 1973, which had stood for 25 years.

While the office settled down to grapple with such matters as the new scales of charges for permits and insurance introduced by the RAC on a per capita basis (which in fact worked well and are still broadly followed) and with a "Blue Book" that presented more complex regulations and requirements year on year, and which were to pose real challenges for the rallyists in the Club, particularly so for those organising the Measham, the calendar of events went ahead broadly unchanged.

The racing scene

At the beginning of the seventies race meetings were four in number, the traditional two at Silverstone, the June meeting at Oulton Park and the fourth meeting which had become well established at Thruxton. However, due to competing pressures from other clubs, it was not to be available for 1973 so a move was made to the much shorter one mile long circuit at Llandow in South Wales. This had been constructed on an

Two stalwarts of the Club's racing scene battle it out at Silverstone in 1977. J T Williamson (nearest the camera) is in the 1923 10500cc Delage, with H P Hine alongside in a 1924/28 Bentley.

ex RAF airfield and by the seventies was becoming very bumpy – perhaps no more so than the circuits on which most of the competing cars had been raced in their youth. However, it took its toll on spokes and suspension items, so no doubt it was a relief to get back to the relative smoothness of Thruxton in 1974, albeit on a very wet day. The weather that year had not been at all good, to the extent that at the spring meeting at Silverstone it was so cold that a marshal from Becketts corner had to be taken to the medical centre suffering from exposure. It was to be the last VSCC promoted meeting at the Hampshire circuit, for in 1975 the Club was to add Donington to the list of venues for its race meetings – returning there for the first time since before the war. But the relationship with Donington was to be far from settled and its appearance on the fixture lists was intermittent for some years. Llandow had also appeared in the Club calendar for 1975, but was then to be dropped and replaced a year later by Cadwell Park; surely along with Oulton Park just the sort of road circuit that perfectly suits vintage and historic cars. As *The Bulletin* report on the August 1976 meeting put it:

> "Most people arrived at Cadwell not really knowing what to expect. To say that competitors and spectators were delighted with the day's racing is an under-statement and it is hard to write this report without lapsing into repetitious superlatives. It is difficult to imagine a more challenging and interesting circuit."

Silverstone meetings were largely made up of five lap handicaps, a selection of named trophy races and an all-comers scratch event. At the spring meetings the G.P. Itala Trophy topped the bill. Up to 1970 this had been won twice each by Amilcar, Delage and Sunbeam Tiger, four times by Bentley and eleven times by Bugatti. Through the seventies and into the eighties the balance was somewhat more even, with David Llewellyn in his 1924 8-litre Bentley emerging the winner in 1971, 1972 and 1973, and then later on in 1978 and 1979. Peter Morley (Bentley Pacey Hassan 4½-litre) followed up the Llewellyn hat-trick in 1974 and 1975 before Bugattis came back into the picture. Bernard Kain was to win in 1976 and 1977 and again in 1983, while Hamish Moffatt in Frank Wall's Bugatti emerged the winner in 1980 and 1981. Another Bugatti in the hands of John Ward won in 1982. The "one-hour blinds", reduced to forty minutes, continued to entertain members driving less exalted machinery.

The second Silverstone meeting each year included the Hawthorn Trophy for Post War Historic Racing Cars, which through the seventies Neil Corner was to make almost his own. His ability to dominate in a wide range of cars was outstanding. In 1971 he won in ERA R4D, in 1972 in a 250F Maserati, in 1973 in an Aston Martin DBR4 and in 1974 in a P25 BRM. Patrick Lindsay, in another 250F won in 1975 but it was back to Corner in Maseratis for both 1976 and 1978 and then in a 3-litre Ferrari Dino 246 in 1982 and 1983. Willie Green had first achieved victory in the Bamford-owned Dino, doing so in 1981 – while S F Phillips (Cooper Bristol) R H Bell (Maserati 250F) and Bruce Halford (Lotus 16) filled in with victories in the intervening years.

Race 1 at the Oulton Park meeting in 1979; the variety that is Club handicap racing encapsulated. From left to right: I Dutton 1929 Morgan Aero – with Mrs A Scott-Moncrieff just behind him in a 1930 Boulogne Frazer Nash. Mrs Di Threlfall glances over her shoulder from the 1930 Austin Ulster, while alongside her on the front row is P N Stott in another 1930 Austin Seven. An ERA lurks in the background.

But a list of victors in a variety of interesting cars paints a somewhat misleading picture of the health of Post War Group 3 Historic racing at the time and concerns started to be raised in the mid seventies. The 1974 Silverstone report pointed out that "at one time we could count on having four or five 250F Maseratis, two Lotuses and an Aston Martin … but today we had three such cars." In the 1975 Summer *Bulletin* Denis Jenkinson likewise expressed disappointment in an article entitled "Historics or Hysterics."

"When we thought up the Historic Racing Car category for VSCC events we visualised a re-enactment of the Grand Prix races of the 1946-58 period, and those of us with not much imagination could see 158 Alfa Romeos battling against 4½-litre Ferraris, with some 4CLT Maseratis and 4½-litre Lago-Talbots thrown in for good measure. What we did not visualise was a DBR4 Aston Martin running away from everything, when that self-same car as a first-line factory entry in 1958 Grand Prix racing could hardly keep up with the also-rans. In addition, we did not visualise an historic 2½-litre Grand Prix car somehow getting away with using a 3-litre engine, nor for that matter did we anticipate a homemade special with a 2-litre Rover engine, joining in with a 3-litre Rover engine installed.

The fields for Historic races are never over-subscribed, which is surprising, for you would think it much easier to keep a post-war Grand Prix car running than an ERA or a Bugatti but it seems that it is not the case. In order to enlarge the scope it was agreed that cars from 1952 and 1953 of the 2-litre Formula 2 of those years, should join in, for all the major Grand Prix races in 1952-53 were run to the 2-litre Formula, as the old Formula 1 had come to a grinding halt. This meant the addition of A-type Connaughts, Cooper-Bristols and others to the Historic field, but in those two years Ferrari had a virtual monopoly, with a few asides by Maserati, and as no-one has produced a 2-litre Ferrari, we can only look at the 2-litre cars that do assemble and say "Well, yes, they did run in Grand Prix races at the time."

However, despite his reservations as to a Tasman series Ferrari Dino and Lockhart's larger engine in the Rover Special he could nevertheless see some merit in what the Club was doing to swell its grids. His article went on to consider the matter in a more positive light.

"At one Silverstone meeting I was standing ruminating on the dismal quality of the entry in an Historic race and happened to be by a very nicely re-built Cooper-Bristol. Two young lads approached and asked if it was exactly like the one Mike Hawthorn used to race. I explained that indeed it was, apart from the colour, and sheer joy came over their faces … and they walked away happy that they had stood by a Cooper-Bristol exactly like the one their hero had driven. They must have been beside themselves when they saw it being driven in the race, and very fast at that."

In a similar way the grid for the majority of the Seaman Trophy races cannot reflect those of the principal races of the vintage and historic eras, but they are certainly made up of extremely interesting cars and are driven by skilful and highly motivated drivers.

The ERA dominance of the Seaman Historic Trophy in the seventies and early eighties was, but for two years, complete. In 1971 Colin Crabbe brought his W125 Mercedes Benz to Oulton, having re-built the car from little more than a pile of bits retrieved from behind the Iron Curtain. Originally built in 1937, the car was little younger than the VSCC and had last been raced in 1939. Before the war the Mercedes and Auto Unions had trounced ERAs at Donington, but on a wet day in Cheshire Martin Morris in R11B was to give the German car a good run for its money, only being overtaken on the last lap to give Crabbe his first ever victory in a motor race. The same result was to be repeated in 1972.

The Mercedes having been sold, the field for the Seaman Historic was left wide open, and Morris was to be the ERA driver who grabbed the chance in an unbroken series of race wins from 1973 to 1977. He came second to Patrick Lindsay in R5B in 1979 before returning as winner in 1982 and 1983, Lindsay having gone on to win in 1980 and 1981. It was not until the Golden Jubilee Year of 1984 that the race was to be

The Hon. Patrick Lindsay, in his signature red shirt, at the wheel of ERA R5B "Remus" at Oulton Park in 1978. The Thailand racing colours of the car recall the years when it was driven by Prince Birabongse "B.Bira", since when it has probably competed in more motor races than any other car.

won by other than an ERA – David Black in a Tipo B Monoposto Alfa Romeo taking home the trophy.

Martin Morris had bought R11B from Peter Hull's brother Douglas and first used it for hill climbing rather than racing. The car's nickname of Humphrey had been given to commemorate Humphrey Cook, whose money had largely made ERAs possible. Essentially strong and simple cars they allowed the skilled amateur to undertake most of the maintenance, as did Morris, who would then tow the car on its trailer to meetings behind his Speed Six Bentley. In all he was to achieve eleven Seaman victories, in 1973 winning both the Vintage and Historic events on the same day, the former in H A Morten's 4½-litre Bentley. Somehow he found time for some historic sports car racing and also provided Neil Corner in R4D with some stiff competition at Silverstone events in the early 70s.

Competition was rather more open for the Vintage Seaman Trophy at the time; the principal contenders, including Hamish Moffatt in Frank Wall's 35B Bugatti, Bernard Kain in a similar car and Ron Footitt in his Cognac Special. At the other end of the size spectrum came the Bentleys and the Bentley derived Specials. Notable among these were Peter Morley's 4½-litre Bentley Pacey Hassan, Keith Schellenberg's 8-litre Bentley Barnato Hassan ("The Whale") and David Llewellyn's 1924 3/8-litre model. Peter Morley, never a small car man, had raced the Napier Lion-engined Sunbeam "Tigress" in the 1970 Seaman race, coming third behind Neil Corner's V12 Sunbeam "Tiger", and in the early eighties emerged behind the wheel of the 24-litre Bentley Napier that, in the hands of Chris Williams, continues to spin its rear wheels and burn rubber at VSCC events. Add Nigel Arnold-Forster's Delage "Torpille" and between them these cars and drivers dominated the Vintage Seaman races up to and including the Golden Jubilee year. Although there was concern about falling grid sizes in vintage racing in the mid seventies this did not extend to the short handicaps and one make races. For example the Oulton 'Nash race in 1974 attracted 24 chain driven vehicles, the race being won by Keith Hill in his Anzani engined model.

Racing at Cadwell quickly established a popular and settled place in the Club calendar, but for Donington stability was slow in coming – and even into the 21st century has been hard to achieve. It became the fifth race meeting of the year in 1979, when it was held in May. The following year it was run in September and in 1981 reverted to May with the second Silverstone taking up the late summer slot. A very thin gate and poor entry in 1982 meant that it was dropped for 1983 as the Club could not do a satisfactory deal with the track management but an invitation to race at Thruxton with the BARC, and at Castle Combe with the BRSCC, happily filled the gap.

Hill Climbs and Sprints

The hill climbing scene was rather more settled with Prescott, and the joint event with the Midland Automobile Club at Shelsley Walsh both well established and attracting good entry levels. Indeed at the 1980 Prescott eleven Edwardians took part. Footitt continued to show his mastery of the vintage category at the Gloucestershire hill, as did Cottam whose Connaught was rarely beaten in the open category. Speed events on the flat were catered for by Curborough, but thanks to the initiative and efforts of Roger Collings a new sprint joined the calendar in July 1981 when the first meeting at Colerne took place.

" What'll she do, mister?"

The first straight line sprint held by the Club back in 1936 at Littlestone-on-Sea was to be repeated in 1937, after which encroaching bungalows (for which, after all, the road had been built) put a stop to it all. Then, after the long wait imposed by the war, the Club was to organise its next such event at Elstree aerodrome on Easter Monday 1946; a hugely popular success. The next sprint, the one-off at Silverstone in 1949 with no spectators allowed, had been a much more private affair. And there the matter had rested – for there was to be a wait of nearly a third of a century before Colerne provided its next classic straight line sprint. An ex RAF Spitfire airfield near Bath, and still used by the Bristol University Air Squadron, it offered a mile long runway of about 60 yards width, the ends of which were joined by the perimeter track, making for a natural return road. Cars ran in pairs but were timed individually. Results were based on times over a kilometre from a standing start, but they were also taken for the standing ¼ mile so that "What'll she do mister" type questions might be answered.

As well as cars a range of members' other interests were on show. A dozen vintage motorcycles gave demonstration runs, riders including Jenks on his Norton; a penny farthing ("ordinary") provided exercise for Sam Clutton and Roger Collings among others, while twelve aeroplanes were also to join the party. These included Patrick Lindsay's Sopwith Triplane and Hamish Moffatt's Currie Wot – a single seater aerobatic biplane of the 1930s.

Rather faster than, when on the "ordinary", Clutton was to cross the sprint finishing line at 95 mph in the Itala, having been paired with another 12-litre Edwardian – Walker's Panhard Levassor – that reached 94 mph. The quickest time of the day was made by a 1955 Maserati which took 24.73 secs to cover the kilometre, going across

Colerne. A wet day in September 1982. Kenneth Neve in the foreground, driving the 1914 TT Humber of 3300cc was to win the Edwardian class on handicap, while Tom Threlfall in the larger engined Theophile Schneider, here seen just ahead, was to win the class outright.

the finishing line at 131 mph. Llewellyn's much heavier 8-litre Bentley covered the kilometre in 25.39 secs, but crossed the finish at 134 mph to be fastest of the day.

Kenneth Neve, in writing up the meeting, reported that

> "quite simply it was by common consent one of the most enjoyable ever. Colerne is in glorious country. It offers all the room in the world for competitors and watchers and … the relaxed programme schedule allowed everybody time to look in at other peoples companionable picnics. There were no loudspeakers to coerce or instruct or entertain, and marshalling was so unobtrusive as to seem non-existent. Controlled informality you might call it. Or VSCC organisation at its very best … Perhaps the success which attended the meeting was the fact that the great British public did not."

The Brooklands dictum of "the right crowd and no crowding" had certainly applied, as it was to do so over the ensuing years. It remained a members only meeting and despite some very wet days (including one when a mini-river across the runway prevented any runs from taking place) continued to be much enjoyed until, in July 2004, the last meeting took place, appropriately on a very damp day, and with a much reduced entry.

When Donington was dropped from the 1983 list of events the gap in the calendar allowed a new hill climb to take place; Wiscombe Park in Devon. The 1,000 yard course up an attractive wooded valley uses the drive that runs up, via two hairpins and a lesser but tight corner after the downhill start, from Wiscombe House. The initial meeting in May that year evoked the atmosphere of Colerne, reminding Peter Hull of "All those meetings we used to have before everyone got so serious about it." There were eleven runners in Class 6 for 500cc single seaters – cars strongly linked with Wiscombe via the Saturday meeting for these cars, that now precedes the VSCC Sunday event. One of these, driven by Warr (but with no further details available), was to make FTD in 49.87 secs. In comparison Harrison's De Dion-Bouton made slowest time of the day in 123.19 secs. But he did at least get up, which several others failed to do. Brian Gray, rear engined in the Hardy Special, was quick, winning his class in 50.73 secs while Moffatt, in the T35B, was the fastest vintage competitor in 51.56 secs. The slow expansion of the Club's hill climbing calendar had thus continued, from the singleton Prescott as established pre-war, via the addition of Shelsley Walsh at the start of the sixties and then, over a decade later, with the inclusion of Wiscombe.

Ron Footitt on the Shelsley Walsh start line in the 1925 Cognac Special- the combination of a GN chassis with an AC engine – with which he had much success over the years, both on the circuits and particularly on the hills.

Trialling developments

Traditions come, and are eventually obliged to go, for in 1971 telegrams from competitors *en route* for the "Welsh" each October were no longer required. Instead till receipts from petrol stations were sufficient to provide evidence of the transit points visited during the Saturday journeys to Presteigne; perhaps in a small way contributing towards BT's decision to abandon telegrams altogether in 1982. In 1973 a new name was to enter the lists of significant hills used on the trial – a single observed section at Pilleth, a few miles west of Presteigne, being introduced. The farmyard and its surrounds quickly became part of the fabric of the event with a second hill, Pilleth 2, being added in 1974 followed by Pilleth 3 in 1975; the crowds that had gathered at the Smatcher now having an alternative and attractive spectating point, and the trial a logical finishing point that was to last until 2000. Meanwhile the driving tests component of the trial was abandoned in 1974, entries having steadily fallen away.

But an even bigger break with tradition was to occur in 1978 when the nerve centre for the trial was moved from the Radnorshire Arms in Presteigne to the Rhydspence Inn near Hay-on-Wye. Various explanations have been offered but it would seem that a change of management at the hotel lay behind the need to find a different base, while the trial itself was to change still more as the requirement for 200 road miles on the Saturday was reduced to 100 miles. This allowed trialling to begin from Rhydspence in the afternoon and a new set of hills in and around Hay to be introduced.

For the 1973 event there had been a brief overlap in the use of both the Smatcher and Pilleth as trials sections, but the iconic and now tamed Smatcher, that had been part of the "Welsh" since 1939, was then to disappear from the lists and not make any sort of return for over twenty years. Competitors with a taste for anagrams for just one year had to be satisfied with the introduction of a hill named Retchams in 1981, this (almost) being Smatcher spelt backwards. But despite the changes and the accompanying murmurs that "things were not what they used to be" the Welsh continued to flourish and entries to hold up. Twelve Vauxhalls competed in 1979 to remind of earlier years

The Welsh Trial, 1974. Nigel Arnold-Forster in his 1925 Anzani-engined Frazer Nash confidently tackles the ford, while his wife Pam watches how to do it as she awaits her turn.

before the advance of Austin Sevens, while seventy-five competitors took part in 1980. These certainly did what they could to maintain tradition for the trial was won by Moffatt in his 1923 T13 Bugatti, while Clarke, Spence, Collings, Threlfall and several other long term stalwarts were among those who won awards.

Support and interest in the driving tests-cum-concours part of the Welsh weekend had been disappointing in the early seventies and a permanent site for them hard to find, so yet another break with tradition had occurred when these were dropped. However, and in part due to the enthusiasm and hard work of Rosemary Burke from the office, they made a brief re-appearance, along with the concours, in nearby Knighton in 1981.

Further north the Lakeland reminded members that there was indeed another trial, the Smith family and friends building up and developing their event over the years. Drumhouse had introduced competitors to a hill on which the drivers of the four-wheel drive trucks that used it on a daily basis were said to get danger money, while new sections on Forestry Commission land were being added to the mix. Five of these,

Drumhouse, the classic Lakeland hill, seen here in 1970 with a Frazer Nash and a pair of Alvises at the head of the queue waiting to tackle its rocky hairpins. The slopes above Honister Pass can be seen beyond.

in the woods above Bassenthwaite Lake, made their first appearance in 1977, and one of the delights of competing in the Lakeland is motoring along the network of well maintained forestry roads linking the sections that provide glorious views of the hills around, and of the lake (on sunny days at least) twinkling below.

The results of the 1982 Lakeland give a clear idea as to how trials fields had developed within the Club over the forty eight years since its first such event early in 1935. Of the 60 entries (just over half of which got up Drumhouse) Austin Sevens were easily the most numerous at sixteen entries and from these was to come the overall winner in the person of Geoff Winder. Nine Frazer Nashes, five each from Riley and Vauxhall, four from Alvis, three from MG and two each from BMW and HRG were accompanied by singleton entries from Lea-Francis (Spence in his special came second overall) and a Ford (the Model A of Threlfall winning Class 2) as well as other single entries from Bugatti, Singer, Humber, Bentley, AJS, Swift, Morris and Wolseley.

Further south a new trial had been added to the Club calendar in 1975. A group of members in and around Somerset had long felt that a trial was needed in the area, so set out to plan one. It nearly happened in 1973 but the fuel crisis of that year put a stop to all competitive events using public roads, so, along with the Measham it was put on hold. 1974 saw the 50th anniversary of Frazer Nash, so the local group, which contained many of the trial planners, ran a one day event on a single site and it is from this small beginning that the Wessex trial was to grow. From the outset they felt that it should be a social as well as competitive occasion, spreading across an early April weekend. After a lunchtime start from a pub at Priddy, a village on top of the Mendips where the locals say that even the devil gets cold, the attractive route, including Cheddar Gorge, eventually got competitors back to Wells. A buffet supper in a private room in the Swan Hotel, just across the road from the Cathedral Close, rounded off the day. On the Sunday morning it was back to trialling, a cluster of sections inclusive of a timed tie-breaker being held in Shipham Quarries. The Wessex, along with the other two trials in the Club calendar of the mid seventies, was to become well established and prove justly popular. Barry Clarke was to win the Wessex in 1978 and 1979 and was then to make it a hat-trick in 1980, his knowledge of Austin Sevens and his expertise in driving them being virtually without parallel. To demonstrate the durability of his Lea-Francis special and his own not inconsiderable skills Harry Spence in his forty seventh year of trialling, was to win the Wessex in 1983, during which Doc Harris, described as "one of the most unchanging sights in post war vintage motoring", was alas forced to retire.

1973–1983

"Yer could tell wun make from anuther in them days, couldn't yer?"

In the spring of 1978 another new trial was to emerge. Scotland had seen several driving tests in previous years but in May Dick Smith, having travelled up from the Lakes to help plan and organise the event, acted as Clerk of the Course at the Club's first Scottish Trial. This was held on one site, akin to a production car trial, a format to be followed for some years – albeit the term 'on site' gives rather a false impression of the 1985 event which was held on a five thousand acre estate, with the very varied hills well spread out and requiring transport sections between them.

The Measham and other Rallies

On a much larger canvas, for in the case of the Measham considerable mileages were of course involved, rallying continued, but increasingly faced with difficulties over authorisation. Modern rallying, involving "plot and bash" route finding leading to high speed motoring along the narrow lanes involved, and usually in the hours of darkness, did not make for good public relations; especially so in the more popular areas for the sport, inclusive of the Welsh Marches. None of which made things easy for the organisers of the Measham. In 1969 there had been problems obtaining route permission from the police but the event did eventually run, after much nail biting from Mike Bullett and his fellow officials; they were rewarded by a good entry of fifty four in 1969, and good weather in 1971. However, route approval problems re-surfaced in 1972, when effectively the roads around Ludlow were put out of bounds. There were difficulties also in 1973, this time with the RAC. But eventually, the date having been moved to February, when it clashed with the marshals' dinner, it did go ahead, with fifty eight crews signing on. Problems simply would not go away, for the winter of 1973/74 saw another oil crisis and a consequent cancellation. Thereafter entries tended to fall away, the sixty of 1975 dropping to forty one in 1976, then, after a small rise in the next year, down to only thirty five. The Club's *Newsletter* of December 1979 carried a gloomy message, reporting the cancellation of the rally for a second year running.

> "The reasons are contained within the *New Rally Rules for 1980* – a publication sent out by the British Motor Sports Council in September … The new rules are extremely onerous and the organisers felt that they would not be able to cope with the new requirements, particularly in regard to public relations work along the whole length of the route … It is unlikely that it will be possible to run the Measham Rally in the form we know it in the years to come, but consideration is being given to some alternative form of competition for the future."

A gloomy article by John Rowley in the 1980 Spring *Bulletin* outlined its thirty year history concluding "… that the Club's most adventurous and challenging event has been ruthlessly destroyed."

However, all was not lost for scatter rallies, neither involving fixed routes nor the demanding public relations requirements that go with them, provided an answer – as did a move to a new area. So on the night of January 17th/18th 1981 the Elcot Night Navigation Rally took place to be won by Peter Binns and his navigator David Filsell in a 1939 HRG. (It is worth noting that well into the 21st century Filsell continues to navigate with distinction in a very similar car, the HRS, built and driven by his long time rallying partner Barry Clarke, and which in effect is an HRG based Special. Rallyists as well as triallists can be very durable). The scatter rally approach was repeated in 1982, returning to Powys. Annabel Jones, who was to navigate her father's Vauxhall 30-98 to a First, reported that it took her a full two hours to plot 16 of the 20 points that could be visited, 15 chosen from them being the target. The clue sheets had been

"SOMETIMES I THINK HE UNDERSTANDS EVERY WORD I SAY"

issued at 10.30pm and at least six crews were still plotting at 1.00am. Navigationally the 1983 event was rather less demanding, being a matter of "plot and bash" to establish the route and target timing rather than regularity to establish the schedule. The disappointingly small entry of 27 sportingly included the 1915 Rolls-Royce 40/50 of Tanner and Close. Marshalling on night events poses the challenge of keeping warm and sometimes involves huddling around a glowing brazier to do so. However, the warmly clad group, so doing near Cheddar were, to the surprise of the competitors, not marshals at all but picketing water workers. Binns and Filsell, this time in a Riley Nine, were to win again, with Cattell and Cork in a Riley Lynx first of the PVTs. Tom Threlfall and his wife Di in a Model A Ford won Class 3.

Further north the Buxton Rally continued, to be joined by the Teesdale which in 1979 also had its share of route authorisation problems. The winners that year were J M Potter and B Hughes in a 1926 AC, a pairing that regularly did well on the rallies of the time. Navigational challenges were clearly growing harder, and none more so than those involving "Squadron Leader Viggles", whose name graced many an Eastern Rally route card in the early eighties, his creator being Clive Bowyer a member from Cambridge. Viggles put his aeronautical knowledge to good use so that navigators had to grapple with details of his airborne observations, compass bearings, the average speeds of aircraft as well as of cars, and the location of often disused airfields to find out where he had located time controls. He did not make an appearance in 1984, when he was reported to have been "an unmourned absentee", but was to return on an Eastern Rally in 2006, still ranked as a Squadron Leader. Navigational expertise had clearly not helped him to gain promotion after more than twenty years.

Driving Tests and the social scene

Navigation of a rather different sort was becoming a feature of driving tests in the late seventies as blindfolds, Le Mans starts and the like were largely discarded and replaced by increasingly complex route finding around a multitude of bollards, ins and outs of "garages" and the stopping astride of lines. Much as rallies were getting harder a more serious approach was slowly replacing the previously carefree gymkhana mood of earlier driving test meetings.

For some time the start of each year had seen tests held at Charterhouse, but they were to move to Thruxton in the early seventies and then, breaking with the southern traditions, to Donington in 1975. But for 1976 it was back down to Hampshire and the army base at Cove before, in 1977, finally settling at Brooklands. With vintage sports cars using at least parts of the old circuit, the site was being used for competition motoring for the first time since 1939.

The winter tests had long been held at Silverstone, where "Tony Bird's tortuous tests" kept competitors thinking as well as driving on the usually bitter December days. The circuit management kept faith with the Club in allowing its otherwise unused facilities to remain operational for the single small winter event, but with entries numbering only in the fifties or sixties it became increasingly disenchanted with providing these, until only the loos were made available. It was clear that the time had come for a move. Malcolm Elder – notable for competing in a top heavy Austin shooting brake that leant at alarming angles around the bollards – happened to mention to Peter Hull that he would keep an eye open for suitable sites in Oxfordshire, where he lived. In the next *Newsletter* he was surprised to see the announcement that Malcolm Elder had volunteered to organise the tests. "Of course you did old boy" replied a laughing Peter Hull on being tackled on the matter, and so it came to pass.

Elder decided that more tests and less waiting were needed. Queuing was too much a feature of the Silverstone events. Also, he felt, a social side to the day was required. The old airfield at Enstone seemed to fit the bill, with plenty of room for tests to be both numerous and well spread out; and with a good pub, the Crown Inn, in the adjacent village.

The first meeting on the new site took place in 1978 and even the old control tower was pressed into service, providing as it did for somewhere where the medical inspections needed for racing licences could be held. Many of the windows were broken or missing, which at least demonstrated that the Club's racers were proof against hypothermia, as well as having the heart, lungs and eyesight that they needed to drive fast cars. At lunchtimes the pub, not unexpectedly, did a roaring trade, while the cars coming down from the tests rather took over the village. There were a number of grumbles and objections at these invasions until one vocal and assertive lady decided to call in the police to deal with a vintage car that had been parked on the grass triangle by the Crown Inn. The honest constable duly arrived and undertook to go inside and identify the miscreant. "Oh yes, that's the Detective Chief Superintendent's car" came the reply. Elder responded, realising PR was needed. Before further events everyone in the village was notified and invited along to watch the tests, and so peace was eventually restored.

After four years the Enstone surfaces were becoming very cut up, so for a couple of years the tests were moved to another ex-airfield, Barford St John. It proved very suitable and as such was used by other motor clubs. As a communications centre a number of aerials were to be found located around the perimeter, one of which fell victim to an errant modern auto test competitor. Permissions were withdrawn and it was back to Enstone.

Both warmer and more leisurely was the rally to the Loire sponsored by Dunlop in May 1980. Thirty cars and about eighty people took part on a tour that took them from Dieppe, through Normandy, across the Seine, to Le Mans, the chateaux country around Saumur, and back via Chartres; the journey peppered with receptions in towns along the way. The well fed and wined participants were accompanied by a yellow Dunlop van carrying their luggage, and another van from Vintage Tyre Supplies, but the spares it carried were never needed. The only mechanical mishap suffered was a seized valve on a Humber, but this was quickly cured. On the way back home the group was to learn that two of their number were on their honeymoon. As they had carried two Dunlop guests in the back of their car for the full five days one must salute their selfless hospitality.

Another essentially social occasion was to occur on New Year's Day 1981, by which date every eligible car within the VSCC had reached the age of fifty, and so the New Year gatherings came into being. Considerable numbers of members and non-members brought out their cars, first licensed pre 1931, to descend on pub car parks around the country. The *Newsletter* reported assemblies at the 'Bell' at Welford on Avon, the 'Folly' at Adstock, the 'Shears' at Collingbourne Ducis, the 'Floating Light' near Oldham, the 'Crown' at Cookham and, of course, the 'Phoenix'. *Motor Sport* reported that the turnout at the latter was "quite staggering". Its report even ran to a coloured picture of the occasion, and looking at it a third of a century later it all seems strangely familiar. The cars are just the same, the pint mugs are the same size, and it is only the flared trouser bottoms that give the game away.

Another New Year's gathering had taken place at the Verzons, just outside Ledbury in Herefordshire, when some forty cars were present. A contemporary report reads that:

> "it was all very nicely wound up when a well known VSCC member took off in his Currie Wot biplane from a nearby field and treated the assembly to some low fly-pasts, a loop, and even a flour bombing display."

1973–1983

The incorrigible Hamish Moffatt was later to feel the wrath of the Civil Aviation Authority.

Now approaching seventy five Clutton, continued to live in the Isle of Man and it was the brainchild of Roger and Judy Collings that a group of members should go out to visit him. Fifty VSCC cars and their occupants left Heysham for a choppy crossing to the island, to enjoy a stay that included watching the Manx Classic Motor Cycle Race, a lap of the closed TT course behind a demonstration Jaguar XK140, driving tests on Jurby airfield, a "mild" navigation event and a trip on the narrow gauge steam railway. A visit was also made to Sam Clutton's house for an organ recital and George Daniels' exposition on the clocks and watches therein.

Few clubs can even hope to match the enormous range of experiences provided by the VSCC, the majority of which could not take place without the organisational underpinnings provided by the office. Peter Hull had been in post as Secretary for just on two years when the move to Russell Road had taken place on 1st October 1973. Tony Bird was well established as Competitions Secretary with Rosemary Burke, effectively, the membership Secretary, while Jim Whyman was also in post. There was then some stability until 1977 when Tony Bird retired, his last official duty being as Clerk of the Course at that year's Prescott. Jim Whyman then took over as Competitions Secretary, but resigned in 1979, his place being taken by Martin Grant-Peterkin on his retirement from the army. Hull, Grant-Peterkin and Rosemary Burke, together with two part-timers, then became the office staff to service an ever growing Club with its ever expanding programme. Peter Hull, along with Tim Carson, had consistently shown that he was primarily a Club member rather than just an employee, once putting a note in the *Newsletter* that if he could not be contacted at the office members could phone him at home of an evening. These three, aided by two long service part-timers, Andrea Green and Sally de la Riviere, were to take the Club up and into its Golden Jubilee in 1984. Under the normal arrangements Tom Threlfall, past Editor of *The Bulletin* and Lycett winner, would have retired from the Presidency at the end of 1983, but it was agreed that he should remain at the helm to see it through its fiftieth year.

The Golden Jubilee Year
1984

When the provisional calendar for 1984 was published the staff at Russell Road must have taken a deep breath. The year ahead was to comprise over three dozen events inclusive of five race meetings, five trials, half a dozen driving tests, four rallies, three Light Car and Edwardian Section events and the Pomeroy, while taking in a very full week at Malvern in early July, where the Golden Jubilee was to be duly celebrated. With approximately six thousand members, of whom six hundred were to attend the Annual General Meeting, then still held in London, the Club at the age of fifty was indeed in rude health. The full calendar was as follows:-

January	Marshals' Dinner
	Driving Tests – Goodwood
February	Mendip Night Rally
March	Pomeroy Trophy
	Annual General Meeting
	Wessex Trial
April	Light Car Welsh Weekend
	Silverstone Race Meeting
	Scottish Trial
May	Northern Rally – Thirsk
	Curborough Speed Trials

	Donington Race Meeting
	Wiscombe Hill Climb
	Boulogne Bicycle Rally
June	Oulton Park Race Meeting
July	*Golden Jubilee Week:-*
	Driving tests – Malvern
	Light Car Rally
	Driving tests – Silverstone
	Navigation Rally
	Driving tests – Oulton Park
	Trial – Malvern
	Scenic run to Prescott
	Shelsley Walsh Hill Climb
	Also in July – the second Silverstone.
August	Prescott Hill Climb
	Shuttleworth visit
	Cadwell Park Race Meeting
September	Madresfield Driving Tests and Concours
	Colerne Speed Trials
	Light Car and Edwardian Rally
October	The Welsh Weekend
	Eastern Rally
November	Lakeland Trial
December	Driving Tests – Enstone

The Golden Jubilee Week

Without doubt the high spot of the year was the week at Malvern, both the town itself, with its relaxed and somewhat old fashioned air and the delightful surrounding countryside, with the Malvern hills separating Worcestershire and Herefordshire, and made up of some of the oldest rocks in England, being ideally suited to the ambience of the Club. Martin Grant-Peterkin, the overall organiser of the week, which immediately preceded his retirement, had selected the Winter Gardens as its administration base. On the Tuesday members drove to the town from around the country and checked in there, while the evening was given over to a party in the nearby ivy clad Abbey Hotel. Next morning only slightly more serious activities got under way with driving tests held on the Three Counties Showground. There were 199 entries to be catered for, while

An atypical competition car on a gymkhana style driving test during the Malvern Golden Jubilee Week. It was one of nearly two hundred taking part in this event. Hancock's 1925 R1 6-30 Daimler requires its driver to have a very long reach to safely drop a ball into the somewhat unstable receptacle alongside.

the tasks involved rolling dice (the score to be remembered after garaging among the cones), the expected fast and slow test, a braking ladder and the balancing of balls on a series of cones. The overall winner was Keith Hill in his 1923/29 Crouch Helix, a car campaigned today by his daughter Susan, while the best Edwardian performance was made by Roger Collings in his 1903 60hp Mercedes, a car that he used for many years. Proceedings concluded with a civic reception in the Winter Gardens that evening.

Thursday was rather more energetic, at least for those who had entered the Silverstone tests, as organised by John Whyman. Of the ninety entrants only seventy three turned up on the day, so perhaps two party evenings in a row had taken their toll; late entries on the day were therefore accepted. The tests themselves involved some quick motoring; standing and flying ¼ mile runs took place on the main Club circuit straight, there was a high speed "wiggle-woggle" between Becketts and Copse and a braking test on the pits straight. L J Stretton in his 1923/29 GN Martyr emerged as the overall winner.

The Golden Jubilee Year

On the same day, in the marvellous weather that was to continue all week, the Light Car and Edwardian Section members enjoyed a navigation rally. The routes (for there were two variants – a long one at 74 miles and a shorter one at 54 miles) designed by Brian Gray took the cars west into rural Herefordshire. Notable among those just following the route were Bill Boddy and Denis Jenkinson in a 1934 Lagonda, while at the other end of the age scale was George Daniels' competing 1907 45hp Daimler. An even older car was Gilbert's 1905 12/18 Riley which also completed the course. Eventually the field made its way to Clehonger and the Finish, where the Collings family generously laid on tea, complete with strawberries and cream. J M Potter in a 1922 AC Empire went home with the Trophy for the best performance.

Come Friday an enormous entry of 150 cars started from the Three Counties Showground on the Golden Jubilee Rally. Organised by Clive Bowyer, who for many years had been involved with running the Eastern Rally, he could not resist bringing back the ever demanding Squadron Leader Viggles, who had a wide choice of disused airfields in the flat lands of Worcestershire on which to base his directions. However, the majority

The Golden Jubilee Week LCES rally. A Talbot 10/23, followed by an 8/18 Humber, pass a sun-soaked marshal as she dutifully records the time of their passing from her lofty perch.

of competitors made it back to a long lunch stop at Worcester Rugby Club, before the afternoon settled down to the less challenging matter of tulip diagrams which took competitors back to the showground. The organisation involved in such an event is all too easily taken for granted. Beyond providing the final instructions and route cards for 150 entrants (reams of paper thus required) the marshals at the time controls around the route all needed location specific instructions, while the caterers at the Rugby Club had to provide for some four hundred plus lunches during the middle of the day. And out of all this came the winner, J F Harris in a 1936 Lagonda Rapide Special.

Also on the Friday the northerners be-sported themselves at Oulton Park. Many of them had wined and dined on the previous evening, where the toast to the Club had been proposed by Anthony Heal, while next morning the competition tackled eight not very serious tests arranged around the circuit. These included the usual "wiggle-woggles", driving around a series of cones with passengers shouting instructions to drivers wearing buckets over their heads, and a final test which involved throwing darts at a dartboard, drivers having to score at least fifty before being allowed to proceed to the finish line. One competitor gave up because she could not hit the dartboard at all, but Patrick Marsh came away with a broad smile having won the event in a 1925 T23 Bugatti.

Saturday was to round things off at Malvern. A trial on the estate of nearby Eastnor Castle had been organised by Hamish Moffatt, with Geoff Winder as his Deputy Clerk of the Course. The day was dry and dusty with conditions far from ideal for trialling, but the final section of the ten tackled was a much needed timed test which was used to resolve the many ties. P J Garland in a 1936 1½-litre HRG was quickest by far, and went away with the Trophy for the overall winner.

Less dusty, and with the sun in its favour, was a scenic run organised by Barry Clarke. A mix of routes, involving pleasant pubs, lovely scenery and 'pick-your-own' strawberry fields, eventually took participants to Prescott where touring ascents were kindly allowed by the Bugatti Owners Club. *The Bulletin* reported on an incident there. "'Sir' said the marshal to the Bentley driver who appeared at the start line with dog beside him and cigar alight 'the RAC would not approve of your dog smoking while ascending the hill'. 'Sir' replied the Bentley driver 'the RAC would not approve of the start line marshal officiating with a glass of beer in his hand'." The day concluded with a very successful black tie Golden Jubilee Ball in the Winter Gardens, organised by Ann Shoosmith; but the week was not quite over.

On the Sunday the short journey to nearby Shelsley Walsh for the VSCC/MAC hill climb was made. Here an extremely large attendance was rewarded with another sunny and memorable day. The memorial that stands at the foot of the hill, commemorating Raymond Mays and his long association with the venue, was unveiled and a selection of cars significant in his life ascended the hill – a Brescia Bugatti, a Riley, the supercharged Vauxhall Villiers, two ERAs and, to cap it all, Rivers Fletcher driving the V16 BRM from the Donington collection. The competitive part of the proceedings saw thirteen Bugattis, a similar number of GN sprint specials-cum-Frazer Nash and five ERAs in action. Fastest Time of the Day went to David Black in his Tipo B Alfa Romeo. Of the specials the original Spider, in the hands of Ron Sant, went extremely well to win the up to 1500cc Vintage class, while other class winners included Tony Stephens in ERA R12C, Martin Morris in the bigger engined ERA R11B and Tom Threlfall as the winner of the Edwardian/early Vintage Class in the Theophile Schneider. As President he had worked extremely hard both in the run-up to the Golden Jubilee week and during the six days involved, so no doubt he returned home well satisfied with the outcomes, while Martin Grant Peterkin could also smile and sit back at last.

The Club, when founded fifty years previously, had identified its objectives as "… to provide competitive … and social events for its members", and during the Malvern week it had clearly excelled in both these respects. Much of the flavour of the Jubilee, and indeed of the Club more generally, was captured in the professionally made video – *The Vintage Spirit*, largely filmed earlier in the year. With the moustachioed Professor Jimmy Edwards as the "reporter", at times accompanied by Peter Hull in an Alvis 12/50, visits were made to the Wessex Trial, the first Silverstone meeting, Wiscombe

Peter Hull, Secretary of the Club for fifteen years between 1971 and 1986, and then briefly in 1988/1989, in characteristic laughing mode. He acted as host to "Professor" Jimmy Edwards who was to compere the video "The Vintage Spirit" made to record the Club's 50th year, conveying him to and from events and around the Malvern showground in an Alvis 12/50.

and the Light Car Rally. Edwards proved excellent in his role, resisting the temptation to play to the gallery and instead asking informed and well chosen questions of the members he encountered and leaving a filmed record that well lived up to its title, with the emphasis being on the people involved. Another permanent record of the Golden Jubilee Year is to be found in the commemorative booklet published that year, edited by the hard working Martin Grant Peterkin. In a series of articles, written by competing Club members, here the emphasis is on the special natures of their particular cars and, along with good photography and Peacop cartoons, it provides another perspective on the Club at that time.

The racing year

There was no shortage of events for the racing fraternity to choose from during the Golden Jubilee year – in addition to the ten speed events organised by the Club there were also invitation races at Silverstone and Snetterton on offer. Dominant competitors, present at most meetings, and very much in the thick of the competition, included the ever forceful Peter Morley in the Bentley-Napier, in stark contrast to Stuart Harper's Morgan 3 wheeler which had started life with a water-cooled MAG engine, but which had later been converted to air cooled power. Small though it was it could give most of the Bentleys a good run for their money when it was going well, albeit Tim Llewellyn was always a hard man to beat in his 3/8 Bentley. Other notable vintage contenders almost always included Ron Footitt in his Cognac and on occasion John Williamson in the V12 Delage which had broken the Land Speed Record at over 140 mph back in 1924. Guy Smith in a single seater Frazer Nash powered by a Speed 25 Alvis engine was also quick throughout the year, especially so on the hills.

In Pre-War All-comers races ERAs had long been in the ascendant but during 1984 David Black's Tipo B Monoposto Alfa Romeo showed excellent form for in addition to its Shelsley victory it was to win the Seaman Trophy at Oulton – the first such Alfa victory for over thirty years. Ever present among the ERAs were those of Patrick Lindsay, who sometimes enjoyed a choice between "Remus" and his ERA engined Delage (which had been converted to 2-litres with a B type engine, rather than its original E type motor), and Martin Morris (R11B) . Fifteen of them were on the grid to compete in the special ERA race at the second Silverstone meeting.

The All Comers scratch races during the year were adequately rather than well supported. In addition to such regular competitors as Alan Cottam (usually driving his

Connaught – but on occasion a Maserati 250F that had been assembled from spare parts and thus was without a continuous history) were the highly competitive Lotus 16s of Bruce Halford, Christopher Mann and Simon Phillips, various but not always numerous Maserati 250Fs, and a number of 2-litre Cooper Bristols and Connaughts. Oddities that appeared during the year included Patrick Lindsay's "Turtle Drilling Company" Special – an Indianapolis car that competed at the second Silverstone in the hands of Neil Corner, complete with advertising decals as had adorned it while thundering around "The Brickyard". With only two gears, and offset to give better balance to the car around left hand corners, it was certainly not a natural for road racing circuits.

"I'd have booked that chap in the Trojan too, but I couldn't catch him"

The Jubilee racing year had started as ever at Silverstone, on a sunny April day with the High Speed Trial, now reduced to forty minutes and a single plug change. Bugattis, not unsurprisingly, dominated the Itala Trophy, but Julian Majzub most certainly was surprised when he capsized his Type 35B on the warming up lap. The race itself was won by Nick Mason in a similar car. The last race of the day – the traditional Survivor's Handicap – was notable for excellent handicapping, the first five finishing very close together, while a report on the race noted that "Peter Morley had the Napier Bentley well wound up and was doing his best to terrify all the innocent people ahead of him".

Curborough, a few weeks later in early May, also saw some large cars in action around the sprint course, Jack Sears in the ex Forrest Lycett 8-litre Bentley winning his class. Brian Gray in the Hardy Special was to win the up to 1000cc racing car class, while Guy Smith (Alvis Nash) had the satisfaction of beating Ron Footitt (Cognac Special) in the pre 1940s racing car class. Fastest Time of the Day went to Cottam in the Connaught.

Curborough had been breezy but the next day, when competitors arrived at Donington, was bleak and bitter, the condition of the circuit was rather disappointing, while the projected race for rear-engined Grand Prix cars had to be cancelled due to lack of support. However, Lou Wickham turned up to race his 12/50 Alvis – having entered the Nidderdale Rally on Saturday 5th May, Curborough on Sunday 6th May and Donington on the Bank Holiday Monday, 7th May – his aim being to compete in every Club event across the year. The most eventful race of the day was that for the Shuttleworth and Nuffield Trophies. David Black stalled the Alfa on the front row of the grid. Bruce Spollon in ERA R8C jumped the start and then spun off, Rodney Felton in a 4 CL Maserati had a monster spin, forcing Stephens (ERA R12C) to take to an escape road, while Hart spun his Riley out of the race. And this was all on the first lap. Once everything had eventually settled down Black made up for lost time and narrowly won from Patrick Lindsay.

Wiscombe in late May was rather quieter, dampened by rain for the second runs, but not before John Venables-Llewellyn in the 2-litre ERA R4A had set a new VSCC record for the hill and with it FTD. Bruce Spollon (R8C) was close behind with Cottam third in the Connaught. Moffatt in his T35B Bugatti was fastest in the vintage class, while Hickey Hickling, a great supporter of Edwardian motoring, won that class in a 1917 Dodge Four.

Oulton Park in June was to be run by Ted Smith, his first event as Competition Secretary of the Club, while the office was also informally represented at the meeting by Rosemary Burke, who won two prizes in the Concours with her Type 30 Bugatti. The programme included a 500cc race, Oulton traditionally being innovative in inviting other clubs to participate, while the Seaman Trophy races provided few surprises; Footitt streaking away in the vintage event to win by nearly three quarters of a lap and David Black winning the Historic Trophy, with the highest ERA, Bruce Spollon, relegated to second place.

Shelsley and Silverstone then followed before it was off to Prescott in August and another win for David Black in the Alfa Romeo. To no-one's surprise Footitt in the Cognac went home with the Vintage award while Threlfall was again the fastest Edwardian. Also in August came Cadwell Park with yet another win for Footitt, but in the Pre-War Racing Cars race Black lost a wheel from the Alfa while still in the lead, giving the race to Martin Morris after a typically fast yet steady drive in his ERA. The Cognac Special, after its earlier exertions, was forced to retire.

The speed season finished in the comparative calm and "clubby" atmosphere of Colerne. In the "ordinary" (penny farthing) bike race Patrick Marsh beat Roger Collings – both future Presidents. George Daniels, in a 1907 poppet valved Daimler, just failed to exceed the national road speed limit by crossing the finishing line at 69.9 mph, while Black's Alfa Romeo was victorious yet again, taking 23.8 secs to cover the standing kilometre. Fastest car over the finishing line was Dean's T59/50 Bugatti at 137.9 mph. Thus, in a happy and relaxed manner, the speed season drew to its close at this most private and laid-back of venues.

Rallies, Trials and Driving Tests

Of all the forms of motor sport organised within the Club that of rallying is the least specialist in terms of the types of car needed to do well. Perhaps this is why the Jubilee booklet made no mention of same – but despite this invisibility the rallyists were out and about during the year, starting out one January night on a partially Cotswold based "Mendip Navigation Rally". The Measham was nearly an unwilling casualty of authorisation problems, for the Gloucestershire Police had initially put a veto on the Club using "their" roads for the Mendip event, but were eventually over-ruled by the RAC. After 140 miles of competition, and as if to demonstrate the wide range of vehicles that can be rallied effectively, the winners emerged as Cattell and Cork with a "clean sheet" penalty free run in their Riley 12/6, the father and daughter team of Tony and Annabel Jones in a Vauxhall 30-98 won the vintage award and the Lees family in a Morris Cowley took home the Jeddere-Fisher Trophy for the best Light Car performance.

Up in the Yorkshire Dales the Nidderdale Rally in early May took competitors some 100 miles through lovely scenery, with the very experienced rallying duo of Glover and

Roberts emerging the winners. Squadron Leader Viggles, after his contributions to the Malvern event, was evidently on leave during the final rally of the year, the Eastern, being replaced by a crow that flew in various directions. Fiats did well, for the rally was won by Toms and Biggs in a 1925 501B with the PVT section going to Cameron and Patten in a Balilla. This was to be the last Eastern Rally organised by Clive Bowyer who stepped down after seven years, to be followed in the role by Peter Glover.

Trialling during the year was in the now well established pattern. The Wessex was dry and saw a tie between Barry Clarke and David Marsh, which without any timed decider, was to stand. The Welsh, still based at Rhydspence, was to be another dry trial and yet another win for Barry Clarke, while the tests-cum-concours element saw Keith Stimson (Riley 9) come away with the Tallylyn Trophy for best performance on the tests (nowadays this Trophy is the principal award for the navigation element of the Welsh) while Green's 2-litre Lagonda won the Concours. Then finally up to the Lakes, where the rain still held off. Breaking with tradition the entry split into two for the start, the well established Wythop Forest being joined by a second venue at the Bridge Hotel, Buttermere, spreading the field so as to reduce queues at the foot of the hills. The main award winners were Geoff Winder (1930 Austin Ulster) and Tom Threlfall (1928 Model A Ford), the latter having frequent competition successes throughout his Presidential year, but not quite to the extent of his achieving a Lycett Memorial hat-trick, following on his wins of 1982 and 1983.

It had been expected that the Golden Jubilee Year would have started at Brooklands, but due to building work at the old circuit the January driving tests were moved to the newer circuit of Goodwood. The gymkhana approach to tests was still being continued for they included gyrations on a skid pan, the use of starting handles to move cars and the carrying of a jug of water during one test, with marks being lost for liquid spilt. The Enstone tests at the other end of the year were rather more serious, photographs of the event showing how rough some of the surfaces used had become. Even the drive at Madresfield had been found to be rather bumpy when the traditional gathering in the lee of the Malverns took place in September. Five tests and a concours were involved, all under the watchful eyes of Jim and Rosemary Adams, who had organised the event for many years. The very good entry of eighty two cars enjoyed a typical mix of serious and not-so-serious tests, with six of them coming away with first class awards. Interest in the concours was fading by this time and there were only five entrants. The expected winner, Neale's Rolls-Royce Silver Ghost, was pipped at the post by Stimson's Riley.

The Golden Jubilee Year

"OH! NO! I DON'T HAVE ANY MORE OF THAT SORT OF NONSENSE SINCE I BOUGHT HIM ONE OF THOSE!"

To complete this survey of the Club at play during 1984 (for at that stage in its history not too many people took too many things too seriously, having listened to the injunctions of Peter Hull that they should remember that they did these things for fun) must come the Pomeroy. Even the weather had remembered that it was a rather special year, for sunshine and blue skies greeted the seventy nine competitors who arrived at Silverstone early on a March morning. The usual mix of "wiggle-woggle", braking and acceleration tests started off the day, with the afternoon taken up by the high speed trials around the circuit. Five out of the previous ten Pomeroys had been won in Bugattis, followed by a trio of "modern" wins (two by a Frazer Nash Le Mans and one by a Reliant Sabre) but the Jubilee event was to see John Horton's 1928 Bugatti T43 winning again, as he had done in 1977 and 1980. It was to be the last vintage win for over a decade, with either "moderns" or PVTs then taking the honours up until 1996.

As 1984 drew to its close the whole Club, members, officers and staff alike, could look back on a quite outstanding year. In several ways it can be seen as the end of an era, especially so at Russell Road where there were a number of significant breaks with the past. While Peter Hull was to continue as Secretary for a few more years his assistant Rosemary Burke had decided to retire. Following the premature death of her husband she had stayed at her post to become a well liked and respected member of the team, her cheerful presence evident at events across the country, as was her hands-on involvement with old cars. She wrote a brief farewell message for *The Bulletin*:

> "I shall be leaving the Club office at Christmas and going to Manchester. MANCHESTER?? Yes, about six miles from where I was born, actually. A bit wetter than Newbury, open skies, sheep and bogs, cobbles and a touch of the Dark Satanics. Lots to do there. I shall miss the office but count myself lucky that I have been part of such a Club. Good luck to my successor and love to you all. Rosemary."

Martin Grant Peterkin, in handing over the role of Competition Secretary to Ted Smith, was to remain in much closer contact with the doings of the Club, quickly making the transition from official to competitor by competing at Colerne in his 3/4½-litre Bentley, and to good effect, being fastest of the larger vintage sports cars.

In June had come the sad news of Margery Carson's death. She had died in hospital shortly following a stroke and heart attack. Together with Tim she had enjoyed thirteen years of retirement just outside Folkestone and their happy partnership, that had so benefited the Club, was finally at an end. Shortly afterwards Carson decided to return to Newbury, where he bought a flat and was able to maintain close contact with old friends and would frequently pop along to Russell Road in order to retain his links with the Club that had long meant so much to him.

Russell Road – The Later Years
1985–1997

In the somewhat cramped accommodation of the ground floor of 121 Russell Road and with the Jubilee Year safely behind them, the staff got down to the task ahead, catering for the needs of the growing membership and running the crowded competition calendar. Up in Cheshire David Thirlby – noted Frazer Nash enthusiast – was settling into the role of *Bulletin* Editor, a post he was to hold with distinction from the beginning of 1985 until handing over to John Warburton in the spring of 2001. Peter Hull, in his last full year as Secretary, was supported by Ted Smith in charge of competitions, while Brian Harcourt-Smith had also joined the team in anticipation of taking over Peter Hull's role in the following year. As well as the physical overcrowding of the office another concern was that of over-subscription of entries for almost all events. A ballot system was tried, together with some slight sifting of entries to ensure reasonably balanced fields within the classes at races and speed events.

By good fortune the top floor of Russell Road came onto the market in 1986 and was purchased by the Club. As Secretary Peter Hull was not to enjoy the extra space so gained, but on retirement he was to get to know the top floor very well when, largely under his direction, it was brought into use as the long needed library and archive. In the early years of the Club's history a handbook collection had been established and from the mid fifties, and for many years afterwards, it was run by Dr Hytten from Aberdeen, who provided a postal loans service for members. Over the years various donations of book collections had been made to the Club and a few books purchased, but with nowhere to properly house them Cameron Millar, Maserati enthusiast and competition driver, took them under his wing until at last the volumes could be properly housed and catalogued.

It often rains in August, as Prescott in 1986 was to remind everyone on the hill; and there were probably quite a few damp eyes in the paddock when at lunchtime a retirement presentation was made to Peter Hull by Sam Clutton on behalf of the many members who had contributed to the parting gift of a generous cheque. After making a short speech of thanks Peter was driven up the hill by Allan Cherrett in the Cherretts' white supercharged 6C 1500 Alfa Romeo. His actual retirement had occurred a few months earlier in May when he had handed over to Harcourt-Smith.

Early in 1987 Russell Road was busy with the dust and noise of builders at work, while Sue Holmes had joined the staff to take charge of accounting and membership matters and to move the Club firmly into the computer age. Unfortunately on personal grounds, Brian Harcourt-Smith found it necessary to resign towards the middle of 1988 and Peter Hull was re-called to fill the breach. He was to serve in this temporary role for some six months into 1989, when David Franklin took over the post. With a history of personal involvement in the old car movement and a background in the insurance industry Franklin proved an excellent Secretary of great professionalism who served the Club well, bringing needed stability to the office until his own retirement some nine years later, at the end of 1997. In the same year as he had taken up his post Neil Murray, well known within the Club as the owner of the Aston Martin "Green Pea" that had competed in the 1922 French Grand Prix, also joined the office staff; first as Assistant Competition Secretary, and then in January 1990 exchanging roles with Ted Smith, whose health was proving troublesome and restrictive.

Poor health was also to rob the Club of its next President – Patrick Marsh, who had followed on from Threlfall at the end of the Jubilee Year. An enthusiastic ERA owner, he had raced the 1½-litre ex-Seaman R1B for over twenty years and in doing so accumulated a vast knowledge of their mechanical aspects and had compiled a set of drawings and notes that together made up what was in effect, an ERA workshop manual that he happily made available to fellow owners. He also trialled a Vauxhall 30-98 and had proved a very useful Committee member of the Club on being elected in 1976. Always full of new ideas he promised to be an excellent President – but he was never properly to recover from a bad fall from the heights of an "ordinary" bicycle while riding in France. First his eyesight deteriorated and, with rapidly failing health, he asked the Committee to appoint a new President and so, at short notice and under these unhappy circumstances, Roger Collings took over the role. Patrick Marsh died in August 1986.

The introduction of 'Blue Forms'

During the 1960s it was becoming clear that standard vintage sports cars were becoming increasingly outclassed in competitions which, combined with rapidly rising prices for good examples, triggered a boom in the re-building and often modification of more "run of the mill" cars, and the conversion of many others into competition oriented "specials". Thus the owner of a car from the first such category might tell a fellow member that "Actually the dashboard isn't quite original yet" while one from the latter might indignantly respond to a question at a pub meet that "Of course it's original. I built it myself". Debates over the PVT list have continued ever since it first emerged, and will no doubt continue to do so for many years to come, while in 1976 the Club decided that a major review was required. Kenneth Neve, as chairman, was to work with Peter Hull and Tony Bird from the office, Mark Joseland and Peter Glover as active vintage competitors, and Denis Jenkinson with his immense knowledge of racing cars built up across many years. In the event the group suggested but a few changes; among them the "65" being added to those Austin Seven models deemed acceptable,

"I DON'T SEE WHAT'S SO SPECIAL ABOUT THAT!"

along with Singer Le Mans, Morgan 4/4s and – most significantly – all ohc engined MGs. Meanwhile competitive and mechanically minded members inevitably continued to develop and modify their cars with increasing insouciance, until it became evident that the Club had to obtain an overview and achieve some sort of control over the situation. Thus, in the late 1980s, Blue Forms came into existence. These required owners to certify that, along with chassis numbers and engine dimensions, six main areas within their cars (chassis, engine crank casing, gearbox casings, back axle casings, front axle beam and brakes) were either original, copied parts to the same design and in similar material to the originals, or non-standard in the case of parts not to the original specification. Accordingly the cars, under the oversight of the Committee, were classified as being either standard, modified or specials – or, in a few cases, hybrid. Sketchy though they were by modern standards, Blue Forms did at least bring some order to the situation, while the Club was careful to point out that: "This Blue Form for the car described merely records that entries for VSCC events will be accepted in respect of this car in its stated form. The issue of this form in no way authenticates the car as being of a particular year, specification or category and must not be used in support of any such claim." Despite this a car with a Blue Form certainly had a desirability that those without could not attain, while members were pressed to register their cars. In the autumn of 1989 what became known as the "Great Eligibility Debate" was held in Birmingham, while at the AGM of the same year the topic had also been discussed. In Birmingham four hundred members – mainly representing the racing fraternity – debated such matters as racing tyre compounds and sizes, wheel sizes, shock absorbers and locked differentials, while a Brescia Bugatti owner (David Sewell) more concerned with the "pur sang" approach, suggested that five specific major components should be nominated, of which three should be original period items. This appears to have been the first public mention of what was to become the partly mythical "three out of five" guidance. The Autumn *Newsletter* of that year pointed out that "it was clear that members wanted a "sort out" among competing cars" and the Eligibility Sub Committee (which was chaired by Barry Clarke) was formed to draw up rules, which were not significantly different to those which had been in existence for many years, but which it was felt "were being interpreted in a more and more creative fashion" as time passed by. With over a thousand vintage and post-vintage cars being used in competitions each had to be considered individually – with opportunities for appeal being provided for disputed rulings. A number of these related to the use of fibreglass wings which were no longer to be allowed, even though some of the offending cars had been so fitted for over half their lives. Over eight hundred forms had been processed by October 1989, when the Eligibility Sub Committee announced that as from 1st January 1990 no entry for any Club competition would be accepted unless the car concerned had been issued with a Blue Form, thus establishing its pedigree.

Aspects of the racing scene

As well as the processing of Blue Forms in the decade following the Jubilee, the office was also kept busy with the organisation of five and sometimes six race meetings per year, within each of which there were typically ten races. Hardy annuals in the list

Road racing par excellence. Cadwell Park 1990. S J Robert's 1927 1500cc Frazer Nash leads R Toone's 1930 1750(s) Alfa Romeo around the Lincolnshire circuit.

of circuits used were Silverstone (with two meetings each year, one in the spring and another in the summer) together with meetings at Oulton Park and Cadwell, at least up until 1993. Donington usually featured in the lists but suffered from not having a fixed place in the calendar, nor particularly good spectator attendance levels. Due to a planning dispute it even had to be cancelled in 1990. Despite this, two Donington meetings were held in 1991, after which it was back to one per year – while in 1992 it was to become home to the Seaman Trophy races.

Moved from Silverstone to Oulton in 1956, these races had been run on the Cheshire circuit with great success. As a new and innovative President, Patrick Marsh had suggested that the profile of Oulton might be raised even higher by running it as a two day meeting – in which format it was to flourish from 1985 until 1992, becoming one of the most popular gatherings in the VSCC calendar. The first of such two day meetings took place over a chilly and showery weekend in early June and included 5 bicycle races (18 competed on 'ordinaries', while the safety bike handicap race had over

A feature of the two day Oulton Park meetings of the 1990s were the bicycle races for both safety and "ordinary" (i.e. penny farthing) machines. Here a group of the latter line up on Clay Hill for the start of their race.

50 entries), 2 concours parades around the circuit, the 100 plus entries including some motor cycles, and 17 actual motor races inclusive of the two Seaman Trophies, not unexpectedly won by Tim Llewellyn's Bentley (Vintage) and David Black's Alfa Romeo (Historic); while Nick Mason was the popular winner of Sunday's All Comers scratch race in a 250F after Mayman – who had won the matching race on the Saturday in a Lotus 16 – spun out of the lead on the last lap. During the intervening evening there had been food and dancing in a marquee, the only problem being that the beer ran out. Marshalling such an extensive programme proved a real challenge but with minor adjustments the 'Oulton two days' settled down to a run of seven years.

1988 was not the driest of these, nor the happiest, as in pouring rain on the Saturday there was a multiple accident after the start of a race going into the first corner. Colin Crabbe and Martin Grant-Peterkin were both badly injured and about eight cars damaged. The race had to be stopped and was re-run with a depleted field on the following Sunday morning. Two of the races at Cadwell that year also had to be stopped after accidents to allow damaged cars to be removed from the circuit.

But natural causes rather than accidents were to result in the deaths of two of the most talented drivers to grace vintage racing at about this time. The Honourable Patrick Lindsay could almost have been lifted from the pages of *Boys Own Paper*. The younger son of an Earl, he had been educated at Eton, playing in the first XI and distinguishing himself as a fast bowler. Seriously interested in painting he joined Christies Old Masters department of which he rose to be head. In due time be was offered the Chairmanship of the auction house but chose instead to remain working with his beloved paintings. He also loved powerful and elegant machinery, collecting both cars and aeroplanes, his collection of the former being boosted when, on a professional trip to India, he was offered the gift of a 1930 Rolls-Royce Phantom by a Maharajah on condition that he drove it home; which he did. Having briefly tried motor racing in modern machinery, he bought Remus – ERA R5B – in 1959, and together they established a quite formidable partnership competing in seventy races and winning thirty of them, inclusive of the Seaman Trophy nine times. He also raced Sir Ralph Millais's Sunbeam Tiger and a number of Maserati 250Fs. He died, aged 58, in January 1986.

In 1987 another famous ERA R4D was to change hands, being purchased by Anthony Mayman. As with Lindsay, Mayman's early interests were in modern machinery and in 1985 he bought Bruce Halford's Lotus 16, winning twice with it in his first season.

R4D needed much attention to turn it into a winning machine and this was certainly achieved, for over half a dozen years in Mayman's hands it proved virtually unbeatable. He won the Seaman Historic Trophy for four years in a row (1989–1992), the Club's Hill Climb Championship in 1991 and 1992, along with records at Wiscombe, Shelsley and Prescott.

In mechanically based sports great success can lead to suspicions being aired and in 1990 Bruce Spollon – then President of the Club – received a letter from another competitor suggesting that R4D's "outrageous performance" was due to modern technology. Mayman voluntarily offered the car for inspection and for it to be sealed following a race. He duly won the Shuttleworth Trophy at Donington, leading from start to finish, the sealed car then taken away to be dismantled and inspected by Mr Rogers, the scrutineer representing the RAC, Barry Clarke and Denis Jenkinson, along with the complainant.

The report proved negative, as the car was found to be entirely in accordance with VSCC eligibility rules. R4D was obviously a very well prepared car and equally well driven, as Mayman proved by winning the Allcomers Race at the same meeting in the Halford Lotus 16. Mayman was to die in 1993, aged only 43.

At the grass roots

While such notable talents as Lindsay and Mayman emerge but rarely, (along with the outstanding abilities of such drivers as Neil Corner who was able to shine in almost any type of car, familiar or otherwise), it is all too easy to overlook the great bulk of competitors who make up the racing backbone of the Club. Competing in fairly modest machinery in high speed trials, five lap handicaps and the one-make races that have featured so regularly at Silverstone, they are at the grass roots of the Club and on which its racing programme ultimately depends.

With determination and application, coupled with sound driving abilities, they can take home some prized trophies.

So it was that Lou Wickham was able to win the Lycett Trophy in 1986 driving his faithful SD Alvis 12/50 Beetleback in rallies, trials, speed events and races before "The Duchess" finally threw a rod racing in 1987, after which he decided to drive a little more slowly. In all he was to campaign this car for close on forty years.

Younger drivers have to learn their trade before rising through the ranks, and there have been few if any younger than Ben Collings who having passed his driving test in the family Züst when just seventeen years old, was on the grid in it for the Edwardian handicap at Mallory Park in 1991 only a week later. Obviously a fast learner, he was to win the Lycett Memorial Trophy in 1993, a feat he was to repeat in 2008.

At the other end of the age scale for many years came C T (Tom) Delaney. Born in 1911 he had the advantage of being a son of the then managing director of Lea-Francis, a firm with a hands-on interest in motor racing. Sammy Davis was enlisted to give him advice and Tom started his racing career at Brooklands in 1930. Using an ex works "Leaf" he achieved sound results before getting married and deciding to put his young family first. After dabbling with aeroplanes and sailing boats he eventually returned to motor racing in 1988 – after a gap of 54 years, again Hyper Lea-Francis equipped. By far the oldest racing driver in the country, if not the world, his last race was to be at the April 2006 VSCC Silverstone meeting, at the extraordinary age of 95.

Carson had died in 1989, when walking to the Newbury office, while Clutton was to do so in 1991. Appropriately he had just arrived at St Martins-in-the-Fields where he was due to inspect and play the organ. His memorial service, attended by a distinguished congregation, was held in St Paul's Cathedral.

Further changes in racing

As if to emphasise the changing nature of the times, the April 1990 Silverstone meeting made the point in a number of ways. The Club circuit, after 38 years in its almost original form, had been altered. Just before the end of the long Club straight, a tight left hander (Brooklands) had been added, shortly followed by a right hander (Bridge), then after a brief wiggle hard right again (New Woodcote) then having re-joined the old Woodcote back to the pit straight and the grandstands. Behind the pits the paddock showed the increasing commercialism that was beginning to be felt in historic racing, while among the cars gathered there were a number of invited pre-1961 rear engined racing cars, entrants in the Mulberry championship for historic racers. Among them were Hannen's Cooper Climax T51, Stretton's similar car and Harper's T53, which were to join battle with as mixed a grid of racers as could be imagined, inclusive of a front engined P25 BRM, a Lotus 16, a Talbot Lago – and going back even further in time, a number of ERAs. At first rear-engined racers participated by invitation only, in races limited to those built before 1966, but eventually they were to

Oulton Park 1990. A representative mix of cars from within the Club. 208: H D Scott-Moncrieff's 1923 4500cc Vauxhall. 173: R Toone's 1930 1750cc(s) Alfa Romeo. 147: P G Cobb's 1928/30 1470cc Frazer Nash.

take part in their own right. Similarly 1950s sports-racing cars began to participate in invitation races at Club meetings, in the same way as Morgan 3 wheelers, competing under ACU rules, had done so for some time.

There was no Oulton Park meeting in 1991, its place being taken by the Club's first visit to Mallory Park – a short and fairly fast circuit that has proved very popular over the years, particularly so in the hosting of Edwardian and Austin Seven races. Oulton did return to the calendar with a two day meeting in August 1992, but this was reduced to a one day meeting in the following year and then dropped out of the calendar until 1996; hence the move of the Seaman races to Donington. In 1994 there were five meetings, the two at Silverstone, one each at Donington and Mallory, plus a new circuit for the Club, that at Pembrey in South Wales. The loss of both Oulton and Cadwell were the results of the owners' insistence on silencing regulations that were unacceptable to the Club, and disagreement over the use of a chicane at Oulton.

1994 saw the opening of the Channel Tunnel, and in that same year the Club was to hold its only racing meeting in France, on the short rather narrow one mile circuit at Croix-en-Ternois, about thirty five miles south of Calais. A shadow was cast over the proceedings when Howard Bevan had a fatal heart attack while practising in his T35B Bugatti. His death required an immediate investigation by the Gendarmerie, this leading to a three hour delay. The races then all had to be shortened before the chastened competitors made their way home. It had proved costly to organise the meeting and the experiment has yet to be repeated. On a more cheerful note 1996 was to witness the return of both Cadwell and Oulton, two circuits of great appeal to vintage racers and spectators alike; and for a time the shape of the racing calendar settled down.

Hill Climbs and Sprints

By the mid eighties the pattern of speed events was well established – with three hill climbs each year (at Wiscombe, Shelsley and Prescott) and two sprints on fairly level terrain (Curborough and Colerne), the first notably curved and the latter wholly straight.

Hill climb venues are invariably in attractive settings; Wiscombe particularly so, but very tricky as Tony Stephens in his ERA was to discover in 1987 and as Julian Gosh found out a year later, when he had a very nasty crash there in the Vauxhall Villiers. A hill that suits nimble cars, Brian Gray in the rear engined Hardy Special often did well on its twisty slopes. Shelsley Walsh is essentially a power hill, so Guy Smith in an Alvis engined single seater Frazer Nash must have been delighted when in 1995 he made Fastest Time of the Day there (albeit the Midlands Automobile Club prefers the term Best Time of the Day) by beating Mark Walker, who had already won at Wiscombe and Loton in the Cirrus engined Parker GN earlier that year. The third hill, long secure in the VSCC calendar, was Prescott, which in 1988 celebrated its 50th anniversary, Sonia Rolt ceremoniously ascending the slopes with her two sons in her late husband's Alvis 12/50. In 1992 a fourth venue joined the VSCC list of speed hill climbs. Earlier invitations from the Hagley & District Light Car Club had brought members to the Loton Park start line, while in 1992 it was to become a Club promoted event. At 1475 yards it remains the longest hill climb on the UK mainland, its deer park setting and paddock stretching up the surrounding slopes, making it ideal for camping and for fine views across surrounding Shropshire and into Wales. Puzzlingly it has often struggled for entries, despite the hog roasts on the preceding evenings as provided by the Baker brothers, Robin and David.

A paddock scene at Loton Park in 1994. No 185 is Mark Walker's formidable 1926 6124cc Parker GN. No 126 is Mrs J A. Walker's 1912 3620 Hispano-Suiza, while Roger Collings stands behind his 1906/16 Mercedes Maybach. Also in shot is some more modern machinery, No 112, a 1935 Bentley and No 149, a 1934 Lagonda.

Hill climbing rewards focus and specialism – and runs of success in the Club's annual aggregate championship are not uncommon. For a time Footitt in the Cognac Special had continued his winning ways, to be followed by Terry Cardy with three such annual trophies in 1987, 1988 and 1989, his mount a T35B Bugatti. Over the next five years the spoils were to be divided between Bruce Spollon and Anthony Mayman, both in ERAs, before Mark Walker took over in 1995 and 1997 – his championship years split by Tony Stephens, whose ERA R12C was to take him to victory in 1996.

On the almost flat surfaces of Curborough and Colerne the sprinting form of speed events continued. No real pattern of success was evident at Curborough although it was another venue that well suited the Hardy Special of Brian Gray that almost always did well there in the up to 1100cc racing car, if not in overall classification.

Quite how an open airfield can become a venue of informality and charm remains something of a mystery, but Colerne managed to demonstrate such qualities over many years. In 1986 Rodney Felton had crossed the finish line in his Monoposto Alfa Romeo at 147 mph, while the 1994 meeting deserves special mention. Almost 2000 members and guests arrived at the airfield on a late April day, drawn not only by the usual free admission but by the promise of demonstration runs from fifteen cars brought along by members of the Aero Engined Car Club. Bill Boddy, its President, had also arranged for Babs – the Parry Thomas car – to be brought along, but it proved temperamental and could not be persuaded to run properly. Someone of an arithmetical frame of mind calculated that the total capacity of those aero-engined cars present that day was some 274-litres. Among the cars owned by VSCC members were the Baker brothers' Hispano engined and Delage based special, the well known Napier Lion engined Bentley and, soon to become very successful at speed events, Mark Walker's Parker GN, powered by just over 6 litres of Cirrus Hermes engine said to produce 250 bhp.

In almost silent contrast the pedal cyclists did their bit, while also on two wheels was Denis Jenkinson with his Norton. Also motor-cycle engined were the 500cc racing cars, while from among 159 car entries Charles Dean in a T50/59 Bugatti was to be fastest across the finishing line at 145 mph. But not even Colerne could delight every year, for in 1995 it was wet and windy, sufficient to persuade Donald Day to do a 360° degree spin in R14B off the starting line.

In 1987 the Burnham on Sea Motor Club had invited VSCC members to travel further west to take part in its seaside sprint along the promenade at Weston-Super-Mare; half a kilometre long in an almost straight line. Thereafter it was to become a joint event, the local club holding its sprint meeting for modern cars on the Saturday, with the Club following on the Sunday. The arrangement was to work well for several years, although costs were to go up, mainly due to the need to provide safety fencing along the sea shore. £1500 was lost on the 1992 meeting, which had also suffered from bad weather on the Saturday. The Burnham Club was unable to get a sufficiently good entry to make its running of the 1993 event a viable proposition – while the VSCC alone could not hope to cover the fixed costs required to run the event, and so, at very short notice, the sprint had to be cancelled. By dint of extremely hard and rapid work by Neil Murray and the office staff at Newbury an alternative event was arranged at the Avon Park Raceway near Stratford-upon-Avon for the same date. Despite lacking the charm of Colerne and the seaside ambience of Weston-Super-Mare, the event at this

The Weston super Mare sprint of 1991. Donald Day makes a typically energetic start in ERA R14B, an ex Bob Gerard car that he has owned, raced and sprinted over very many years.

drag-racing venue was well received by competitors, relieved no doubt that they had been provided with at least somewhere to put their machinery to the test.

The Boulogne Bicycle Rallies

Which club event has attracted its largest ever entry and oldest competing vehicle? Almost certainly one of the Boulogne Bicycle Rallies, and probably that of 1991.

Prior to the First World War a triangular circuit of roads to the east of Boulogne had been used for the Coupe de l'Auto races and would no doubt have been all but forgotten had not an Englishman, one Francis Pickett, made a fortune from dismantling high explosive shells left over from the war and dealing in the resultant scrap metals. From the profits he invested considerably in the Boulogne area, among other things building a casino and hotel on the coast towards Calais, as well as his own extravagant house above the town. Among Francis Pickett's business associates was Archie Frazer-Nash and, no doubt encouraged by him and seeking to enhance his reputation among the locals, this "King of Boulogne" had the roads that formed the old 23.22 mile circuit re-surfaced and in 1921 organised a speed week upon them. British entries were encouraged by Frazer-Nash and by 1923, when sprints as well as races took place, such notables as Parry Thomas, De Hane Segrave and George Eyston were among those competing. Indeed in 1926 Segrave marginally exceeded 148 mph during a sprint. However, the popularity of the speed week was undermined by two fatal accidents in 1928, and so the Boulogne Grand Prix and its associated events were abandoned.

To commemorate their 1925 successes on the circuit the Frazer Nash Section of the VSCC, which had enjoyed a successful "raid" to Boulogne in 1975, thought it a good idea to organise a Speed Week along the lines of those held in the 1920s. This was planned for late May 1978 and although hopes for a hill climb and sprints came to nothing, a little sand racing at Hardelot, fifteen miles further down the coast, was organised. In all twenty two British entries, combined with a dozen French Vintagents, made up the rally entry – albeit Frazer Nashes were scarcely to be seen with only a single one turning out. Barry Peerless – vintage motorist, cyclist and Francophile – discovering that a day trip with bike on the P&O ferry from Folkestone would cost but a few pounds per person – encouraged twenty four cycling VSCC members to accompany him on the trip to Boulogne on the Sunday. They joined with the rallyists at Hardelot for lunch and after a few cycle races on the sand got back to the ferry port in time to catch the boat home that evening.

However, among their number, which included Peter Hull, the Club Secretary, were those who decided that to ride around the Grand Prix circuit would make for a worthwhile day. Not all of them managed the full lap, for cafés and bars along the route provided a powerful distraction, while others diverted and got as far as Hardelot. But the seed for the Boulogne Bicycle Rallies, had been sown.

In the following year nearly fifty bikes, including ten from the Veteran Cycle Club, among which were two "ordinaries" (penny farthings), cycled around the old Speed Week circuit on a pleasant early summer's day. Predictably Peter Hull's Sunbeam bike was considerably slower than Seagrave's Sunbeam car had been fifty years earlier.

The entry went up again in 1980, with almost eighty participants taking part, among them Barry Peerless who must have been delighted by the health of the child he had helped to nurture. He was rather late leaving the boat on which, due to unpredictable waves, some of his blood had been spilt as he had cut himself shaving. Trying to catch up with the main party on his Rudge-Whitworth he pedalled away furiously, until his thirst just had to be slaked with a suitable beverage. This achieved, he got to the top of a steep hill, lay down on the grass and dozed off. He was woken by two motor-cycle policemen, who then tried to get him into the ambulance that stood waiting nearby. While he had been sleeping, two cars had managed to have an accident at the top of the hill and the police, seeing blood from his shaving wounds, thought that he had been part of the same collision. Peter Hull recorded that a 1865 Boneshaker took part in this event, while young Harry Colledge, son of the then Light Car and Edwardian section competition Secretary, not quite eight years old, magnificently managed to complete the twenty three mile lap.

In 1991 the amazing total of five hundred bikes took part, inclusive of "ordinaries", tradesmen's bikes with baskets on their fronts (including the postman's bike that had once delivered letters to the Carsons), family bikes with children's seats at the rear, tricycles and tandems. Their riders showed equal diversity, clad in anything from sports jackets, shirts and ties on the one hand to old rugger shirts and shorts on the other. It was around this time that the following *cri de coeur* appeared in the Club's *Newsletter*.

> "The office has been contacted to see if it can help trace a certain Sarah who went on the Boulogne Bike Rally. She was at the lunch stop at Alincthun talking to a young Frenchman called Michael Froay. She would be in her teens and is quite small and very pretty. Michael is eager to correspond

with her, presumably to improve his English. We have the note which he left pinned to the door of a house where Sarah seems to have enjoyed some refreshments with friends. The letter is marked Urgent!"

P&O withdrew their ferry to Boulogne in 1993, but after some difficulties, arrangements were made with Seacat to carry the bikes on the relatively cramped catamaran they then used on the route – then in 1994 would-be participants were advised that group bookings were no longer possible. But despite such minor hiccups the event continues as a now well established yet totally informal feature of the annual club calendar.

2002 saw the twenty fifth anniversary of the original Hardelot gathering that had started it all. Boulogne joined in the occasion with morning coffee, croissants and orange juice being served in the courtyard of the Chateau Museé, under the benign and approving patronage of the Mayor, before the 200 riders (14 on high bikes) set out on their journey around such parts of the circuit that still remain suitable for use by pedal bikes. Dual carriageways and roundabouts have inevitably changed things by reducing accessibility but the basic outline of the Grand Prix circuit still provides the focus.

Numbers have dropped away since the heroic days of the early 1980s, but the Boulogne Bicycle Rally continues to delight its aficionados who typically number from fifty up to a hundred each year. Various alternative routes, catering for the less energetic and those propelling children as well as themselves, have been devised, so that on the last Sunday in May each year VSCC cyclists may yet be found at lunchtime resting and chatting on the village green of Alincthun, half way round the route, with a few of the braver ones even taking a swim in the river Liane on their way back to Boulogne.

Demonstrations of the natural affinity that seems to exist between interesting bicycles and vintage cars – much in the same way that there is also an affinity between the cars and light aircraft – have not been confined to France. Bicycle races were held at Oulton Park during the two day race meetings of the 1950s, Prescott still provides up-hill bicycle racing for all ages on the Sunday mornings before the cars take over, the runway at Colerne has been host to pedal power, while in 1994 the Madresfield drive saw bicycle racing taking place at lunchtime while the less energetic looked on and enjoyed their picnics as the competitors pedalled by.

> *From **The Bulletin** – Autumn 1988*
>
> *A letter to the then Editor, David Thirlby, from Dorinda & Lucille Thirlby.*
>
> *"Dear Father,*
> *You are well aware of the high standing in which your daughters hold you. But we have felt that we should have remonstrated with you before about the sexist, anti-feminist Ludwig cartoons which your distinguished cartoonist, Lionel Stretton, produces ... It's no use you pretending that you do not input ideas to your cartoonist ... or denying that Mrs Bear, whenever she appears is always shown in a pretty poor light".*
>
> *(It is apparent from the adjacent cartoon that even Mrs Bear eventually got fed up herself).*

The Club at Sixty

In 1994 the Club was to reach sixty years of age. On New Year's Day a dozen or so social gatherings took place in bars and pub car parks around the country, the fourteenth year that they had done so, with those at the "Phoenix", the "Verzons" in Herefordshire and the "Old Thatched Inn" at Adstock in Buckinghamshire among the hardy annuals on the list.

The competition calendar for the year was made up of the following Club organised events, together with an invitation class at the Brighton Speed Trials.

January	Measham Rally
	Driving Tests at Brooklands
February	Herefordshire Trial
	Pomeroy Trophy
March	Derbyshire Trial
	Exmoor Fringe Trial
April	Silverstone Race Meeting
	LCES Welsh Weekend
	Colerne Sprint
May	Curborough Sprint
	Wiscombe Hill Climb
	Northern Rally

Ludwig - The Bear

	Scottish Trial
	Loton Park Hill Climb
June	Silverstone Race Meeting
July	Shelsley Walsh Hill Climb
	Malvern Jubilee Week:-
	Driving Tests
	LCES Rally
	Cornbury Park Sprint
	Navigational Rally
	60th Birthday Trial
And also in July	Mallory Park Race Meeting
	Pembrey Race Meeting
August	Prescott Hill Climb
	Donington Race Meeting
September	Madresfield Driving Tests
	Kentish Rally
	LCES Driving Tests
October	The Welsh Weekend – Trial and Rally
	Eastern Rally
November	Lakeland Trial
December	Driving Tests at Abingdon

The racing year

The racing schedule for 1994 was to comprise five meetings (two at Silverstone and one each at Pembrey, Mallory and Donington), with ten races at each of these. With race promotion becoming an ever more expensive business, meetings needed to appeal

Two highly talented VSCC racing drivers at work. Neil Corner in the 1960 Ferrari Dino – as fitted with a 2990cc engine used for the Tasman series of races – ahead of Anthony Mayman in Bruce Halford's 1959 2495cc Lotus 16 at Oulton Park in 1987. The Lotus was eventually to come home first following a hard fought race, in which Corner had spun out of the lead in the closing stages.

to as wide an audience as possible, in order to generate the required income to meet the costs. Post war racing cars and the sports-racing cars of the fifties were rightly perceived as crowd pullers, as was shown at the April Silverstone meeting when the weather became quite awful and it started to snow. Instead of retreating home, as normally they could have been expected to do, the spectators shivered and waited for the 10 lap scratch race for post war sports racing cars – not wishing to miss the sight of Sytner's and Brooks's D type Jaguars battling with Pearson's Lister Jaguar which, after a hard fought race, it eventually won. The meeting was also notable as the first time that a rear-engined car had won a VSCC race – before then they had only competed in invitation races – when Rod Jolley in a Cooper came home a comfortable first in the post-war single seater race. However, a balance had to be struck in race programmes to ensure that there were still plenty of opportunities for the grass-roots clubmen to compete, with ten scratch races and eleven short handicaps being run across the season, in addition to the inclusion of a race for road going sports cars at Pembrey. 500cc racing cars had been invited to Pembrey and Mallory in the Bob Gerard Trophy race for pre and post war racing cars.

A number of one make races were also run during the year. At Silverstone there was an all ERA race, won by Ricketts in R1B, at Pembrey a 6 lapper for Frazer Nash and GN based cars, while Donington hosted a Morgan 3 wheeler race under ACU rules.

It was to be an ERA year on the hills. Spollon (R8C) was fastest at Wiscombe and Loton, Ricketts (R1B) at Shelsley and Day (R14B) at Prescott – with Bruce Spollon winning the Club's aggregate Hill Climb Trophy.

Mallory Park 1994. C J Hancock's 1935 955cc Fiat (no 158) and A E Risley's 1931 1495cc (s) Aston Martin (no 132) battle it out.

The 60th Birthday Week at Malvern

The organisers, John Bridcutt and Martin Grant-Peterkin (the latter able to bring his 50th anniversary experience to bear), decided that the formula that had worked so well before was in little need of major change. Near on 2000 members participated in one way or another during the week and approaching 1500 cars in all made some sort of appearance. About 650 of these had been entered in at least one event, Alvis being the most numerous, with 65 taking part, a little ahead of the Austins which had 55 representatives, and Riley with 52. There was a good turn out of Frazer Nash at 47 – a very high percentage of the small numbers ever made – while 35 Vauxhalls were also entered. An E type 30-98 Vauxhall was to win the Concours, for which there had been 45 entrants.

A touring assembly, starting from the Gaydon Motor Museum, brought many of the participants to Malvern, while others towed caravans to get there. A hill walk on the Malverns themselves reminded members of the penetrative abilities of good Worcestershire drizzle, on the same day of which there was also a rather damp cycling tour. The Tuesday driving tests, devised by Malcolm Elder, supported by David Marsh and Grant-Peterkin, attracted an amazing two hundred entries and, with twenty very varied tests to be tackled, generated four thousand test results for processing. Sixty marshals kept the whole thing going so efficiently that the tests were completed by the mid-afternoon. The Light Car and Edwardian Section navigation rally attracted 98 entries, with a noisy Cyclecar evening held in one of the larger showground halls. Geoff Winder organised a Trial, and Mike Tebbett a Navigation Rally for 136 competitors – all of whom appreciated the leisurely 90 minute lunch break.

Such events were very much in keeping with the spirit of the VSCC, while the sprint held at Cornbury was redolent of pre-war Club competition, being held up the drive of a large house on a fairly basic surface of flints and rolled tar, deemed suitable for Edwardians and sports cars only. A grey day turned to rain in the early afternoon but then cleared up enough to allow Julian Bronson to make FTD in his supercharged Big Four Riley. No one minded when proceedings had to be halted to allow a tractor to cross the course and later when a Post Office van went up the drive to collect the post. It was almost back to the mid thirties.

And as before, the week was rounded off with another successful Ball, again organised by Ann Shoosmith.

Developments in trialling

Certainly the oldest and most revered trial in the Club's calendar is that of the Welsh, and based at Rhydspence it was to continue there until 1986. The driving tests and concours components of the weekend were attracting smaller and smaller entries at this time and so were soon to be dropped. 1987 saw the happy return to Presteigne and the Radnorshire Arms, where a new manager had indicated that he wanted the Club back, while two years later the 50th anniversary of the event was celebrated, inclusive of 200 miles on the Saturday and the introduction of *en route* filter controls for scrutineering. The Welsh must have been a significant element in the Radnorshire's cash flow in October 1991, for that year there were two sittings for the pre-booked Saturday suppers, free drinks provided by Sotheby's, the sponsors, from 6.30pm until 8.00pm, dancing and a disco, and a Max Hill film show. Sleepy triallists then had to get up to face the observed sections on the Sunday.

> *From **The Bulletin** report on the 1990 Welsh Trial:*
>
> *"Its Hamish Moffat! The small blue Bugatti buzzed up from the Pilleth farmyard through the trees, swung right and then furiously stormed the sharp left up to the final climb.*
>
> *Suddenly they stopped. Despite frantic coaxing the Bugatti would move no further. "You're boiling" shouted an observer from the crowd. "You're on fire!" cried another. Moffat leapt out and threw off the bonnet "Fire!" Bystanders threw earth onto the blazing engine. The fuel pressure was cut off. Someone rushed for a fire extinguisher. Our hero grabbed a worn but much-loved Barbour and threw it over the engine as though it was a blazing chip pan.*
>
> *The extinguishers arrived and the fire was soon out. The smouldering jacket was retrieved. "Well done" yelled someone. "It's all right" replied our hero, "it wasn't my jacket."*

At about this time there was considerable debate about the length of the run-in required on the Saturday. A letter went out to 195 regular triallists asking for their views, of whom 23% of the respondents argued strongly in favour of the retention of the traditional 200 miles. A true English (or should it be Welsh?) compromise emerged, for in alternate years either 100 or 200 miles had to be covered. In 1997 (a '100 mile' year) Smatcher returned to the list of hills being used, a trials section in the wood parallel to the original track having been devised. The trial was now under the oversight of George Shetliffe who had taken over in 1996, while alongside him David Filsell organised Sunday's navigation rallies. These seem to have had a rather chequered history in earlier years, sometimes filling in for the driving tests, but they became a regular feature of the Welsh weekends from the late eighties onwards. At first the rallyists were required to complete the Saturday road mileage, but this requirement was eventually dropped on the grounds that the rallying element of the weekend was sufficient evidence of the roadworthiness of the competing cars.

Down on the Mendips the "Wessex Trial" continued, until difficulties in finding suitable sections caused it to be postponed for 1992. The gap was filled by a new event, the "Herefordshire", initially organised by Rodney Felton and Hamish Moffatt, the original intention being for it to be based at Eastnor Castle, but the Verzons Hotel – just outside Ledbury – was to become its base – while the hoped for return of the "Wessex" did not come to pass. Meanwhile the "Derbyshire Trial" (organised by John Harris, after whom it is now named) had been introduced in 1987, its Peak District location using several of the classic hills frequently climbed on long distance MCC trials, while in 1993 came the final trialling addition of the decade, with the introduction of the "Exmoor Fringe" organised by Graham White and Patrick Adams. Along with the very popular Lakeland, and the enjoyable but rather distant Scottish, the Club's trialling calendar had been built up to six events per year, which have thus continued over the years.

Ludwig - The Bear

Rallies and Driving Tests

As the Welsh remains the Club's iconic trial, so it is that the Measham is the most significant and challenging in its rallying year. From 1981 to 1988 organisers, feeling it was unrealistic to try and comply with the demanding Public Relations requirements of the RAC Competitions Department, had resorted to running the January night events as scatter rallies, with no fixed routes. It is too easy to dismiss them all as lightweight apologies for the real thing, for many of them were demanding rallies, challenging to

A very well known car driven by a VSCC stalwart; Mark Garfitt's 1937 Frazer Nash/BMW 319/55 at Lanthwaite on the 1983 Lakeland trial. During over forty years of ownership he has covered in excess of 230,000 miles in the car, rallying, racing, sprinting and trialling it with considerable success, and winning the Thoroughbred Trophy eight times. He also organises social and competitive events for the Club and has been Clerk of the Course of the Herefordshire Trial for many years.

both drivers and navigators. But they were not the real Measham. After several years in and around the Mendips a return to the Midlands was made in 1985 but still in scatter form, and it was not until August of 1987 when the *Newsletter* announced the glad news that "for 1988 it is planned to again run a full blooded Measham Rally – 190 miles from Loughborough to Grantham and back" and warned of the considerable PR that would be required. But the organisers of rallies for modern cars had shown it *was* possible to comply with the stringent regulations and thanks to the determination of Stephen Harvey the event was to go ahead, with 69 competitors congregating at the start. The half way halt, courtesy of the MOD, was in the warmth of a large heated hanger on the edge of Grantham, where mobile catering was also on hand. Thanks to Harvey, and to Jim Adams who had organised the many marshals, the Measham was back. To show how long ago all of this took place none of the competitors shown in photographs of the event are seen wearing the LED head mounted torches now *de rigeur* for night rallying. For the three years from 1990 until 1992, under the watchful eyes of the Tebbett brothers, Mike and Paul, the event moved back nearer to the Welsh Marches, with a start in Hereford, after which it was up north to the Thirsk area, to be organised by committed rallyists John Potter and Brian Hughes. With ex Sunbeam works rallyist Ian Hall in charge, it then returned to Hereford before venturing into Worcestershire. In 1998, after a gap of 25 years, it returned to the Long Mynd – when to show how fickle entrants can be, only 32 of them made it to the start.

By the mid eighties a relatively stable pattern of three annual rallies had emerged. The Measham in its "scatter" format started off the year, followed in May by a Northern Rally (Derbyshire or Yorkshire based) and concluded with the Eastern in the autumn. Following its 1988 return to its traditional format, the Measham then became a somewhat peripatetic event, moving around the northern and west midland counties, while further south Dick Patten and Robert Britcher had introduced the Kentish rally in 1990, which was to feature in the Club's rallying calendar for a decade. The team that had organised the Eastern Rally for many years was to step down after the 1996 event, which was to be run as a night rally in 1997. In that year the comparatively low-key navigation rally that had been part of the Welsh weekend for several years was given more emphasis than before and has since become a permanent feature of the Club's rallying calendar.

A "loss" incurred at about this time was the demise of watch boxes, the Club having purchased a set of sophisticated digital chronometers for use by marshals. Over the years different *Bulletin* editors have had very different views on the use of verse in the pages that they control, but fortunately David Thirlby was to allow Tim Cork's piece on Watch-Boxes to be published in the spring of 1996 – the extracts below providing an informed retrospective of this now almost forgotten way of timing rallies.

> "The watch-box was once the navigator's friend
> A small black cube with a painted end
> Within which the watch sat, face up for inspection.
> Remembered by all with degrees of affection
> The sealing ceremony, with gas board pliers
> And little lead seals, and sharp little wires …
> The sought after box with the well scratched lid
> Behind which the true time could often be hid.
> Some rascals had also perfected the feat
> Of dropping the watch under the seat.
> After huffing and puffing the box would be found
> And the required minute had somehow ticked round …
> … I'm afraid the system is now past its prime.
> Sorry, dear watch box, we've had to call time."

While navigators grappled with the complexities of route finding and time keeping, it was the drivers who were navigationally challenged on some of the driving tests devised by Malcolm Elder each December. These continued at Enstone until 1993, with the final *Bulletin* report by "JBH" – (from a venue that a few years earlier had been described in another article as "a fearful place on the top of the Oxfordshsire Wolds") – written in telegraphic style …

> "Late as usual – lovely Oxfordshire countryside – diabolical morning weather – pub lunch – warmth – contentment – drowsiness. Oh yes, the driving tests – Malcolm Elder relaxed supremo – mud – medical tests – more mud – Surprise, surprise, beautiful sunny afternoon – drive home – warmth – contentment – drowsiness. Then remembered to write report. Ten tests well spaced out around airfield. FTD Mahany's 1939 HRG. The other first class award to David Marsh (Bugatti). A special commendation/commiseration to marshal John Ingham who spent his day riding in every one of the eighty two starters vehicles in Test 10, to check on the minimum number of gear changes. He ended up plastered in mud, literally head to foot."

The tests moved from Abingdon in 1994 to Upper Heyford, a Transport Command airfield familiar to Neil Murray who had spent two years serving there in the RAF. Kipping inverted his Austin 7 during the day and it poured at lunchtime, but otherwise all went well, participants relieved that there had been a nearby pub in which to eat and get warm. In 1995 the tests were moved to Westcott, "another windswept airfield", when pleasingly the entry reached 104.

As a change from such flat surfaces Brooklands, inclusive of banking and aeroplanes in the background, continued to play host to the New Year driving tests, providing a "local" event for the numerous members living in the south-east; while in Worcestershire each September Madresfield continued to play host to the comparatively decorous driving tests still held there.

But be it a race, a hill climb, a rally or driving tests marshals are required, for it is on these worthy volunteers that the Club's competition programme ultimately depends. Nothing can happen without them.

MG, Riley, Bugatti and Austin – a few of the wide range of cars waiting on the Brooklands banking for the start of the New Year's Driving Tests in 1997.

Marshalling

In October 1936 the Club set out to run a speed trial on a newly found course at Littlestone-on-Sea near New Romney in Kent. Here was half a mile of wide well constructed concreted road running parallel with the sea, intended to serve the adjacent building estate under construction. In contrast with the majority of speed trial courses of the time, the surface was quite magnificent, while a strong entry of fifty cars boded well for the event.

However, the meeting very nearly did not take place, for by the advertised starting time of 1.30pm only three marshals had arrived. Clutton, who had found the course, later expressed his reactions in a terse piece in the Autumn *Bulletin*.

> "If competitors can be punctual it is difficult to see why marshals cannot also arrive to schedule, and had there been a full list of starters, or a finer day to encourage more spectators, it is quite probable that the meeting may have been held up indefinitely. As things were, it was only by superhuman efforts that the meeting was got under way by 2 p.m. It is an entirely mistaken notion that committees possess magical powers to run events without any outside assistance, and unless the other members of a club are willing to pull their weight it might as well shut down straight away. Even viewed from a purely selfish point of view it is a profound truth that if you cannot yourself compete in an event, the next best way to enjoy it is to feel that you have in some way actively contributed towards its success.
>
> You said what? You said that was quite enough preaching thank you? La! The impudence of the creature."

And the situation remains much the same, with many a Chief Marshal writing, telephoning and emailing in the run up to an event in an attempt to raise sufficient helpers to allow the competition to be safely run. While the bureaucracy of marshalling has, as with most other things in life, increased with signing-in sheets at all events, orange overalls at speed events and, nowadays, training courses as well to remind of the seriousness of the undertaking, it essentially remains fun… as Alan Winn, writing in a *Bulletin* in the 1980s, tells of the "Secret Life of Adrian Marshal". In doing so he also tells us quite a lot about life in the Club at the time.

"Jan 22, Sunday
Today, I have decided to become a marshal. This is a momentous moment event in my life. For the last time I have stood around watching other people doing things. It was Fred's fault, Fred marshals all the time. He came up to me today at the driving tests, all covered in watches and pens and pads and things, made some comment about my being as useful as an udder on a bull, standing there watching. I think he was cold and tired. Anyway, afterwards when we were in the bar, and I didn't have anything to talk about having done, and everybody else did, Fred said I should marshal, and then I would, and I wouldn't get stuck for buying all the big rounds. I think he was right.

Jan 25, Wednesday
Rang the VSCC office. I told Ted (Smith) I wanted to be a marshal, and he asked if I meant for the Measham. Had to admit I hadn't thought of the Measham. Nobody from here goes to that – it's too far away they say, and anyway their cars aren't right for it, apparently. I told Ted that, and he said if their cars weren't right they should get better cars or come in the modern and marshal. He has sent me a form.

Jan 28, Saturday
I have filled out the form. Fred says I shouldn't bother with all that, as he just rings up the office a few days before an event and says 'Need any marshals?'. I check with Ted, who said something about if all the old fools did that we'd never know whether we could run the meetings.

February 22, Saturday
Panic! I have read all the instructions again, and the sheet of notes for marshals. As a result I have spent all day tramping the streets of Surbiton, trying to find a non-nylon anorak in a colour other than bright yellow or red (we are not supposed to wear clothing the same colour as signal flags, or made of man-made fibres which melt when heated). Fred came round this afternoon and said 'Don't be bloody silly – you can use that grotty old Barbour I keep in the back for spare passengers'. Why didn't I think of that? He says Silverstone's freezing in March, and have I got gloves and waterproof trousers, a warm hat and wellies? Am I marshalling the Pom, or joining Scott on his way to the Antarctic?

February 28, Monday
Will I ever be ready? There's stacks of kit in the car. Bert came round to borrow my Araldite (the white plastic gearlever knob's fallen off his Mayflower) and cracked the old joke about Scott and the Antarctic. I graciously declined his offer of a trip to the pub on the grounds that I have to get up early in the morning. Besides which, I can't find the stopper for the Thermos – Fred says I should take it full of soup or coffee. He also suggests taking a picnic in case I get stuck out somewhere and don't have time for lunch.

March 1, Saturday
Lunchtime, its fine but freezing. The Mars bars and coffee ran out by 10a.m. and my feet are frozen – I forgot the thick socks. It was better while Test A – the high speed slalom – was underway. I was in charge of the marker cones at the far end and three cars spun into them, so I had some running around to do. Fred's right, you're much closer to the cars and action out there – but I notice the crafty sod's got a job in the results room, with a heater and pleasant female company. Half the other marshals on my test arrived in Vintage cars – I'd thought it was just people who didn't have one, or didn't have one running, who did it. In a way I wish I'd brought the Riley – but I did meet a marshal with a Lynx who'd got the brake adjusting screw I needed.

March 2, Sunday
Too tired and too cold to write this yesterday: we had finished by 4 o'clock, but after we'd had a couple of jars in the paddock bar and then stopped for dinner on the way home, it was quite late. Mabel (the wife) wanted to know why I hadn't rung and said I'd be late, and I knew we always go out on Saturday night and why did I want to go to sleep. I tried to tell her what I'd been doing, and how exciting it was watching squads of post-war Ferraris and Cobras mixing it with Bugattis though Woodcote. As a track marshal, I didn't have to do anything at all. I thought this was a bit of a letdown, but the BMRMC rescue marshals said that was the best way for a day to be. (I forgot: the club paid me £3.00 for turning up, to pay for lunch. I have saved my first marshal's armband.)

March 5, Wednesday
I have just been to the AGM. Met lots of the people who were marshalling on Saturday – some of them are on the committee. Had a good chat and a laugh with one of the chaps who spun into my cones at the Pom, and we had a beer later. Ted says he's sent through my instructions for the Wessex Trial: I thought it was weeks away, but apparently it's on the weekend after next. What am I going to do? I haven't booked a hotel, and it's a two-day event. Maybe I'll ring and say I'm ill, but Fred says I'm a wimp if I do.

March 13, Thursday
I'm in luck. Fred's found me a room in a bed-and-breakfast in Cheddar, so the Wessex is on. We're going down tomorrow night (Mabel's coming too: says it's OK as long as she doesn't have to cook on Saturday night!) I have had to borrow her a pair of wellies and a hat. Apparently we will be working in a quarry, and have to be there by 9 on Sunday morning. We have bought a bigger Thermos, and are taking a huge picnic.

March 15, Saturday
It's raining! Water everywhere, and guess who didn't bring a brolly, so we're sitting in the car to dry out while we wait for more cars to appear. Not many people are getting up our hill, so there's lots of rushing around pushing them up to the turning point at halfway. I'm knackered. M is a bit grumpy but OK – she's sitting at the bottom keeping cars in line for the start, and has somebody's umbrella to stand under most of the time. I always thought trials drivers were mad, but they all come up and say 'you must be mad standing here in the rain all day …'

March 16, Sunday
Thank God, it's fine again – well, at least it's not raining. Had a splendid night last night in the pub. Apparently one of the insurance brokers (John Scotts) puts up a barrel of free beer for drivers and marshals at trials, and there was some left for us when we poured ourselves in. Slept like a log, and difficult to get up and back to the quarry for 9 this morning. Had an easier hill, and most people got up it: it's great seeing people's faces when you give them maximum marks. A pity more people don't marshal, as we were quite busy – but I saw a lot of the marshals from the Pom were here as competitors. Home now, and a whole month before Silverstone …

April 14, Monday
Still no instructions for Silverstone, so phoned. Ted says they were sent out last week, but I'm on trackside duties again anyway, and would I be there by 8.15. Not again!

April 15, Tuesday
Instructions have arrived. This time they include two free tickets and a paddock car pass, so M is going to come. She's always refused to go back to Silverstone since we had to leave the car on the outside and carry the picnic over the bridge in the rain to where Bert's car was.

April 19, Saturday
Have we been busy this morning! They were really short of marshals first thing, and when I got to my post (Runway Crossing – the other guys say it's the VSCC's Siberia) the observer in charge wanted to know if I could flag. Had to admit I never had, but he said I'd have to learn how to use a yellow sometime, and it had better be now. Fortunately, it was quite simple – I just had to wave it if there was an incident in my sector, or hold it up stationary if the next yellow down the track was being waved. The hardest part was concentrating on looking just that one way, and not turning round to watch the cars coming. ERAs sound magic in full cry down Club Straight! The observer gave us all a briefing before practice started … practice went on for ages, but I only had to use the yellow once. The blue looks like more fun.

April 20, Sunday
The afternoon was even more hectic. More flag marshals arrived so I was restored to the ranks – but then they found they needed more marshals in the pits for the 40-minute blind. Each car had to come in at some point and change a spark plug, and there had to be a marshal for each couple of pits to make sure it was done right. Had to report one of 'my' drivers for overshooting his pit and reversing – the other one with a Bentley had heaps of trouble with his leather bonnet straps and then dropped his plug.

After that, things died down, and I spent the rest of the afternoon on pitlane spectator/mechanic control. People get a bit cross when you stop them from hanging over the pit rail trying to take photos, or want to rush over and see what's happening when a car comes into the pits, but if you're polite they seem to be OK. As long as you keep one eye on them, the pit counter's a great place to see the racing from – the big cars coming out of Woodcote are really impressive.

April 23, Wednesday
My doctor is a secret marshal! I went to see him today, and while he was writing out my prescription he said 'Didn't I see you on the pit counter at Silverstone on Saturday? I was taking a break from being MO at Copse at the time'. I knew he had a 2-litre Lagonda that he takes to the pub on fine Sundays, but didn't know he was active. Perhaps he'll do me a cheap medical sometime…

May 2, Friday
Instructions for Wiscombe are here – Ted's notes point out that they're still short of marshals, so I think I'll ask Bert if he wants to come.

May 3, Saturday
Bert has agreed to come to Wiscombe. Worried about not knowing what to do, but I assure him that us experienced marshals will help him out.

May 12, Monday
Wiscombe was amazing! We were on the startline, so I was able to talk to all the drivers as they came up. Got a ride up the hill with the clerk of

course and steward in a 4.3 Alvis at one stage – it looks like a super hill, so maybe I'll enter next year. I'm told that when entry lists are oversubscribed for certain events, priority will be given to people who have marshalled. I must fix the Riley's brakes at last.

December 16, Tuesday
'The President and Committee of the Vintage Sports-Car Club request the pleasure of your company at the Club's Marshals' Dinner at the British Racing Drivers Club Suite, Silverstone Circuit …' The Club has invited me to dinner! I didn't know about this: apparently they invite the people who have done the most marshalling – flag marshals, course marshals, doctors, timekeepers, lap scorers, results secretaries, number painters, the lot – and me. I have accepted.

Such carefree days of the 1980s were not to last for much longer, with growing recognition of the responsibilities and the liabilities of event organisers, and the need for a more professional management of risk.

Marshals training for speed events within the Club got underway in the 1990s at the Pomeroy meetings – classroom sessions in the mornings being followed by practical trackside training during the High Speed Trials in the afternoons. Non-speed event marshalling also requires specific skills and a number of training sessions, mainly in the early 2000s, have been organised as far afield as Derbyshire, Exmoor, Prescott and the Lakes, but the emphasis has to remain on speed event training.

The Motor Sports Association is generous in its support of training programmes and the recognition of Registered Marshals, while the training and eventual licensing of Clerks of the Course and Stewards is considerably more rigorous. Even small non-speed events, as well as rallies and trials using almost forgotten country lanes or forestry tracks, have to meet a multitude of requirements and be granted appropriate permissions. The days of turning up to take part in a "follow my leader" trial, or arriving a bit late at a race circuit to be handed a yellow flag and perhaps a fire extinguisher and told to "get on with it" are now long gone.

But no event, however great or small, can hope to function without that body of volunteer officials and marshals on whom the Club continues to depend.

The Marshals' Dinner

In February 1955 the following announcement appeared in the *Newsletter*

> "Invitations are to be sent to those who have consistently helped to make Club events such a success, but inevitably some helpers have been overlooked due to incomplete lists of marshals etc. Will any member therefore who has not received an invitation and feels qualified please notify the Secretary who will be only too pleased to include him in the list. Owing to the large numbers involved it has been regretfully decided that this must be a stag party and we shall have to find some other way of thanking our lady helpers."

No doubt the diplomatic skills of the then Secretary, Tim Carson, were well up to the task of fending off any would-be attendees who had insufficient marshalling background to qualify for a free dinner – while back in the 1950s the majority of women were sufficiently quiescent to not demand equal treatment. After all it was still a world in which men played cricket while their womenfolk prepared tomato sandwiches back at the pavilion and it was highly unlikely that the membership of the club would see things differently. Indeed the women were overlooked in the following year and the year after – and indeed on many more as the promise to "find other ways of thanking our lady helpers" failed to materialise. Eventually a solution did at last emerge. Lady marshals and other female helpers who had made a significant contribution to the club in the previous year were to be sent a ten shilling Boots Gift Token instead! And so the "boys night out", inclusive of risqué jokes within the after dinner speeches, could continue unrestrained while the women (who had probably heard most of the jokes anyway) could remain unembarrassed – but also unfed.

In 1973 Angela Cherrett joined the Committee, the first woman to do so post war. She successfully put forward the case for a "ladies only" dinner and so, from the mid 70s onwards, a small group of women marshals met annually in central London at a variety of restaurants, where no doubt the range of their menus was considerably more varied than that enjoyed by the men.

When the marshals' dinner was first mooted there was some discussion as to what should be on the menu – and who better to ask than past president Laurence Pomeroy, whose reputation as a *bon viveur* and gourmet had gone before him. "Nothing to beat good old English steak and kidney pudding" came his bluff reply … and the tradition continues to this day. One of the more arduous duties of current Competition Secretaries is to ensure the suitability of the puddings prior to the event, so as to avoid the unhappy situation that once occurred when the anticipated steak and kidney pudding was nothing of the sort. Removable lids of puff pastry rested on top of individual dishes containing meat beneath. In the mid 50s the dinner was held in the City at comparatively small restaurants – in 1956 at Pimms in Bishopsgate Street. *The Bulletin* report of the time, no doubt written by Clutton, was short and to the point.

> "There was a minimal amount of speaking. Pomeroy (then one of the Directors of the Club) addressed the crowd for exactly six minutes, eight seconds – managed to include a slightly technical joke too. The bar remained playing to capacity for the rest of the evening."

With the growth of the club the numbers invited to the dinner rose and it became necessary to find a larger venue. Anthony Heal, true to form, came to the rescue, making the restaurant at his Tottenham Court Road premises available to the Club.

For some years the ladies continued to dine separately and the tale is told of the ever-gentlemanly Peter Hull going to collect a small group of them from a restaurant in Soho in the club's minibus rather than having them wander down the doubtful streets that night. Having parked the minibus he walked down a short passage to what he thought was the restaurant door. "I have come for six ladies". "Well" came the dumbfounded reply, "I don't know if we can manage that, but I suppose we could try". A much embarrassed Hull turned to see that the restaurant door was behind him.

By the late 1970s the club was yet bigger, the marshals more numerous and the membership less London and home counties centric. The dinner was moved to Silverstone and steak and kidney pudding was consumed in one of the hospitality suites while those with caravans and motor homes could park them in the paddock. And at last the anachronism of separate dinners was ended, with the ladies allowed to join the gentlemen to dine.

Now the dinner moves around the country, as befits a national club, usually held in the same weekend at the same venue as the Annual General Meeting.

The VSCC is not short of myths, one of these being that to qualify for an invitation to the dinner one must have marshalled at least six times – and although in practice this level of commitment generally is required the mechanism for determining the invitees is rather different.

First, reference is made to the signing-on sheets. The office staff collect the data, rank members in order of marshalling frequency and then invite approximately 350, inclusive of senior officials such as Stewards and Clerks of the Course, to attend. Normally about half of those invited are able to do so and eventually sit down together to enjoy their traditional steak and kidney. But what about the vegetarians? Although a vegetarian option is always made available experience (unsurprisingly) has shown that the vast majority of members are happily carnivore. In a club that places tradition high up the list, it is now well established that it is the youngest member of the office staff who proposes the loyal toast at the conclusion of the dinner.

Closing Down the Kremlin

Affectionately known as the Kremlin, and even with the additional space provided on the top floor, the office at Russell Road was clearly becoming too small. In his President's report of 1996 David Marsh – brother of Patrick who ten years earlier had so sadly died during his own Presidency – was to write that:

> "It is clear that with the continuing wish of our members for more events the Club office at Russell Road has exceeded saturation point and we need to look for more suitable premises. We have spent a good deal of time and energy, principally with the excellent help of John Malyan, to find a new home and we hope that very soon we will be able to settle in a new office which will offer proper space and facilities for our staff and be much more member friendly."

The search centred on Oxfordshire, seen as an ideal location, being near to the centre of events and close to the homes of many of the 6700 membership. The Russell Road premises were put on the market and fortunately were to sell quite readily, while The Old Post Office in Chipping Norton was purchased accordingly. Malyan, a Club member who frequently competed in his Frazer Nash BMW, masterminded the refurbishment and fitting out, so that all was ready well ahead of the forthcoming move. The first floor flat above the new premises was to be let.

Inevitably the move was to lead to a number of staff changes. In 1996 Robert Ellis had joined the staff as Assistant Competition Manager to Neil Murray, whose place he was later to take, while in 1997 Steve Allen joined the staff, to become responsible for accounts and membership. Sue North (Sue Holmes as she was before her marriage – on which day Roger Collings and Neil Murray had helped convey the bridal party in Züst and Sunbeam respectively) could not make the move, while David Franklin after nearly nine years as Secretary, was to retire. The new team at Chipping Norton was to include Neil Murray as Secretary, Robert Ellis as Competition Secretary, Sadie Wigglesworth in charge of membership liaison and Public Relations, with Steve Allen taking care of the accounts and membership records. Peter Hull, who had made weekly visits to the Club library while it was in Newbury and where he had worked with John Willis, was also obliged to step down from looking after that side of things, his place in Oxfordshire to be taken by Nick Walker.

The move itself was quite low key and informal, but involved much work for Neil Murray, Robert Ellis and Steve Allen. At Chipping Norton all had been made ready ahead of the move, so that by dint of multiple staff car journeys – sometimes with what was known as the blue "pig trailer" in tow behind – equipment and papers were carried to Oxfordshire. Back at Russell Road, vacated after a quarter of a century, a big skip took care of the rest.

The Club opened for business in Chipping Norton on 5th January 1998.

Chipping Norton and beyond
1998–2014

Specialist knowledge and experience had inevitably been lost when David Franklin and Sue North had retired at the time of the move to Chipping Norton, but with Neil Murray as Secretary, Robert Ellis as Competition Secretary and with Steve Allen looking after accounts and membership – following a few months initiation at Russell Road – there was a sound foundation on which to build. The competition department in particular was hard pressed in the first year at the Old Post Office, with a heavy burden falling on the shoulders of its Clerk, Lesley Jeal. A key appointment was to be made in July 1998, when Bob Wimmer became Assistant Competition Secretary, from which position he was to be promoted some two and a half years later to become Competition Secretary – a post he was then to hold until his eventual retirement at the end of 2008.

John Malyan, as architect in charge, had made an excellent job of turning the Club's new base from being a post office into an effective suite of offices, inclusive of the old sorting room which was to become the library. Nick Walker was appointed as Librarian, and following a first degree in Mechanical Engineering at Cambridge and a career in business, his interests in things mechanical had found expression in the writing of a number of motoring books. A man who got on with things, he was obviously a wise choice and his commitment to the task was to be demonstrated by his completion of an Open University Masters degree in Information and Library studies, the insights and knowledge gained allowing him to be the key figure in the conversion of the

Club's wide ranging collection of books, journals and photographs into a first class motoring library and archive. Walker was to die in 2010, but the library – in what is now named the Nick Walker room – houses one of the country's best motoring libraries and, staffed by a team of volunteers, is a resource of real value to members and other enquirers on virtually any aspect of motoring and motor sport across the years. Membership meanwhile was continuing to slowly rise, from 6900 in 1998 to reach the 7000 mark a year later. Since then, with minor fluctuations, it has remained fairly steady around this figure, standing at just above the level at the end of 2014.

Developments in Racing

Into the twenty first century the Club's competition programme has tended to diverge. While there has been comparatively little change in either the number or nature of the rallies, trials and driving tests being run, significant changes have occurred on the racing front. The 50th anniversary of the Club's first meeting at Silverstone took place in April 1999, with a good entry of just over 280 cars. While the backdrop to the racing was one of the periodic re-building programmes that have affected Silverstone over the years, the Itala Trophy was tradition personified, and a very good race. Tim Llewellyn's 3/8-litre Bentley led the 35B Bugattis of James Diffey and Julian Majzub off the line, with Majzub closely challenging the Bentley by the second lap. He was almost alongside when he span and Llewellyn did the same in sympathy, but managed to retain his place while Majzub, who had stalled, got out to re-start the Bugatti and attempted to catch up. Diffey was now a safe second, but only until a conrod broke on his 35B and so Llewellyn led Giles home in the Cognac Special. After such classic vintage racing the rest of the meeting continued in the same traditional vein, together with a somewhat processional 1950 sports car race and a 12 lapper for post war racing cars, as was typical of the programming of the times.

But in order to draw larger crowds of spectators and generate the increased income needed to pay for the every rising costs of promoting a meeting, novelty and publicity were needed; Julian Ghosh (President from 1999–2001) being among those who realised the financial imperative to do so. The Donington meeting later that year featured a demonstration of a 1938 Mercedes Benz W154, driven *con brio* by John Surtees, with a 1998 Mercedes powered McLaren and a similarly powered Penske also lapping the circuit. In 2000 the paddock was crowded with the "trailer city" that accompanied the post war racers to meetings, the races including an Historic Grand Prix Car Association (HGPCA) race, to be won by a rear engined Cooper, and another 50s sports-racing car race, while there was a demonstration of racing motorcycles and a 500cc car race. Also at the circuit a pre-war Auto Union was on display, but it did not run.

However, in 2001 – when a joint 2 day meeting with the HGPCA was held – Auto Unions did run; a Crosthwaite and Gardiner 1936/37 V16 C type and a 1938 V12 D type. There were also demonstrations by a pair of Audi Le Mans cars and a four wheel drive Audi Quattro rally car. Add in the 2¼ hour endurance race that included an AC Cobra and E type Jaguar on the grid among the vintage and PVT sports cars, and it was certainly not a typical VSCC event as they had been known, while the Seaman Trophy races, once seen as the main feature of the Donington meetings, were slipping down the billing. Ghosh, when interviewed by *Motor Sport* at about this time, made it clear that he recognised that "he walked on a knife-edge as he balanced the commercial pressures with the wishes of Club members" but that "the Club's bigger race meetings at Silverstone and Donington helped support the less profitable events at Cadwell Park and Mallory." Thus the high profile "See Red" meetings were to follow at Donington.

Oulton Park, after a six year break, was to return to the Club's racing programme in 2005. Although it was very successful in the first year of its return, the meeting was later to suffer from falling grids and increased costs and, before long, it was again to be dropped from the calendar. By 2010 there were five race meetings each year; the April

Chipping Norton and beyond

Silverstone meeting, the two day "See Red" event at Donington, plus racing at each of the three "Parks" – Cadwell, Mallory and Oulton. Although the Oulton meeting of that year had proved very enjoyable on a lovely summer day, economics were against it, so that in 2011 Pembrey was to take its place. A small friendly circuit in South Wales its two day events involve a sprint and a (much enjoyed) team relay race on the Saturdays – the "clubby" atmosphere very much in contrast to the "See Red" meetings at Donington. The last of these was to be in 2011, so that for 2012 the five meetings promoted by the Club were to be the one day meeting at Silverstone in April, the well

2005. Variety in makes and ages at Oulton Park. 147 – the 1913 Peugeot of Clive Press. 46 – the 1928 supercharged Austin Seven of Jeremy Flann. 155 – the 1927 SD 12/50 Alvis of Tim Fletcher. 62 – the 1937 monoposto Austin Seven of Nick Hayward-Cook.

established Cadwell and Mallory meetings along with Pembrey – and at last, after decades without one – a VSCC race meeting in the east of the country, at Snetterton.

While the Itala Trophy race was able to remain at its long term home at Silverstone the Seaman Historic and Vintage Trophy races were to be moved yet again, in this case from Donington to the new race meeting in East Anglia, while Silverstone was to become a two day event, inclusive of a range of invitation races. In 2013, with

220

uncertainties over the availability of Mallory, Donington, as a one day event, was reinstated to the calendar for 2014; while the Snetterton experiment of 2012 had proved a success, popular with competitors and spectators alike, since when it has settled into the calendar.

The "Spring Start" at Silverstone, following in Donington's footsteps, became a two day meeting in April 2013, with the crowded paddock containing entrants for invitation races for the Historic Grand Prix Association, the Fifties Sports Racing Car Club, the Formula Junior Historic Racing Association and the 500 Owners Association. *The Bulletin* report concluded with a cautionary note.

> "What the Club's founding fathers would have made of the event is hard to surmise, but it seemed a long way from their original intentions. If this type of meeting is the road down which the Club is to go, there may be a need for some hard thought about the Club's future aims and objectives."

However, the 2014 Silverstone meeting must have pleased traditionalists in that the first event of the meeting was a well supported 30 minute High Speed Regularity Trial, inclusive of a plug change along the way.

Sadly the GP Itala Trophy race, later that afternoon, was to end in tragedy. Young Garry Whyte, well up in the field and driving the 1921 GN Gnome special with gusto, slid off the circuit, overturned, was thrown out, and later died of his injuries. The race had to be stopped. The Pembrey meeting of the previous August had also reminded all those involved that motorsport can indeed be dangerous when due to an accident another race had also to be stopped. Nicholas Rossi, in a single seater 1957 Lotus, overturned and suffered serious injuries. The Snetterton meeting of the same year saw the third of this unhappy cluster of major accidents when, during practice, Steve Jewell in a 35B Bugatti hit a barrier at speed, and soon after was to die; the fatality inevitably casting a pall of gloom over the abbreviated racing that followed. Fortunately such occasions are rare, but a salutary reminder of the ever-present, yet knowingly accepted, risks involved in motor racing.

Spirits were however lifted on the second of the two days at Silverstone in April 2014 by the appearance of 9 ERAs and an ERA Riley on the grid to celebrate the 80th birthday of the marque, with Mark Gilles in R3A coming home the winner, in this, the first race of the afternoon. At the other end of the day, the last of the 21 race programme, came a Set 3 race – for standard and modified pre-war sports cars, these ranging in size from the 4-litre Talbot Lagos of Marcus Black and John Guyatt down to the Austin 7 Ulster of John Everett and the MG Montlhery of Barry Foster, with Andrew Mitchell in a 1937 1½-litre HRG coming home the eventual winner.

During 2008 the Racing Sub-Committee of the Club, a small group comprising active and former racers, had developed a structure within which competition cars could be categorised and their races organised. Three new racing "sets" were introduced in 2009 and subjected to scrutiny at a pair of "racers forums", held so that those involved could express their views and make suggestions for improvements. Some "tweaks" and refinements were made for 2010, since when racing within the Club has been to the same broad pattern. Each race meting contains a mix of named pre-war Trophy races, together with invited grids from other branches of historic racing. Thus the 50s sports racers, the 500cc and Formula Junior cars and those from the HGPCA are absorbed within a VSCC meeting, having paid an agreed fee for the inclusion of their grids – the contracts involving a certain amount of dedicated practice time, a race of a certain length and even the provision of winners' garlands. The Club has a guaranteed income ahead of the event while the invited clubs, rarely large enough to run a meeting in their own right, have an established event within which they can race their cars.

The sets themselves cater for the wide range of competition cars found within the Club.

- Set 1   Vintage racing cars
- Set 2   Pre 1961 front engined racing cars
- Set 3   Standard and modified sports cars
- Set 4   Special sports cars
- Set 5   Provides for 2 short scratch races at each meeting
- Set 6   Provides for 2 short handicaps at each meeting

Set 3, providing for standard and modified sports cars only, is rightly popular and invariably attracts full grids of the types of car that would have seemed very familiar to the Club's racing fraternity of the early post war years. Among competitors in the Set are those who take part in the Owner, Driver, Mechanic series co-ordinated by John Guyatt and who, by definition, are "do it yourself" entrants – their own cheque books, spanners and steering wheels inclusive.

Although a body of opinion within the Club has understandable reservations about the incursions of the "invited" racers they do at least provide the financial support for otherwise potentially uneconomic events such as the smaller race meetings, the Loton Park hill climb and the Pomeroy Trophy; the latter without spectator income would otherwise struggle to cover the circuit hire costs on its own. These have steadily risen from the days of the late 1930s, when a sprint venue along a drive could be hired from as little as five guineas (£5.25p) for a meeting, to current levels where the daily hire charge for the smallest of circuits is in the order of £12,000, and can rise to as much as £20,000, or sometimes even higher for a large one. To such charges need to be added a number of fixed costs, inclusive of time keeping services, breakdown and rescue vehicle hire, doctors, paramedics and ambulance charges; while among the variable costs are such items as the per capita MSA fees for competitors, payments on agreed scales to scrutineers, handicappers and time keepers, and the purchase of awards and garlands for the winners.

In the early 1960s, when pre and post war historic racers were beginning to appear in Club events – ERAs followed by Connaughts and Cooper Bristols, and then such front-engined classics as 250F Maseratis – the VSCC was virtually alone in providing a competitive arena for these cars.

The appeal of such "nostalgicars" to the general public was clear to see and in response the number of events for historic racers, as promoted by other organisations, grew rapidly. Such names as the Coy's Historic, the Goodwood Revival and the Donington Festival, together with the Gold Cup meeting at Oulton have become part of the national racing calendar – while on the continental mainland, with historic meetings taking place on such circuits as Spa, the Nurburgring, Monaco, Angouleme and Le Mans, the early dominant position of the VSCC has been lost. The imperative to reach out across other sectors of the historic racing scene thus informs its thinking, with acceptance of the need to be ready to spread its reach and be ready to welcome other specialist clubs to its race meetings.

Over this period the hill climb calendar had remained more stable, Wiscombe, Shelsley Walsh, Prescott and Loton all continuing, with the sprints at Curborough and Colerne doing likewise. 2004 however was to be a year of change in that it saw the final Colerne meeting and the introduction of an autumn sprint at Goodwood, the lap of the circuit providing a very different sort of challenge for the drivers, while Pembrey has since been added as another circuit-based sprint. From the start line at Goodwood,

Wiscombe Park in May 2007, and Tony Stephens prepares to leave the line in ERA R12B. Fourteen of the Bourne built ERAs were present at this meeting, paying tribute to the great ERA driver Martin Morris who had died in the previous year. But on a day of very changeable conditions the fastest time was to be made, not by an ERA, but by a Frazer Nash in the hands of Jonathan Cobb.

just after the chicane, competing cars are lined up in batches of five, being individually released at ten second intervals to commence a lap of the circuit, with no overtaking allowed. Should anyone catch up and be baulked by a slower car they return to the start and are then later allowed a further lap. Times of between 100 seconds to 120 seconds for the circuit are typically achieved; but on a soaking wet day in October 2013 a good twenty seconds were added to these when Fastest Time of the Day went to Sue Darbyshire in her nimble Morgan Super Aero. In achieving this she beat such sprinting stalwarts as Rob Cobden (Riley Falcon Special) Ian Baxter (Bellevue MG) and James Baxter (ERA R4A).

A rather shorter sprint was added to the list in 2007, when a Centenary Sprint was held at Brooklands, to commemorate its opening in June 1907; since when it has become a regular feature of the Club's calendar as part of the two day Brooklands Double Twelve Festival (inclusive of driving tests and a concours) as organised by the Museum. Using part of the test track built by Mercedes Benz on the old airfield site, its twists and turns take a fast car in the order of 40 seconds to cover.

Curborough in May 2001, and Chris Williams begins to light up the tyres of the 1929 24000cc Napier Bentley. He was to cross the line at the end of the short finishing straight at 82 mph, severely challenging the limited braking of this heavy car, and needing all his skills to bring it safely to a stop. The class for such Unlimited Cars was to be won by Robin Baker in his similarly massive Hispano-Delage which, along with the Napier Bentley, presented considerable driving challenges around the narrow and twisty Staffordshire sprint course.

While circuits and speed venues may come and go, a certain amount of continuity may be found the in the names of the winning drivers across the years. Having sent his entry forms to Chipping Norton rather than to Newbury Julian Majzub was to win the Itala Trophy in 1998, before making it four in a row 2003, 2004, 2005 and 2006. He also won the Seaman Vintage Trophy in 2003 and 2005. G W (Geraint) Owen, usually campaigning a Type 35 Bugatti, having won the Seaman Vintage Trophy in 2002 repeated the feat in 2009 and 2010, while also winning the Itala Trophy in 2008 and 2009. Among the historic racers the name of David Morris (ERA R11B) with Seaman victories in 1999 to 2002 inclusive, followed by further wins in 2005 and 2010 stands out, while Mark Gillies (ERA R3A) along with Mac Hulbert (ERA R4D) have continued to demonstrate the abilities of the Bourne built cars across the years.

On the hills outstanding names have been Bruce Spollon, with three more years in which he won the aggregate Hill Climb Trophy, Rob Cobden in his Riley Falcon Special who was to win in 2007 and 2008, followed by an almost unbeatable James Baxter in his single seater Frazer Nash across the years from 2009 onwards.

Despite being seriously ill from soon after the start of the decade James Diffey stands out as an extraordinarily talented driver of the period, shining in both races and trials, usually in his hard worked Brescia Bugatti. He was to win the Pomeroy Trophy four times in all, in BMW saloons and a rather less likely Mark 3 Ford Cortina, while his 2005 duel with James Baxter at Oulton Park – in 1937 Alta sports and Alfa Monza respectively – will be long remembered. Diffey was to win the aggregate Lycett Memorial Trophy twice before be succumbed to cancer in 2007.

Four Iconic Events

Apart from the races and hill climbs no VSCC calendar would be complete without the inclusion of four iconic events, all long standing and all, in their very different ways, part of the very fabric of the Club. The Measham has always come right at the beginning of the year, and involving nearly 200 miles of rallying in an often open vintage or PVT car, it provides a unique and demanding challenge – 1999 had taken the rally up north again with a start at Leeming in Yorkshire, with John Gill heavily involved in its organisation. It was then to move into Lancashire for another three years. The rallying team of John Potter and Brian Hughes were to get to know the roads of the county very well by winning in their Alvis 12/50 in all of the three years that it was held there, and then doing so again in 2005, when the event moved down to Wiltshire and a Swindon start. Following three years there it was not to move far, just east to Basingstoke in 2010, being won by Barry Clarke and David Filsell in an Austin Seven saloon. This incredible pair of vastly experienced competitors was still competing in 2014, coming back from Durham (the event having moved north again) after another night in the Austin Seven saloon and with yet another Measham award. Another pair of regulars, usually finishing well towards the top of the field, have been Mark Garfitt and Dood Pearce in the former's Frazer Nash/BMW 319/55.

Well established partnerships, accumulating considerable experience and expertise over the decades, are clearly of benefit in rallying as the results of several well known competitors have shown. John Potter and Brian Hughes must be able to lay claim to being one of the most seasoned of such duos; John, by the end of 2014, having competed in 131 VSCC rallies, with Brian alongside him for 93 of these – with 40 wins testifying to their effectiveness. In contrast Annabel Jones, a doyen of the navigational fraternity and multiple winner of the Club's annual Navigators' Trophy, is peripatetic in her approach and has successfully guided a wide variety of drivers in a wide variety of cars to victories over the years.

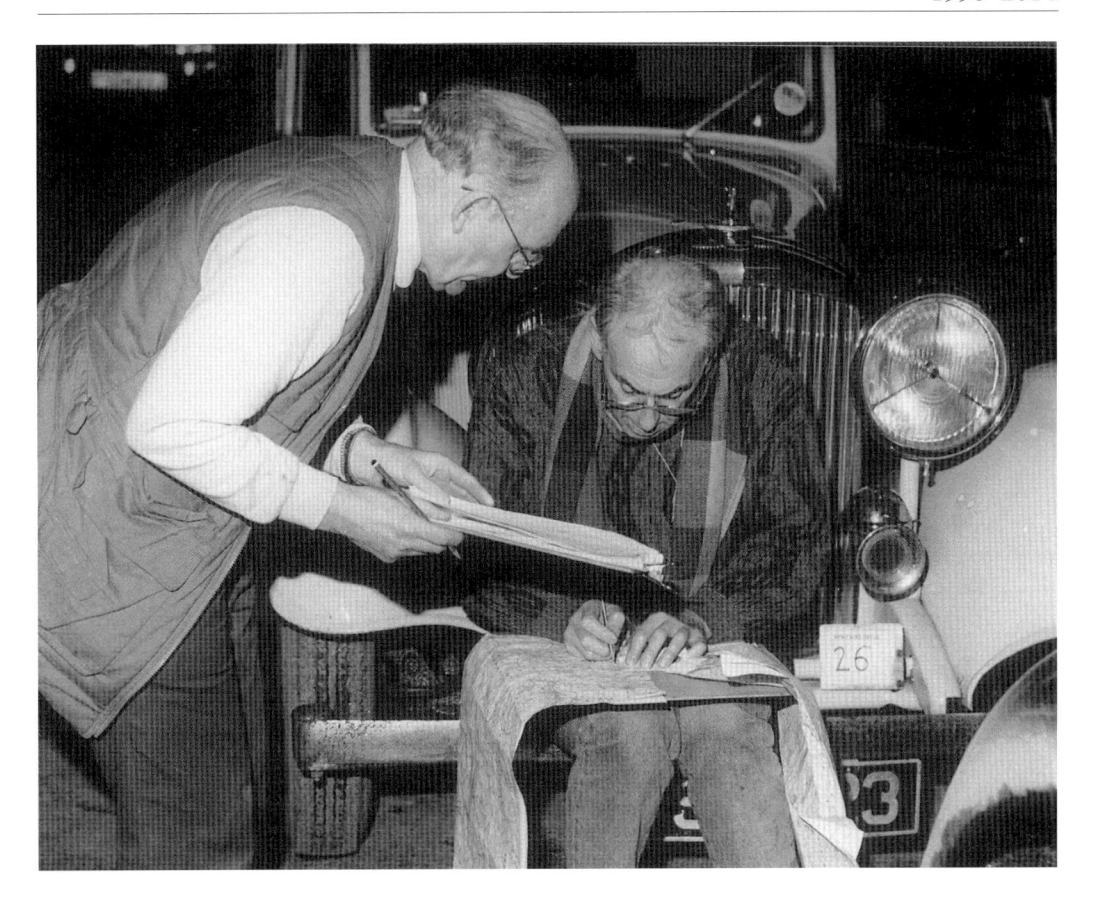

At the half way point on the 1988 Measham Rally. Ray Edge (for many years the Club's Chief Marshal) and John Warburton (The Bulletin Editor from 2000 until 2007) plot the second part of the route. Their 3.5-litre "Derby" Bentley, despite its bulk, has proved a very effective rally car, carrying its owner to the Club's Rally Driver's Trophy in 2011, 2012 and 2013.

The Pomeroy, confined to the chilly Northampton uplands of Silverstone in February, with subtle changes made to its scoring system over the years, was to become something of a Frazer Nash benefit, especially so between 1998 and 2011. Within these fourteen years two of the victories were in PVTs – a 1934 Super Sports and a 1938 Frazer Nash BMW – while in eight other years vintage 'Nashes emerged as winners. The outstanding driver was Patrick Blakeney-Edwards with four victories, a hat-trick in 2007, 2008 and 2009 and a further victory in 2011 in a rare 'Nash saloon. Tom Threlfall had observed in his report on the 1997 event that "Posterity will have to judge whether it advanced the progress of the search for the Ideal Touring Car significantly. It probably (as ever) did not." But the Pom remains great fun for the participants and a good way of blowing away some of winter's cobwebs, and if it has been won in some unlikely "high speed tourers" it cannot be won by a poor driver.

Chipping Norton and beyond

Above – The Pomeroy Memorial Trophy of 2010, with a typical mix of cars from across the years. Those shown include the Mille Miglia Frazer Nash of Andrew Hall, which was to win a First Class award, the 4½-litre Bentley of Nigel Batchelor and the Triumph TR2 of Charles Gillett. Meanwhile the V12 Lagonda Le Mans Replica of Alan Chandler lines up for the corner ahead.

Below – Late August 2014, and a perfect English summer's day. Ami-Louise Sharpe – 1912 3-litre Sunbeam Coup de l'Auto – rolls towards the start of the Slow-Fast test at Madresfield. The three young men on the right took it in turns to walk alongside cars on the slow section to ensure that no use was made of either brakes or clutch. In the background the Malvern Hills and Madresfield Court watch over the scene

In complete contrast late summer days, usually in September, continued to provide a very different kind of diversion for Club members. The Madresfield organising teams – that of the long serving Adams, followed by Paul and Chrissie Tebbett, with Bob Watt continuing to compute the results – have done their best to devise different ways of providing relatively gentle competition on a very straight drive; changing MSA (Motor Sports Association) requirements trimming the length of the once full blooded final sprint, but otherwise making little significant difference. The Concours for competing cars became a self-judging affair ("Which car would you most like to take home?") while a concours for the cars of spectating members ("Which car has given the judges the most pleasure to see?") was introduced in 2012. Although the winners have usually changed from year to year, Rob Gibson achieved a unique hat-trick using a Wolseley Hornet Special in 2011 and 2012 and an Austin Seven Special in 2013. He then made it four in a row with another Austin win in 2014. Along with its delightful setting, the relaxed air and picnics at lunchtime, are annual proof that history can repeat itself.

At first glance the Welsh weekend has changed very little over the years, with even The Smatcher having returned – albeit in altered form – in 1997; but more significant changes were ahead for the trial. In 1998 the first use of a section at Cwm Whitton, a little to the north of Presteigne, was made with a second hill there being added in the following year. In 2000 there was more fundamental change as the farm at Pilleth changed hands and no longer could be used for the final cluster of hills. Cwm Whitton was to come to the rescue, taking over this role in 2002, since then both trial and rally finishing at the farm here. In the intervening year – 2001 – there could be no rally, as there was a Foot and Mouth epidemic that prevented the use of public roads through essentially agricultural areas. With great determination Paul Tebbett and George Shetliffe set forth to arrange a trial wholly within the confines of Radnor Forest, the conifers and forestry tracks providing the backdrop to the sections, with baths of disinfectant for wheels and boots at the entrance. The Welsh reached 65 years of age in 2004. The local landowners, and others in the area who had been so co-operative in their support of the trial, were invited to the Radnorshire for a dinner to thank them for their enthusiasm and tolerance of an event which holds a special place in the affection of almost all of those in and around Presteigne, a celebration that was repeated in 2014 to mark the 75th anniversary of the event.

The entry for the trial of 1998 had shown how much trialling had changed and how specialist it had all become. The Harry Bowler Memorial Trophy for the best

Above – The father and son team of Peter and Martin Jelley in their Austin 16/6 check in at a Time Control on the 1999 Welsh Rally. The three marshals, from left to right, sign the competitors' time card, read out the time of arrival from the rally clock and enter the details on the control's record sheet.

Below – Modified and Special Austin Sevens have dominated trials entry and award lists for many years, and particularly so around the start of the millennium. Here, a typical example of their number, Ian Patton's Ulster, tackles the mud of "Sipping Cider", a section on the Herefordshire Trial in the early spring of 2010.

performance of the event was to go to Barry Clarke in a 1928 Austin Seven, while Ian Williamson in an ex Cream Cracker MG from 1935 was on the same number of penalties. It was Clarke's sixth win, to which he was to add yet another in the following year. First Class awards went to three competitors, two of whom were in Austin Sevens, Second Class awards went to six competitors, all of whom were in Austin Sevens, while Third Class awards went to nine competitors five of whom were in similar cars. Of 18 awards overall 72% went to the little cars from Longbridge – albeit few, if any, were unchanged from the days that they had left the factory.

The great Club triallist Leslie Winder had been anticipating such developments as long ago as 1951 when, in a letter to *The Bulletin*, he had written:

> "My own opinion is that a proper hill should be a proper road from somewhere to somewhere else, if at the same time it is the sort of road over which the driver of 25 years ago might have driven so much the better … I hate to see vintage machinery developing into glorified trials specials which they will if really grassy muddy sections are employed…"

However, with the passage of time "proper roads" have largely been sanitised, and trials sections have had to be devised that will challenge the new breed of motor car being used to try and climb them. The Vauxhall 30-98 entries, once so common, have almost completely died away (Jeddere-Fisher had rolled his in the 2006 event) while Model A Fords have come to dominate the long wheel base class. There were 22 of these on the 2011 Trial, with only Paul Jeavons being a regular (and successful) 30-98 triallalist in recent years. In the short wheelbase classes modified and special Austin Sevens are constantly to the fore, with such names as Dave Dye and Don Skelton standing out. But neither the men nor the Austins always get their own way, as Louise Bunting (GN Touring) with a hat-trick of wins on the Lakeland Trials of 2012, 2013 and 2014, was to show.

The rallying element of the Welsh weekend continued to demonstrate that almost any sound vintage or PVT car could do well in the right hands. (Against a certain amount of opposition the latter were allowed to compete in the rally from 2008, but the trial remains open to vintage cars only). In 2007, a year when the triallists were again confined by Foot and Mouth to Radnor Forest, the rally, which was allowed to happen as it did not directly cross any farm land, was won in a Bentley, in 2008 in a Daimler, in 2010 in a Fiat Ballila, in 2013 (to show that they refuse to be held down) by a 1928 Austin Seven Chummy, and in 2014 in a Riley Lynx. The Vintage Welsh Rally (to give it its full official title) broke with tradition in 2014 by starting near the Gloucestershire–Herefordshire border, only reaching Wales in its closing few miles. Longer than usual, the rally itself was well received, but the pressures to return it to its Welsh homeland were great.

Rallies, Trials, Tours and Tests

In addition to the Measham, the Club typically holds four or five other navigational rallies each year. These are well spread out across the country, but surprisingly have not reached the south west. They normally remain for a three year run in an area before moving on. Thus the Lincolnshire Wolds, the Forest of Bowland in Lancashire, the Derbyshire Peak District, as well as the roads of Kent, Wiltshire, Berkshire, of the old Rutlandshire, and around Malvern have included those that have played host to route boards, time controls and PR notices in their time. In 2002 a new rally was to join the lists for a three year stint; the Cotswold as organised by Derek and Gilly Howard-Orchard. As well as attracting higher entries than usual (78 in the first year – nearly double that found on many Club rallies) it quickly became noted for its delightful lunch stop settings. The privately owned Longborough Festival Opera House near Stow-on-the-Wold was the half-way halt in 2002, then in the following year the rally paused for breath and sustenance at the Rendcomb Aerodrome Club – the base for the Utterley Butterley stunt fliers – while in 2004 (albeit at the wrong time of year for the snowdrops for which it is nationally renowned) by the lawns of the Hall at Colesbourne Park. Vintage Sports-Car Club rallying reaches lunch stops that other rallies rarely reach.

Not to be outdone the Light Car and Edwardian Section usually manages some memorable settings as part of its summer rallies. Notable years included 2005, when the rally was based at Little Nash near Presteigne – the home of Roger and Judy Collings. After a barbecue and bonfire on the previous evening the rally itself (the entry including the 1908 Itala driven by George Daniels, with the Rolt family Alvis 12/50 in attendance) wound its way to the magnificent setting of Stanage Park and Castle for a picnic lunch. Then back to Little Nash for tea on the lawns of the attractive garden. It was another glorious summer's day in June 2014 when the LCES met near Rugby at the Warwickshire home of Peter Stevenson, whose grounds include a lake, complete with steam launch and around which runs a miniature steam railway. Here participants could camp and enjoy such delights on the previous evening and where the rally (ably organised by 'French' Dave Crouch and Andy Fox) concluded for tea and the results.

This rally, along with several other such events in the opening years of the 2000s, included a touring category for entrants who preferred to follow the route but without navigational challenges, while other tours were either free standing or, in the case of the Exmoor Fringe, linked to the trial. 2011, partly due to encouragement from Tim Cork, was a particularly rich year for tours. They were held in Three Counties (in this case Herefordshire, Shropshire and Gloucestershire), Derbyshire, Yorkshire, Norfolk and (the King Billy Tour) in South Yorkshire. The summer also saw a Brittany Tour with the diverse collection of cars taking part including a 1912 Renault, an Austin Seven Chummy, a couple of vintage Bentleys and two 1932 Rolls-Royces. Some years before, in 2003, a more strenuous tour – the Pyrenean Challenge – had taken the 17 starters to an altitude of 6935 feet on the Col du Tourmalet, a key climb on many cycling Tours de France. Other overseas tours have included Burgundy and Ireland.

Away from tarmac surfaces a new event was to be added to the calendar in 2006 in the shape of the Cotswold Trial; a return to an area in which the Club had run its pre-war Gloucester Trials. Setting out to cater for novices it included a Class Zero for these, that attracted over thirty such entries, and comprised a number of driving tests as well as a trials section at Prescott. As the trial has developed the Prescott connection has been steadily strengthened, the event now starting and finishing there, with a clutch of hills located on the slopes adjacent to the hill climb itself; while the now re-named Novice (rather than Zero) class continues to attract high numbers. Other significant changes on the trials scene have included a new team to run the Lakeland Trial following the retirement of the Smith family. Alan Couper and John Gill now head this up. An innovation in 2014 was to require competitors to visit hills in a set order, rather than allowing them to choose their own order – and hence the most favourable timings as to when to tackle sections – which in their judgement might get either easier or harder as the day progressed. This certainly kept the event moving well, as did the prohibition on walking the sections before they could be attempted.

A re-location affected the Winter Driving Tests in 2010. After their years at Enstone, Abingdon and then Westcott, they were moved to St George's Barracks on the outskirts of Bicester, where the surfaces were generally smoother; but the temperatures were much the same, with a sprinkling of snow to welcome competitors and marshals on their first visit. The tests demonstrated the usual Elder complexities and subtleties, and are likely to continue to do so, as in 2014 Mark Elder took over the role of Clerk of the Course from his father Malcolm, who had organised them for so many years. The site was also changed, moving just down the road to the historic motoring and aviation centre, Bicester Heritage.

Four Anniversaries

The Club was to mark a run of significant birthdays across the years 1999, 2004, 2009 and 2014 when in turn it reached sixty five, seventy, seventy five and eighty years of age.

Malvern was to be the focus for the 1999 celebrations based, as was the usual practice, at the Three Counties Showground, where there was plenty of room for camping, caravanning and driving tests on the service roads. George Shetliffe, together with Paul Knill-Jones, took on the organisation and in its basics the programme was much to the now familiar pattern – but two events within it were to stand out. Paul and Chrissie Tebbett organised the first ever "Homes and Gardens" day on which a number of local members opened up their garages, gardens and, in one case the 7¼" gauge passenger carrying railway around their grounds, so that participants could follow their own routes to visit a number of domestic, horticultural and mechanical delights. Hamish Moffatt's home, with vintage aircraft, a private landing strip, a small lake replete with steam launch, not to mention his vintage cars, was surely the brightest star in the firmament. Equally memorable was the cyclecar climb up the Olde Wyche Road. Arguably the steepest residential road in England, reaching 1 in 2.8 at the top, it had been used as an observed section on early reliability trials. Although normally closed to all motorists except residents – who then may only use it downhill for access – permission had been obtained for its use, for two hours only, by a gathering of cyclecars, with various GN models dominant. The climbs went ahead with the organisers, headed by Bob Jones, terrified by both the number of spectators squeezed along the road and the energy with which the participants attacked the hill. Mike Bullett, who against all the odds managed the climb in his AV Monocar, got what was probably the loudest round of applause. Shetliffe was not over surprised to later receive a letter from the Police Superintendent of the local Traffic Department explaining that "A number of complaints have been passed to me … I am told that two pupils (from the local school) were basically held prisoner in a garden on the Olde Wyche for an hour while their parents searched for them". No doubt from such safe surroundings they had enjoyed watching the cars go by. However, with great magnanimity, he concluded the letter with "I do not wish to prevent the event from re-occurring".

The sprint held along the drive of the nearby Whitfield estate must have seemed tame in comparison, albeit with a cattle grid to add interest to a variety of fast and slow corners, while earlier in the week there had been a vintage fly-in and gathering of OMs at Defford. A dozen aircraft arrived, in rather better weather than at the end of the week when the Utterley Butterley wing walking team flew in over the Malvern showground, but in the thundery downpour could scarcely be seen.

For the 70th anniversary celebrations the Club moved north to Harrogate. As well as a "Homes and Gardens" rally on new territory and with eleven venues that could be

The 65th Anniversary celebrations of the Club in 1999 included a fly-in to Defford airfield in Worcestershire where the gathering of cars, inclusive of a number of OMs as seen here, was joined by a dozen aircraft. Among these was G-ACDJ, a DH 82A Tiger Moth, built by de Havilland in 1933.

visited, the Ridings Rally, inclusive of some challenging navigation, took 90 competitors over to Blubberhouses unused by the VSCC since the early fifties. During the week there were two speed events, a sprint on the airfield at Elvington with its adjacent air museum as a distraction, and a hill climb at Harewood on the long and multi-cornered course there. John Gill, overall organiser of the event, was rewarded for his efforts by the appreciative response of members concluding their week at the 70th Anniversary Dinner and Dance.

The calendar for 2004 shows how extensive the Club's programme had become over 70 years, and the wide range of activities involved.

January	Brooklands Driving Tests
	The Measham Rally
February	Exmoor Fringe Trial with Tour
	The Pomeroy Trophy
March	The John Harris (Derbyshire) Trial plus Tour
	Herefordshire Trial
	LCES Welsh Weekend
April	Scottish Trial
	Silverstone Race Meeting
May	Northern Rally – Derbyshire
	Curborough speed trials
	East Anglia Tour
	Boulogne Bicycle Rally
June	Silverstone Historic Festival race meeting
	Eastern Rally –Lincolnshire
	Cadwell Park race meeting
	LCES Summer Rally – Cotswolds
July	Shelsley Walsh hill climb
	Colerne speed trials
	Mallory Park race meeting
August	Prescott hill climb
	70th Anniversary week in Harrogate
September	Cotswold Rally
	Madresfield Driving Tests
	Donington race meeting
	LCES Driving tests
	Loton Park hill climb
October	Welsh Trial and Rally
	Autumn Sprint – Goodwood
November	Lakeland Trial
	Driving tests – Westcott

75 years of the VSCC was to be celebrated, with a return to Malvern in August 2009. The "week" spread over ten days, had started at Prescott and included over thirty

events, while in the background were Richard Houlgate and the hard working Chipping Norton staff to keep everything running smoothly. Steam featured strongly with another of Herefordshire's passenger carrying miniature railways, the Kyre Valley, to be encountered on the Homes and Gardens event, a day trip on the standard gauge Severn Valley Railway on offer, and yet more steam at the end of the Cyclecar gathering which assembled at the Downs School where a miniature steam railway could be sampled. The navigation rally organised by Dick Wilkinson – who for several years had been in charge of the equivalent Welsh event – challenged many a navigator as the maps he provided for them were from the Cassini Historic series of the OS, as originally published in 1919/20. Remarkably the lanes of the area had changed very little in the intervening years; but perhaps the most memorable of the days was the 'fly-in' to Shobdon airfield where an estimated three hundred vintage cars gathered and where both vintage and modern aircraft were to be seen both on the ground and in the sky above.

Until 2014 the name of Peterborough had featured little in the annals of Club history, so it was to the surprise of many that it was chosen as the base for its 80th birthday celebrations. The East of England Showground, sufficiently spacious to host a number of competitive events as well as accommodating tents, caravans and the parking needs for a week of VSCC activities, proved a highly suitable base – all under the very effective organisational oversight of Gemma Price of the Club's Competition Department. The week followed on from the usual Prescott meeting, where an additional day using the longer extended hill climb course had been included, and which was blessed with good weather. Some twenty events, covering a variety of tastes – inclusive of a jazz piano concert and a beer festival – took place, notable among them being a "first" in the shape of an Autosolo. This all-forward driving test competition was won by a Riley in the hands of Andrew Craven, while Marcus Croome, who had come all the way up from Cornwall, went away with a 1st Class award won in his 1904 Wolseley. The entry for the Acorn Rally was both large and diverse, with 100 cars ranging from a 1925 Trojan Utility at one end of the performance scale to a Frazer Nash/BMW 328 Sports at the other. Kevin Lee and Annabel Jones, navigating in her family Vauxhall 30-98, went away as the winners. Robin Baker in the 11760cc Hispano Amicar Special was quickest in the Anniversary Straight Line Sprint held on the nearby Santa Pod Railway, while in contrast a LCES Tour and a Treasure Hunt provided for more gentle entertainment. The largest entry of all was for the 3 Ms Scatter Tour, with 200 cars setting out to visit some of the Mills, Manors and Motorhouses (as well as many other interesting sights) in and around the area. After a final day of festivities on the

A calmer side of Club life. An Alvis and a Lancia take their rest by Moulton Mill near Spalding – the tallest windmill in the country. It was visited by many of the 200 entrants who took part in the 3Ms Tour (Mills, Manors and Motorhouses) that formed part of the 80th Anniversary Celebrations based at Peterborough in August 2014.

showground members made their way home with memories of a satisfying week of motoring through the pleasantly attractive countryside and villages of that corner of England.

Staffing and other developments

Back at the office a number of staffing changes have inevitably occurred over time. In mid 2000 Neil Murray retired from the Secretaryship, his place being taken by S A M (Stuart) Pringle, who was to remain with the Club for a little over five years. Joining him in the following year was M G (Mike) Stripe, appointed as "Events Manager", the need triggered by the increasing administrative demands made by high profile race meetings; while in February Bob Wimmer became Competition Secretary in succession to Robert Ellis, in turn to be followed by Richard Winchester in 2009. On the increasingly important public relations and publicity front Gillian Carr, no mean competition driver in her own right, was to follow Sadie Wigglesworth, while in May 2001 Gill Batkin had joined the staff as office administrator, assisting the Club Secretary and co-ordinating the production of the monthly *Newsletter*.

In the late 1940s a number of brief information sheets had been circulated to members, in early 1953 these settling down to become regular *Newsletters*. In March 1965 they started to be issued in A5 format, the now familiar booklets first appearing in black and white but later including colour. Month by month these bring news of forthcoming events, cars for sale, any changes in regulations and indeed information on the whole range of issues and interests effecting the doings of the widely diverse Club. Through its pages members could thus learn of such changes as the move of the Winter Driving Tests from Westcott to Bicester in 2010 (buildings being planned for the former site), of changing locations for the rally programme, of cars for sale and the latest scores counting towards the Club's aggregate awards.

There is an apocryphal tale of a pre-war motor club in Surrey that had more trophies than it had members, but the VSCC with just on seven thousand members, and some one hundred and twenty trophies – of which thirty seven are for annual aggregate awards – still has some way to go.

While the *Newsletter* is true to its name *The Bulletin*, as well as containing reports on recent events, also allows for a much more reflective and analytic approach towards the doings of the Club.

The Bulletin

A dictum, that has long been part of the perspective shared by its Editors, is that "*The Bulletin* is the glue which binds the Club together". Indeed for many of its seven thousand members it is the only contact that they have with its activities and their view of the Club is both formed and maintained by its tone and content. The first of the eleven Editors that there have been so far was the ever influential Sam Clutton who (aged only twenty five when he took on the role) adopted for modern tastes a somewhat naïve and forced "jokiness" that would grate with a modern readership, but which no doubt appealed to those for whom it was originally written. In later years even Clutton admitted that he shuddered at some of his earliest utterances.

The mission of the BBC – to inform, educate and entertain – is not far off the unstated yet implicit aims of *The Bulletin* while Michael Elsom, its Editor from 1979 to 1984, in the issue that celebrated its 250th edition in the winter of 2005, stood back to take an overview of what he felt it should set out to do.

> "*The Bulletin* represents the Club – it is the platform for placing what the Club does and thinks before its members. Of course the multitudinous events show the active side of the VSCC, and show it to be a thriving organisation providing enjoyable motor sport at all levels. But it is in the reports of these events, the exchange of views contained in its pages and the historical articles that the wider picture emerges. Despite the increased number of magazines catering for vehicles of all ages, which VSCC members enjoy, no-one with a serious interest in pre-war motoring can afford to cancel their subscription to the VSCC. The exchange of views in *The Bulletin* is vital and keeps people in touch with the issues of the moment – even in the age of websites. You only have to look at the Editorial and correspondence pages to appreciate the wide range of views on absolutely everything from eligibility to events co-ordination …
>
> It is primarily as an historical record that *The Bulletin* is special – because whatever you may think of the VSCC from time to time, it is a very special Club. It is a very special Club because, even now, it does not take itself too seriously – however hard it is sometimes to realise that. Just as the Club rises above the interests of its individual members, so *The Bulletin* smoothes them out and presents a wider picture. It does so in a

very special way because of the skills of its contributors and its editorial team."

In the same 250th *Bulletin* other previous Editors had been invited to share their memories and their views. Sandy Skinner (Editor 1970–1973) recalled the era when Verstage of Basingstoke were still the printers, as they had been for very many years, and when John Stanford (Editor 1956–1966) was forced to apologise for the late publication of an issue as a goat, belonging to the local sub-postmistress, had enjoyed eating the proofs. He also recalled how Nigel Arnold-Forster (Editor 1954–1955 and 1966–1970) had rashly published a learned article on 250F Maseratis by Denis Jenkinson assuming that a piece by someone of his journalistic stature surely did not require close editorial scrutiny. But Jenks normally worked under the watchful eye of Bill Boddy, who ensured that anything verging on the libellous was subject to the editorial blue pencil. A non-member, mentioned unflatteringly in the article, sued – and without any defence a grovelling apology and damages were required to settle the matter. Tom Threlfall (Editor 1973–1979) recalled the day when the preparation of an issue required "pasting up" – a tedious process involving scissors and cow gum to physically assemble the mock-up pages – and of his eventual move to computers and floppy discs. Inevitably, and rightly so, each Editor has had his own penchants and style. While Threlfall, unlike most of his predecessors, did not make much use of cartoons his own work was almost always introduced by his "trade mark" use of well chosen and usually erudite quotations. In contrast David Thirlby (Editor 1985–2001) was evidently fond of cartoons for the "page three" work of Lionel Stretton and his creation Ludwig the Bear was to enliven many a *Bulletin* over the years that he was in charge.

Thirlby also recalled how:

> "After four years of producing *The Bulletin* I fell out with the printer of the time, chiefly because I was not treated as an Editor but as a contributor. I have always been a member of societies that are concerned with the industrial past, especially with links to locomotion. One of these societies was the old bicycle movement. I have never forgotten the day I received a copy of their magazine, which had changed overnight from a Gestetnered news-sheet to a well laid out publication, with all the advantages of the printing revolution then taking place on the back of desk top publishing. I got in touch with Brian Hayward, a Committee member of the Veteran

Cycle Club, but much more importantly the MD of Quorum, the printers in Cheltenham. He said that my Amstrad computer with Locoscript was obsolete – and there was I thinking I was right at the cutting edge of modernity. Brian said I had to have a PC and Ventura Publisher. Sensation.

This was the opportunity to change everything. Talking of walking on egg shells: the tact and diplomacy I utilised frightened me, but it was all a waste of time and unnecessary since Sam Clutton was all in favour, as was Roger Collings, the then-President. And the Committee agreed.

I am still amazed how easy it all was. Quorum printed the first issue and now (twenty-two years later) the same company prints a large proportion of the Club's publications in addition to *The Bulletin.*"

The other big change that took place in Thirlby's time was a substantial increase in *The Bulletin* page size, this going up by just over a third in the spring of 1990. The original page size that had been used from the earliest of the post-war *Bulletins* was no longer feasible for the task in hand. The number of events to be covered had steadily increased, alongside an increased use of photographs, while to squeeze it all in the number of pages had gone up to over a hundred per issue, while the size of the typeface had been reduced to the point where a number of readers understandably complained. The Editor apologised to "those aggrieved members who have put up bookshelves to hold *The Bulletin* through to the twenty first century" – but now, after nearly a quarter of a century, only a few are said to still regret the change, while the current size has proved itself well nigh ideal. Also on Thirlby's watch a few colour photographs crept in during the mid nineties, followed by a coloured cover in Autumn 1997. These then became a regular feature, while the proportion of colour used inside steadily increased.

The next Editor, John Warburton (2000–2007) used his tenure to particularly good effect, *The Bulletin* being awarded the prestigious Brigham Award of the Society of Automotive Historians, doing so in company with the American publication *Vintage Motor Sport – The journal of motor racing history*. The co-chairman of the selection panel for this international award wrote "*The Bulletin* of the Vintage Sports-Car Club represents the highest standard of historical automotive publishing, both in content and presentation. The consistent quality suggests a staff that knows and loves their profession."

A wide range of articles accompanied the traditional reports, one notably initiating a lively debate on the enduring topic of eligibility. He also introduced the cartoonist Apsley to a wider and appreciative audience. In 2008 Warburton was followed by John Staveley who continues to uphold *The Bulletin* traditions, inclusive of accurate and entertaining reporting, informed historical articles and notably high photographic standards, while in Quorum, the printers, the Club is fortunate in having a firm with a commitment to the special interests of the VSCC.

In the closing months of 2014 *The Bulletin* was to lose two outstanding names from those who have made significant long term contributions to its development. David Venables, Assistant Editor for over twenty years was to die in October, shortly afterwards to be followed by David Thirlby, under whose editorship he once had worked.

Correspondence

The correspondence columns of *The Bulletin* regularly remind readers of the huge range of interests and genuine erudition that exist within the Club. An insoluble problem (for it is within the nature of the beast and cannot ever be fully resolved) is how to conduct a written debate in a magazine that appears at quarterly intervals. By the time that the reply to an earlier letter is printed matters will, more often than not, have moved on. With the coming of the internet, and the Forums to be found on the Club's website, topical debate can and does take place, but seldom are the postings as carefully thought through as are the letters published in *The Bulletin*. The printed work maintains an authority beyond that of on-screen communication, while successive Editors have the challenge of selecting letters that relate to enduring topics and matters of principle.

Thus letters on eligibility have been a recurring theme over the years, with far from all members satisfied as to the wisdom and impartiality of the Committee. Hence in the winter of 1964 a letter from Kenneth Wright appeared suggesting that …. "the title of the Vintage Sports-Car Club is now utter nonsense (a more accurate nomenclature would be the Pride and Prejudice Car Club) and that unless the executive likes the bonnet of his car, or it is a pre-1931 job, entry to the "elite" calls for money, influence or a seat on the Committee!" Needless to say this letter generated a number of responses, both supporting and opposing his views, and debating an appropriate title for the Club; which, not unsurprisingly, still remains the same. Sometimes *The Bulletin* Editors have initiated debate themselves as did the article "Eligibility Blues" by John

Warburton and his Assistant Editor David Venables in the winter of 2003. This, as intended, stimulated a range of thoughtful letters as befitted the very thoughtful and balanced article on this perennial topic.

The first letter to appear in a *Bulletin* after the war was in June 1946. It was from pre-war member D A ffrench-Mullen writing from the RAF Club in Piccadilly.

> "Dear Sir, with effect from about October 1937 I had the pleasure of being a member of the Vintage SCC, although contributing little beyond undistinguished loyalty and an Austro Daimler which usually became temperamental and arrived too late to take part in any events. During the last five years I was a prisoner of war and since my return have decided to take up residence in Eire …. Under the circumstances I am parting with regret but also with relief from the Austro Daimler and would like to give it to someone who will cosset it with the solicitude to which it is accustomed. I say "give it" but there is one snag – the garage bill for the war at one shilling and sixpence a week works out at about fifty pounds. I have not dared to visit the car for fear of having to pay the bills… Should you hear of some dauntless spirit who would like the car I will gladly produce all the particulars."

The next letter to appear, this time actually under the heading 'Correspondence', was not until December 1948. Jack Fairman (later to distinguish himself in long distance sportscar racing, especially with the works Aston Martin team – and appropriately for a VSCC member being the last man ever to start a Grand Prix in a front engined motor car; albeit the Ferguson with four wheel drive) wrote about the superiority of vintage machines over modern cars in terms of their durability.

However, this singleton letter could not be said to be the beginning of a correspondence column. Nor could the sole letter that appeared in the May 1949 *Bulletin*. A. C. Whincop had written to the then Editor, Sam Clutton, protesting "most strongly against your abuse of your office by utilising it to make a vindictive personal attack on Mr Gilbey in the last issue of *The Bulletin*. I have discussed the attack with a number of members and we are of the unanimous opinion that your conduct in this matter is deplorable". Clutton's report on a visit to the British Grand Prix (a party of VSCC members having gone up by coach) had contained the following:-

"Funny – they must be putting on a safety campaign display in the middle on the Grand Prix" – "Oh! No, its only Gilbey on his Maserati". "By jove! That chap coming round now seems to be in trouble" – "Oh! No its only Gilbey again on his Saturday afternoon potter". "Hello! Here's honest Sam Gilbey still driving with steady judgement to ensure finishing" – "Wouldn't an Austin Ruby have been more comfortable and gone just as fast?"

True to form, Clutton was loathe to apologise, his riposte to Whincop's letter reading "The Editor is jealous of the reputation of British drivers, especially in international events where foreign competitors are apt to judge the skills and courage of British drivers by the performance of anyone with an English name".

Single letters continued to appear intermittently into the early 1950s until, under the Editorship of Ronald (Steady) Barker, the beginnings of a correspondence column started to emerge. Under the heading "The Editor, Dear Sir …" five letters, each on a different topic, appeared in September 1951 – while in the Christmas *Bulletin* of that year a clutch of letters responding to an article by Bill Boddy about his Clyno showed what could be done.

Groups of letters, typically three per issue, continued to be published, usually without any overall headings, and often on unrelated topics until the early 1960s. Then, under the Editorship of J E Stanford, "Correspondence" began to be published regularly under this heading, and so continues to this day.

Over the decades the range of topics has been quite immense. To state a few at random. "Frazer Nash 'orgies' at Mayfair Hotel" (Summer 1953). "Dwindling Edwardians at our events" (Spring 1959). "Genuine Lucas vintage oil lamps" (Autumn 1963). "Most neglected car award" (Autumn 1970). "Sponsors and hospitality" (Autumn 1980). "Measham winners. Saloons precluded" (Summer 1990). "Trials classes need to be reviewed" (Autumn 2010) and "Simms Magneto grub screws" (Spring 2011)… and so on.

One wonders if Peter Hull, when he reviewed the book *Lagonda – a history of the marque*, in the winter of 1978, expected a passing observation on spelling to generate some memorable correspondence. He commented on finding just one misprint in nearly five hundred pages, but only awarded nine marks out of ten for the spelling of "kilometre" as "kilometer" and "louvre" as "louver". In the following *Bulletin* a letter from Barclay Dodd, a member then living in Mexico, defended "these quite acceptable spellings in a country changing to the metric system rather than la système métrique". The letter concluded "*A small prize – in old pennies and half pennies – is offered to the first member who can inform the Editor which art or science uses the louver as a unit of measurement. Answers should be sent on a sheet of Jeyes double ply under a plain brown wrapper not later than April 2nd 1980.*"

Well ahead of this carefully chosen deadline, Bill Marshall from Hampshire rose to the challenge, his letter being published in the Autumn *Bulletin* of 1979. While we do not know if he won the prize, he certainly had a claim to expect some sort of award.

Dear Mr. Editor,

In 28 years' membership, I have not yet had a letter published in *The Bulletin*. This could be a record if it were round with a hole in the middle. I have written twice before but neither was published. "Too Rude" you said "for our sensitive members".

This letter however is in reply to your request for information on louver, for which you offered your actual money. You wondered if they were units used in science or the arts. There are of course four sorts of louvers. Firstly those immortalised in "Sons and Louvers". This variety occurs in 57 different attitudes as described by the calmer of the two Sutra playboys, and by Ketelby in his Persian Garden, or something. This sort of louver is measured in blocks of sex, where two sexes make a duzzen. Duzzen what? Duzzen matter. Whether this variety is art or science is dictated primarily by technique. Secondly they are a sort of plant-pod or dried up marine creature (picture if you can, Chris Pack sans Plymouth gin for ten years). Used by the more masochistic instead of a sponge. Definitely science. Thirdly, they are the habitués of a certain French art gallery which shall be nameless unless you can extract some advertising revenue from it. Herein is displayed a picture of some grimacing poppet and a statue without arms. Can't think why they don't repair it. Reminds me of the tale about the three-headed, one legged man without arms standing at a 'bus stop. "Allo, allo, allo", says the conductor, "you look 'armless enough – 'op on". Definitely art, and the score was one all. A fourth but possibly not final category numbers those unfortunates (including myself) who, like Godfrey in "Dad's Army" need to match intake with outflow, millilitre for millilitre. A great handicap for one whose formative years were dominated by the products of the Newcastle Brewery, and who remembers with affection his C.O's announcement of a future P.U. "Food will be retailed at one and tuppence per pint". The word in this context is derived from the French, who, in reply to "Where's he gone" would reply "vers le lieu" terminating the phrase at that point with commendable sense of delicacy. Hence "Lieuvers". A fairly arty expression, applied to this scientist which evens out the score at two all.

Should this solution merit the prize, please forward the coins wrapped in the label on a full bottle of Newcastle Brown – the label should not be removed from the bottle. Re-reading the competition regulations I realise that I have not typed my entry on Jeyes double ply. I did consider stealing from my employer some of his continuous stationery (now there's a contradiction in terms) which is marked periodically "Supplied for Government Service". Despite all the cutbacks in Government expenditure, it is quite untrue that recent consignments have been overprinted "use both sides".

Some members, in fact rather a lot of them, write more soberly about their cars, though not many from the rank and file can compete on automobile terms with that sent to Tim Carson at the Club office in 1956. R D Ford then lived in Venezuela and tells us something of his range of vehicles, and of some of the problems that can beset even the wealthy among our members.

"I can advise you that my "stable" has not changed since my last letter of 2nd March 1955. I still have the following cars:

1928 Minerva boat tailed open phaeton
1929 Speed-6 6½-litre Vanden Plas Bentley
1933 4½-litre Invicta, 100 miles per hour four-seater model
1934 Alfa Romeo, Type 8C two-seater sports
1934 Hispano-Suiza 9.7-litre V-12 drophead coupé. Van Vooren body.
1936 Duesenberg JN 8½-litre convertible phaeton, 8 cylinder, 32 valve, 265 hp

>   1937 Phantom III Rolls-Royce, sports, 4 door Barker sedan
>   1938 57S Bugatti, 3.3-litre two-seater coupé
>   1940 540K 5.7-litre Mercedes Benz two door sports coupé

> … the Alfa Romeo has been completely rebuilt … and the engine is like a fine watch. I drove the car a few months ago in California and, at 40 miles per hour, by flooring the throttle, the rear wheels could be spun on a dry pavement. It has incredible get-away, but of course not much top speed, as it was designed for road racing … The Hispano-Suiza was originally the property of Rainier III of Monte Carlo. My wife has the car as a regular every-day car when she is in the States and it performs beautifully, incredibly powerfully and quietly … The 57S Bugatti I have here in Caracas with me is I must say close to my favourite car. It is, as all Bugattis are, temperamental, but it is a beautiful thing … The Duesenberg is an incredible car giving some 265 horse-power. It is quite noisy and runs rather roughly until it reaches a speed of 60-70 miles per hour when it levels out and runs beautifully up to practically any speed between 100 and 140. It will do 95 in second gear which gives you an idea of its tremendous potential. It is certainly one of the gems of my collection and, strangely, my only American car …

> I am at present trying to build a garage for the cars on some property I purchased in 1954. Unfortunately I ran up against a city zoning law which refuses to allow more than a four-car garage on any individual piece of property and I have had to go through a lot of legal work to get a special concession to allow me to build a ten-car garage. I hope this will be finished early in April and meantime the cars are housed in San Mateo, California where I have an excellent French mechanic who checks each car once a week to be sure that it runs properly and that they are well maintained. Yours sincerely,"

And at the other end of the spectrum, with a concern for Club history, came a letter from Bob Watt – a stalwart Midlands member and for many years associated with Madresfield – querying which Club event has the longest history.

> "I beg to differ (gently) from the statement in the Winter 2004 *Bulletin* that the Welsh has the longest history of any Club event. It is true that

the first Welsh was held in 1939, but the second did not take place until 1950. If you ignore gaps like this Donington is even older, since the first Club event there was held in July 1937, followed by meetings in 1938 and 1939, but then followed a long gap until the driving tests in 1974, with the current series of race meetings starting in 1979.

If however you prefer to look at the length of continuous history, Prescott was first held in 1938, and has been held every year since 1946, just beating Madresfield (1947) by one year; that is unless you feel that the loss of Madresfield in 2000, due to the fuel protests, should count."

Some views from The Old Post Office

Few people are as well placed to obtain an overview of the Club as are those who occupy the Secretaryship. They see Presidents and Committee members come and go, the membership in all multitudinous forms – old fogeys and junior members alike – while across the secretarial desk flows a never ending stream of challenges and issues. Mike Stripe was to serve nearly nine years in this role before leaving the Club in the summer of 2014, and before his departure was invited to share some of his thoughts on the constantly evolving task. In particular he noted "an ever growing commitment to legislation, the steadily growing number of Club members and events, a resultant increase in staff both employed and volunteer, and all the self governance issues that these bring with them." Unsurprisingly high on the list of matters likely to cross his desk were those concerned with eligibility. To use his own words:-

"One perennial topic of debate is the list of Post Vintage Thoroughbreds accepted by the Club or, as it is usually known, the PVT list. It's one of those topics which comes up time and again and polarises opinion but it took a while before it was ever considered. It was Edwardian cars that first exercised the eligibility debate. Classes for Edwardian cars were introduced in 1936. At the time, even these cars were comparatively young and it was not until the early post-war years that post-vintage cars were accepted for competition, initially at the discretion of the Committee, such resolution being passed by an overwhelming majority at the 1945 AGM. The debate, about what should and should not be included, has been high on the members' chattering list ever since. Recently, the Committee even considered opening up the Club's car eligibility to the 1950s or 1960s. Die-hards will be pleased to know that the discussion did not last long but it was one that the Committee felt they should have.

Beyond the PVT list, Eligibility generally is a constant and challenging boiling pot. Fashions change over the years. For example, I often baulk when I am told that the Club raced much nicer cars in 50s and 60s than it does now. This is a common perception but I think it simply means that we saw more 'well-known' cars than we do today. What many overlook is that their preparation often resulted in cars that bore little resemblance to the original, with fat tyres and telescopic shock-absorbers being just two examples of commonplace things that made that era much less attractive. There is little doubt that the cars we see competing today have a much closer resemblance to 'proper' pre-war motor cars than those that competed 40-50 years ago and the Eligibility Sub-Committee (ESC), all volunteers, have done a splendid job of bringing this aspect of the Club's ethos back on to the straight and narrow. It is an unforgiving minefield, of experts and opinions that could test the patience of the most gentle of personalities, and every Club member should be grateful for what the ESC do – even if they think they are wrong. The simple truth is that they *are* right, for they are the ones charged with making the decisions; often seeking confirmation from the main Committee where there is any doubt.

I've been told many, many times that, as Secretary, I must stop so-and-so from lifting the body off that wonderful old saloon and converting it into a sports tourer. Saloon cars, no matter how desirable, are far less likely to be regarded as sports-cars than are touring cars, so a natural conflict arises immediately. I might agree with the sentiment of protecting rare saloons but I wonder what jurisdiction the complainers think the Secretary, or the Club, has. Perhaps it is the statement in the Eligibility of Cars rule that says, "It is not acceptable to turn a sports car into a fake Historical Racing Car or a saloon car into a sports or touring car". What this means is that, if the Club knows that this is what has happened, the resultant car may not be accepted for Club competitions and therefore will not be issued with a Buff form. Regrettably, it does *not* mean that the Club has the authority to prevent such things from happening. This leads on to a

"THAT SETTLES IT ; EVEN THE THREEPENNY BIT UNDER THE CARPET IS A REPLICA"

wider consideration of the benefits of a 'Buff Form'. It is a simple fact that while 1,500 different cars may appear in VSCC competitions in any one season there are at least four times as many as that which have been issued with a Buff Form. The truth is, of course, that many see the possession of a Buff Form as a clear endorsement of the car's provenance. Regrettably, they seem to be right, even though the Club is adamant that the Eligibility Document is published by the VSCC solely for its own purposes to regulate the use of members' cars in VSCC events and competitions and that it does not confer on or constitute authenticity to any car; nor does it imply any proven historical provenance for a car. What's more, the Eligibility Forms and Passports are not to be used for any trade or commercial purpose. So 'Currently with Buff Form', the only phrase that we will willingly allow in adverts for VSCC eligible cars, means that the current owner has a Buff Form that allows him to run the car in VSCC competitions. Nothing more. That said, we do keep an eye on trade adverts and try to prevent misuse of Buff Forms for trade and provenance purposes."

The Club Secretary is line-manager for the staff at Chipping Norton, and frequently is called upon to justify their number.

"All too often I hear that the Club is over-staffed. It is certainly true that, over the years, the number of employed staff has grown. However, it has not been unjustified as both the number of members and the number of sporting events that the Club runs has increased inexorably. In its 80th Anniversary year the Club has about 7,000 members and will need somewhere in the order of 45 permits from the governing body (Motor Sports Association) to organise competitive events. Even allowing for the army of volunteers that organise events locally and help out on the day, this amounts to an extensive workload for eight people to manage. In the early days virtually all events were organised on a much more informal basis by volunteers, and many smaller motor clubs operate in this way, even today. However, usually such clubs concentrate on a few events in a single discipline whereas the VSCC holds competitive events in virtually all motor sport disciplines; an almost unique and extremely satisfying status. This requires levels of expertise not found elsewhere from a dedicated staff, many of whom work 20 or more weekends every year. The Old Post Office is also self-sufficient. How often have we heard the question "Don't you have someone to do that for you?" Well, no actually, we don't. That is why we all stuff envelopes, why we all answer the 'phone, why we all load the van, why we are always last to leave the venue, and so on. More importantly we must all ensure that the Club complies with every bit of legislation governing small to medium sized businesses, including accounts, health and

Chipping Norton and beyond

At the start of another Club year: The New Year's day gathering at the Verzons Hotel near Ledbury in Herefordshire as seen in 2003. 107 vintage and PVT cars were in attendance, representing 31 different makes in all.

safety (in the office and at events), personnel management (or Human Resources as it is usually known these days), the sport – and everything else. We are also landlords, contract negotiators, deal makers, sounding boards and "where the buck stops". That said, we are supported by a band of enthusiastic, energetic, knowledgeable and generally helpful Committee members. In fact they outnumber the staff by at least two to one and their strategic control of the Club is key to its status and effort. They are all volunteers and they have corporate responsibility for everything that the Club does. It is the Committee and Staff who rejoice in sharing the joy and rewards of success, but they also have to cope with the depths of tragedy that our sport sometimes brings. The breadth of that responsibility and authority may be easily overlooked, along with the sheer amount of work that must be done, and we simply cannot please all of the members all of the time, even though we try. Getting it right for the majority, most of the time, is the usual outcome and we get blessed few genuine complaints. I would certainly argue that the Membership gets good value from its Club staff."

Upon Mike Stripe's departure, he having been the twelfth Secretary of the Club, the search was on for his successor. In the interim Steve Allen – the last remaining link with the Russell Road staff, and only recently retired from his post as Accounts and Membership Secretary – returned to The Old Post Office on a part-time basis as Acting Secretary. Early in December 2014 the new Secretary, Dave Salmon, was to take up his post.

Challenges and Issues Ahead

At the age of 80 the VSCC can be seen as being in good shape, still fulfilling the original objectives of its founders who in 1934 had set out "to provide competitive events for owners of cars five years old or more and social events for its members". The outstanding men who were to nurture and develop these ideas over the early years left the Club a legacy on which it has been able to build. Well led, with some excellent Presidents, it has been able to adapt to changing circumstances in a pragmatic flexible (yet sometimes reluctant) manner, while in the years ahead it would seem that such evolution must proceed apace.

Over many years the ever pressing and central issue of Eligibility has exercised members minds, been debated over many a pint and taken up much space in the pages and correspondence columns of *The Bulletin*. In a very real sense there are no answers for "what is truth on one side of the Pyrenees is error on the other". There is an inherent illogicality in an arrangement that allows some of the poorer cars from the 1920s to have automatic admission to the Club, while some far better cars from the 1930s have been excluded. In accepting this the PVT list has been steadily expanded, while if it continues to do so for long enough the situation may eventually be reached when all cars built on or before 31st December 1940 have become eligible. But a strong body of opinion will argue otherwise, believing that discernible quality must remain the yardstick for admission. Wisely the Club has consistently included the phrase "with the Committee's approval" in the relevant documentation, with the Eligibility Committee making the final recommendation as to what should obtain.

For the racing fraternity a large vocabulary, and a complex of ideas behind these words, often exercises their minds. Original or fake? A facsimile, a replica, a reproduction or a re-creation? What do these terms actually mean and when does applied mechanical ingenuity become cheating? Again there are no easy answers. The VSCC is not a preservation society, largely existing for competition between its eligible cars. But when does a car stop being the one that its builders originally made; for competition wears out cars and components need to be replaced? A letter in the Summer 1989 *Bulletin* clearly made the point. "I do not believe that technically there is a totally original racing car that has been 'used in anger' that has not had some major or minor accident repairs or modifications since the day it was made ... any car more than twenty years old has been modified from original in some way – at least several times – to keep it competitive". Thus many of the much raced ERAs that take part in the Club's event have had virtually all their major components replaced over the years due to honest wear and tear or accidental damage.

As a result they may be considered as almost a form of toolroom copy cars – albeit ones with a continuous history. ("A fine broom this; only one new handle and three new heads in the past five years!") The Eligibility Sub-Committee was asked to consider the matter of allowing toolroom copy cars to take part in VSCC racing, and in February 2013 published some of its thoughts. "Grids of truly original cars inevitably have grown smaller with the passage of time. Several significant racing cars have been sold overseas, while other are seen by their owners as too valuable to race. Some events – for example the Goodwood Revival meeting – permit copy cars, and some high quality examples already exist, and it is clear that many of our members, and spectators in general, enjoy seeing such "period" racing. While "specials", which have been permitted by the Club from its outset, provide excellent racing they should not come to dominate grids, so given careful supervision exact copies, without anachronistic features or modifications should be allowed." The matter remains under review, while it is interesting to set such a proposal against a statement made by the Committee in 1997.

The manufacture of new cars

"As members may know the Committee has been approached for its views ... on the acceptability of the manufacture of "new" vintage motor cars. The Committee is firmly of the view that, although other clubs may wish to accept such cars ... we should not seek to change (our eligibility rules) in order to accommodate newly built cars."

Ludwig - The Bear

There are of course no clear answers, while the wisdom of the Eligibility Sub Committee in this difficult task remains crucial to the future of the Club.

To build a replica 1920s sports car, while technically achievable, might produce a vehicle of great utility but which would be well nigh impossible to use on the road in terms of legislative and licencing requirements and the need for Individual Vehicle Approval (IVA). Toolroom copy cars, should they be embraced by the Club, will thus be confined to the circuits and speed event venues, while members road going cars will inevitably remain much as they are now, in either standard, modified or special form. Fortunately the range of spares and replacement parts available from specialist firms is extensive, making motoring in a 1920s or 1930s vehicle relatively straight forward – as long as this is allowed on the public highways,

Everyday motoring has changed rapidly in the early years of the 21st century. The certainty of most production cars having an internal combustion engine at the front, a manual gearbox and a prop shaft to drive rear wheels has long since gone, while electrical charging points for hybrids and battery reliant city cars continue to spread. Even the 2014 crop of Formula 1 racing cars were hybrids, as was the winner at Le Mans. It is against such a background that the old car movement must work for the unfettered use of its vehicles on public roads, where increasingly they might be seen as out of step with the norms of the times. Already available fuels have become less "vintage friendly" while the abandonment of MOT requirements for historic vehicles adds to the feeling that they are being pushed to the fringe. The Club's membership of The Federation of British Historic Vehicle Clubs – which exists to uphold the freedom to use historic vehicles on the road, and is the initiator of the spring "Drive It Day" – is therefore likely to become increasingly important.

Within the Club there are also challenges. Membership has remained relatively stable over recent years, but as *anno domini* takes its toll there needs to be a steady flow of new members coming in. A number of recruitment initiatives have been tried, inclusive of a Club stand at its own events and at the major classic and historic motor shows, while it is reassuring to see a good sprinkling of young faces among competitors, particularly among the trialling fraternity. There is however a growing concern that the age of marshals (with an associated reduction in their mobility, as can often be needed in trials) has been steadily rising. Thus far, and sometimes with the assistance of members from other clubs, a crisis has been avoided – while in some ways there is consolation to be found that, even in the 1930s, a shortage of marshals was not unknown.

Over the years it is inevitable that there will be an ebb and flow in the relative popularity of the various types of event. In the early days of the Club there were concerns that trialling – contrary to expectations- found little support, but now the opposite is the case with the entry lists for trials very often over-subscribed. In contrast 2014 saw some falling off in the number of racing entries, in part explained by increased competition from other Clubs promoting historic racing, and exacerbated by conflicting calendar requirements that exceptionally meant that three of the Club's five race meetings had to be squeezed into a seven week period, mid-season. Rallying is supported by a relatively small hard core of enthusiasts, but as the Acorn Rally held as part of the 80th birthday celebrations at Peterborough showed, given the right place and timing big entries can be achieved. The introduction of the easier Champagne Class has also helped make rallying more attractive to a number of members. Driving tests have also seen something of a recent resurgence, with the Winter Tests at Bicester attracting a large and enthusiastic entry. While the Light Car and Edwardian Section events remain ever popular and well subscribed.

Of the multitude of Clubs in the motoring firmament surely none can compare with the VSCC? This was recognised at the 2014 International Historic Motoring Awards ceremony, hosted by *Octane* magazine, at which it won that for the Club of the Year. The citation referred to the exceptionally wide range of events that were run – over 50 in the year, albeit boosted by the Peterborough celebrations – while the equally wide range of cars that find a home in the Club is truly amazing. Where else could one hope to participate and compete in such diverse vehicles as, perhaps, a 1905 De Dion Bouton, an Austin Seven saloon, an Alvis 12/50 tourer, or an ERA with a Grand Prix podium finish to its credit? Enjoyment levels at events are high, their settings usually delightful, while the pub meets (sixty nine at the last count) provide an important part of the social underpinning.

Aware of the various challenges ahead the Club has shown itself able to adapt, while crucially retaining its unique ambience, grounded in a mutual enthusiasm for old motor cars and the pastime of motoring for its own sake. George Daniels, with his deep love of fine mechanisms, wrote that "The survival of the mechanical watch is ensured by its qualities. It is historic, technical, aesthetic, useful and even amusing." Had he added "and sometimes infuriating" he could well have been describing the characteristics of a vintage car.

Tom Rolt, writing of the Club in his autobiography *Landscape with Machines*, published over forty years ago sums up a situation that has dated very little and largely reflects the spirit of the Club today.

> "Although I have since been concerned in the birth of other clubs or societies formed for one object or another, in no organisation other than the VSCC have I found such good company or made so many lifelong friends. I have often wondered why this should be. It seems that the vintage car attracts a type of mind that is peculiarly congenial to me. It is not by any means a one-track mind, but one with an exacting appreciation for fine craftsmanship that is by no means confined to motor cars. But there is nothing solemn or portentous about this appreciation for it is combined with a keenly ironic sense of humour that is quite free from malice and is capable of laughing at itself. It is due to this detachment and light-hearted tolerance that the VSCC can organise its affairs and its events with a degree of efficiency combined with a complete absence of friction, empire-building or officiousness which, in my experience, is quite unique

among voluntary associations, whatsoever their object. Despite the fact that its membership has grown eight-fold in recent years the Club still retains the character impressed upon it by that handful of people who used to foregather at the Phoenix thirty-five years ago."

Ad Multos Annos

"They also serve who only stand and wait". The Marsh family Austin Seven Chummy, as seen at a Welsh weekend in the early 1960s. Sally Marsh reads a Sunday paper while the dog Ella, with a fine disregard for the detail of Milton's verse, sits obediently by.

Appendices

Presidents

S C H Davis	1936 – 1937	T J Threlfall	1981 – 1984
F Lycett	1938 – 1947	C P Marsh	1985 – 1986
L Pomeroy	1948 – 1950	R A Collings	1986 – 1989
E K H Karslake	1951 – 1953	B Spollon	1990 – 1992
C Clutton	1954 – 1956	B M Clarke	1993 – 1995
H P Bowler	1957 – 1959	D R Marsh	1996 – 1998
K Neve	1960 – 1962	J P Ghosh	1999 – 2001
J W Rowley	1963 – 1965	P L Glover	2002 – 2004
R Barker	1966 – 1968	M R Grant Peterkin	2005 – 2007
P A Mann	1969 – 1971	R L Ballard	2008 – 2010
N M Arnold-Forster	1971 – 1974	A K Stephens	2011 – 2013
B B D Kain	1975 – 1977	T P Kneller	2014 –
J W T Crocker	1978 – 1980		

Secretaries

C P L Nicholson	1934 – 1937	B Harcourt-Smith	1986 – 1988
E T Lewis	1935 – 1936	P M A Hull	1988 – 1989
T W Carson	1936 – 1939	D L Franklin	1989 – 1997
A S Heal	1945	N F Murray	1998 – 2000
T W Carson	1946 – 1971	S A M Pringle	2000 – 2005
P M A Hull	1971 – 1986	M G Stripe	2006 – 2014

Editors of *The Bulletin*

C Clutton	1934 – 1937	N Arnold-Forster	1966 – 1970
R Watkins Pitchford	1937 – 1938	A M D Skinner	1970 – 1973
C Clutton	1938 – 1951	T J Threlfall	1973 – 1979
R Barker	1951 – 1953	M R Elsom	1979 – 1984
R Gibson Jarvie	1953 – 1954	D A Thirlby	1985 – 2000
N Arnold-Forster	1954 – 1955	E J Warburton	2000 – 2007
J E Stanford	1956 – 1966	J R C Staveley	2008 –

Annual Aggregate Awards

The Club's major trophy the Lycett Memorial Trophy is awarded to the driver gaining the most points during the year. Different cars may be used but all must be either Edwardian or Vintage.

The original trophy – a large silver rose bowl – was given by Forrest Lycett and accordingly named the Lycett Trophy. This was so awarded until 1959. After Forrest Lycett's unfortunate death in 1960 (sadly he was run down) the premier aggregate award became the Lycett Memorial Trophy. This is a large silver salver, strikingly engraved with a picture of Lycett's well known 8 litre Bentley (which ironically was not built until after the vintage qualifying date of 31st December 1930) and which has been awarded from 1960 onwards.

From then on the original Lycett Trophy has gone to the runner-up, but from 1984 onwards it was decided that it should be restricted to the driver gaining most points driving only one Edwardian or Vintage car across the year.

The Lycett Trophy

Year	Trophy Awarded to	Year	Trophy Awarded to
1935	D Monro	1951	P J E Binns
1936	M Chambers	1952	J G Vessey
1937	C Windsor-Richards	1953	P J E Binns
1938	C Windsor Richards	1954	P J E Binns
1939	C Windsor Richards	1955	P J E Binns
1946	J V Bolster	1956	R E B Noble
1947	C R Abbott	1957	N Arnold-Forster
1948	J V Bolster	1958	P J E Binns
1949	J Jane	1959	G G McDonald
1950	J W Rowley		

The Lycett Memorial Trophy

Year	Trophy Awarded to	Year	Trophy Awarded to
1960	M J Bradley	1980	H F Moffatt
1961	J W Rowley	1981	T C Llewellyn
1962	B M Clarke	1982	T J Threlfall
1963	N Arnold-Forster	1983	T J Threlfall
1964	G R Footitt	1984	A D Jones
1965	N Arnold-Forster	1985	A D Jones
1966	B B D Kain	1986	D R Marsh
1967	B B D Kain	1987	J P Ghosh
1968	M T Joseland	1988	R A Collings
1969	J A Griffiths	1989	L J Wickham
1970	J A Griffiths	1990	R A Collings
1971	J A Griffiths	1991	P Blakeney-Edwards
1972	N Arnold-Forster	1992	Miss A M Jones
1973	N Arnold-Forster	1993	B J A Collings
1974	N Arnold-Forster	1994	J S Baxter
1975	B B D Kain	1995	J S Baxter
1976	J P Ghosh	1996	C R Marsh
1977	B B D Kain	1997	J M Potter
1978	T J Threlfall	1998	J F Diffey
1979	T J Threlfall	1999	J F Diffey

2000	*P L Glover*	*2008*	*B J A Collings*
2001	*D R Marsh*	*2009*	*G W Owen*
2002	*J Gill*	*2010*	*G J Graham*
2003	*D A Buck*	*2011*	*D Cawley*
2004	*R Parsons*	*2012*	*D Knight*
2005	*K T Mycock*	*2013*	*C Gillett*
2006	*G P Frank*	*2014*	*S A Blakeney-Edwards*
2007	*R A Collings*		

Over the years there have been several multiple winners of the Lycett/Lycett Memorial trophies, a challenge becoming progressively harder to achieve as the Club calendar expands. Four drivers have achieved hat-tricks:-

C Windsor-Richards – 1937, 1938, 1939

P J E Binns – 1953, 1954, 1955 … and two other wins in 1951 and 1958

J A Griffiths – 1969, 1970, 1971

N Arnold-Forster – 1972, 1973, 1974 … in which years he was also Club President. He had two previous wins in 1963 and 1965

Three wins have been achieved by R A Collings – 1988, 1990 and 2007, while his son B J A Collings has won twice – 1993 and 2008.

A notable pair of "two wins in a row" were achieved by T J Threlfall – in 1978 and 1979 while editing the Bulletin in 1978, and in 1982 and 1983 while serving as President.

To date Annabel Jones – in 1992 – remains the only lady to have won, her father A D Jones having previously done so in both 1984 and 1985.

The Thoroughbred Trophy

Following the acceptance of Post Vintage Thoroughbreds into the Club it emerged that there was a need for an aggregate trophy to cover such cars. This takes the form of a silver bowl and it has been awarded annually since 1955.

Year	Trophy Awarded to	Year	Trophy Awarded to
1955	Dr Harris	1985	M R Garfitt
1956	Dr Harris	1986	M R Garfitt
1957	W F Moss	1987	I J Hall
1958	A J Gibson	1988	B Spollon
1959	L S Michael	1989	D Taylor
1960	A S R Charnock	1990	P M H Stringer
1961	D H Coates	1991	W J Mahany
1962	A S R Charnock	1992	W J Mahany
1963	P Waller	1993	W J Mahany
1964	Dr Harris	1994	T C Rides
1965	B Sismey	1995	J P Bronson
1966	F G Giles	1996	J P Bronson
1967	E R Fuller	1997	J P Bronson
1968	B Sismey	1998	A R J Abraham
1969	D P Harris	1999	T A Watson
1970	K Knight	2000	M R Garfitt
1971	P J E Binns	2001	R G Wadman
1972	P W Still	2002	M R Garfitt
1973	F G Giles	2003	M R Garfitt
1974	I Wolstenholmes	2004	W J Mahany
1975	C R Newton	2005	W J Mahany
1976	C R Newton	2006	W J Mahany
1977	D J P Edwards	2007	W J Mahany
1978	S G Harvey	2008	J B Guyatt
1979	S G Harvey	2009	N Thorp
1980	N H S Lees	2010	D Pryke
1981	N H S Lees	2011	D Rushton
1982	M R Garfitt	2012	D Pryke
1983	M R Garfitt	2013	D Pryke
1984	M R Garfitt	2014	J B Guyatt

Multiple winners of the Thoroughbred Trophy have also emerged, the first hat-trick being achieved by M R Garfitt in 1982, 1983 and 1984, while his winning streak continued into 1985 and 1986 to make it five in a row. He then returned as the winner in 2000, 2002 and 2003.

W H Mahany also achieved a hat-trick – 1991, 1992 and 1993, and returned with a run of four wins in 2004, 2005, 2006 and 2007.

In between these runs J P Bronson achieved a hat-trick in 1995, 1996 and 1997

The Light Car Trophy

Awarded to the member putting up the best performance using a Light Car in VSCC competitions during the year.

Year	Trophy Awarded to	Year	Trophy Awarded to
1952	J A R Grice	1972	Pam Arnold-Forster
1953	C J Whisker	1973	Clive Hamilton-Gould
1954	Leslie Winder	1974	Clive Hamilton-Gould
1955	Leslie Winder	1975	Peter Gledhill
1956	J D Rogers	1976	Peter Gledhill
1957	J D Rogers	1977	Jack McEwan
1958	John Milner	1978	Peter Gledhill
1959	John Milner	1979	Barry Clarke
1960	H J A F De Salis	1980	Tony Jones
1961	Patrick Marsh	1981	Branislav Sudjic
1962	Ian Cardy	1982	Di Threlfall
1963	Patrick Marsh	1983	Tom Threlfall
1964	Patrick Marsh	1984	Tom & Di Threlfall
1965	Keith Hill	1985/86	No award
1966	John Milner	1987	Mike Bartlett
1967	Mrs Jane Hill	1988	Tony Carlisle
1968	Patrick Marsh & Gill Cardy	1989	Mike Kipping
1969	Tony Griffiths	1990	Andrew Hall
1970	Tony Griffiths	1991	Simon Colledge
1971	Tony Griffiths	1992	Simon Colledge

1993	*Andrew Tarring*	*2004*	*Richard Prest*
1994	*Alex Marsh*	*2005*	*Paul Rogers*
1995	*Andrew Tarring*	*2006*	*Matthew Bell*
1996	*Roger Thorpe*	*2007*	*Matthew Bell*
1997	*Clive Hamilton-Gould*	*2008*	*Keith Hill*
1998	*Richard Wills*	*2009*	*Clive Hamilton-Gould*
1999	*Clive Hamilton-Gould*	*2010*	*Christopher Dallas*
2000	*Richard Wills*	*2011*	*Matthew Bell*
2001	*Clive Hamilton-Gould*	*2012*	*Richard Prest*
2002	*Clive Hamilton-Gould*	*2013*	*Gerry Michelmore*
2003	*Clive Hamilton-Gould*	*2014*	*Clive Hamilton-Gould*

With nine wins, inclusive of a hat-trick, and across forty plus years, the name of Clive Hamilton-Gould stands out among the winners.

Two husband and wife sucesses are also worthy of note. Keith Hill won the Trophy in 1965, to be followed by his wife Jane just two years later. In 1982 Diana Threlfall was to win, her husband Tom doing so in the following year, while together they were to win in 1984.

Bibliography and Sources

The main data base used has been the set of Vintage Sports-Car Club *Bulletins,* running from June 1946 (Volume Five, No 1) until Winter 2014 (No 286), which forms the Julian Fall collection. Prior to March 1937, when the first printed *Bulletin* appeared (as Volume Three No 2), duplicated *Newsletters,* with not entirely consistent numbering, were used to keep members in touch with the Club.

The collection of *Newsletters* housed in the Library at Chipping Norton contains these early communications, as well as those that appeared post-war at somewhat irregular intervals until 1953, after which matters settled down so that by 1965 they became monthly booklets mailed to members, being in the current format from January 1967. These have proved very useful in telling of the on-going plans and the "nuts and bolts" of Club life, whereas *The Bulletin,* with its concentration on event reporting, tends to deal with the finished products.

The early *Minutes* of the Club's Committee have also been accessed, their emphasis tending to be on decisions, rather than the details of discussion, but of great interest nevertheless.

Among the many journals and magazines consulted have been:

Autocar   *The Motor*   *The Light Car*   *Bugantics*   *Motor Sport*

Bibliography and Sources

Other sources that have contributed information and insights have included:

Books.

Cork, Tim (Ed)	*Light Car Journey*	VSCC, 2007
Gardiner, Juliet	*The Thirties*	Harper Press, 2010
Hull, Peter	*The History of the VSCC*	Cassell, 1964
Hull, Peter	*The VSCC Golden Jubilee Book*	VSCC, 1984
Hunt, Julian	*Motorsport Explorer*	Haynes, 2012
Laycock, Bridget	*1908 Itala – a celebration of 90 years*	Unspecified, 1998
Neve, Kenneth	*A bit behind the times*	Grenville, 1988
Priestley, J B	*English Journey*	Gollancz, 1934
Rolt L T C	*Landscape with Machines*	Longmans, 1971
Setright L J K	*Drive On!*	Palawan Press, 2002

Booklets.

The VSCC Golden Jubilee Programme Booklet	1984
The VSCC 65th Anniversary Commemorative Programme	1999
The VSCC 80th Anniversary Booklet	2014

Videos.

The 50th anniversary video	1984
"7 Days in Harrogate". The 70th anniversary video	2004

An additional, and very useful, resource has been the collection of race, sprint and hill climb programmes as housed in the Club's archive.

Photographic credits

Ferret Fotographics:	17, 32, 34, 41, 74, 75, 76, 119, 132
Max Hill:	70, 82, 83, 87, 97, 100, 104, 115, 124, 125, 130
Roger McDonald:	Frontispiece, 121, 134, 135, 142, 144, 146, 149, 151, 152, 153, 165, 166, 168, 181, 182, 186, 188, 196, 197, 201, 204, 220, 224, 225, 227, 228 bottom, 230 x 2, 235, 238, 252, 259

Bibliography and Sources

Peter McFadyen Photography:	228 top
VSCC archive:	25, 72
Richmond Pike / VSCC archive:	79
Bob Stallard / VSCC archive:	55
Studio 3 / VSCC archive:	111
Studio 3 / Ferret Fotographics:	139
Brian Galbraith / VSCC archive:	190

Thanks are also due to Arthur Davis for his line drawing of The Old Post Office as appears on the rear of the dust jacket.

Index

A

Abbot C 61
Abecassis G 62
Abingdon Driving Tests 195, 204, 233
AC 33, 48, 87, 151, 158, 166, 219
Adams J ix, 202
Adams (Mrs) R 173
Adams P 200
Adstock 87, 88, 160, 194
Ahern J 100
AJS 154
Alfa Romeo 32, 35, 48, 69, 75, 77, 79, 86, 97, 100, 113, 115, 133, 147, 168, 169, 172, 178, 181, 183, 186, 189, 247, 248
Alfonso Hispano 26, 53
Allard S 41
Allason J H 15
Allen S ix, 215, 217, 253
Alta 48, 68, 226
Alvis 9, 10, 15, 16, 23, 25, 30, 33, 37, 40, 41, 48, 52, 56, 57, 58, 59, 66, 68, 69, 74, 86, 91, 93, 94, 100, 110, 111, 121, 133, 153, 154, 168, 169, 171, 184, 187, 198, 211, 220, 226, 232, 238, 257
Amilcar 9, 10, 112, 114, 143
Anglo-American Rallies 93
Annual Aggregate Awards 7, 239
Apsley (Cartoonist) 243
Arnold-Forster N 77, 96, 120, 134, 147, 152, 241, 261, 262, 263, 264, 266
Aston Clinton 12, 16, 17, 24, 101
Aston Martin 13, 22, 27, 31, 48, 117, 126, 144, 145, 178, 197, 244
Audi 219
Austins ii, 2, 4, 8, 9, 22, 23, 48, 58, 69, 88, 97, 98, 99, 110, 118, 119, 132, 136, 144, 153, 154, 159, 173, 179, 186, 204, 220, 222, 226, 229, 230, 231, 232, 233, 245, 257, 259
Austin Seven Car Club 8
Austro Daimler 244
Autocar, The 3, 269
Autosolo 237

Auto Union 30, 36, 219
Avon Park Raceway 189
Ayers Capt A J 99

B

Badgery T W 58, 90
Bagshot 43, 45, 46, 52, 54, 56
Baker brothers (D & R) 187, 189
Baker R 225, 237
Ballot 31, 40, 106
Barford St John 160
Barker "Steady" R 88, 261, 262
Barnato-Hassan 79, 147
Baron A 12, 18
Batkin G ix, 239
Baxter J 224, 225, 226
Bean 101
Beaulieu 130, 133
Becke Powerplus 41
"Beelzebub" 13
Bell R H 144
Bendall C J 83
Bennett Sgt 128
Bentley 4, 5, 9, 13, 15, 16, 22, 26, 27, 32, 37, 39, 48, 52, 56, 57, 58, 61, 62, 67, 68, 73, 76, 77, 79, 86, 93, 96, 97, 98, 100, 101, 103, 104, 105, 109, 110, 112, 113, 114, 122, 126, 142, 143, 147, 150, 154, 167, 169, 171, 175, 183, 188, 189, 210, 218, 225, 227, 228, 231, 247, 262
Bentley Drivers Club 122
Berry J 114
Bevan H 187
BHW 40, 41, 77
Bicester Heritage Centre 233, 234, 239, 256
Binns P 87, 91, 96, 99, 125, 157, 263, 264, 265
Bira Prince 62, 114, 146
Bird (Tony) A P 133, 141, 159, 161, 179
Birks A 25
Bishop G C 84
Bisley 54, 55, 56, 57, 58, 78, 84, 95, 129
"Black Bess" 13, 18, 100
Black D 147, 168, 169, 171, 172, 183
Black M 222
Blakeney-Edwards P 92, 227, 263
Blight A 93, 127
"Bloody Mary" 26, 28, 53, 68
Blubberhouses 84, 118, 235

Blue Forms 179, 180, 181
BMV 37
BMW 22, 48, 120, 154, 201, 214, 226, 227, 237
Boddy W 5, 19, 45, 59, 64, 87, 166, 189, 241, 245
Bolster J 16, 26, 28, 53, 54, 64, 68, 116, 263
Bolzano 131
Boorer D E 117
Boulogne Bicycle Rally 164, 193, 236
Bowen Sir J 40
Bowler H P 9, 13, 15, 16, 27, 30, 35, 37, 39, 43, 46, 52, 56, 58, 105, 126, 229, 261
Bowler M 131
Bowyer C 158, 166, 173
Bramshill Speed Trial 17, 20
Bridcutt J 198
Brigham Award of the Society of Automotive Historians 242
Bristol Motor Cycle and Light Car Club 44
Britcher R 202
Brittany Tour 233
BRM 144, 168, 185
Broad J 97
Brocklebank S S 17
Brooklands 2, 13, 19, 20, 28, 33, 40, 59, 61, 64, 69, 92, 105, 112, 150, 159, 173, 185, 194, 204, 224, 236
Brooks T G 11
Brooks (Tony) C A S 114
Broxton Rally 126
Bruce Spollon ix, 62, 171, 172, 184, 188, 197, 225
Buckle Air Commodore N R 95
Bugatti ii, 12, 13, 17, 18, 22, 27, 30, 31, 32, 33, 35, 37, 39, 40, 41, 48, 52, 53, 60, 61, 62, 68, 73, 76, 77, 78, 94, 96, 97, 98, 100, 110, 111, 112, 114, 117, 119, 126, 127, 130, 134, 142, 143, 145, 147, 153, 154, 167, 168, 171, 172, 174, 180, 187, 188, 189, 199, 203, 204, 218, 221, 225, 226, 248
Bugatti Owners Club 27, 33, 167
Bulletin, The vii, viii, 10, 11, 12, 13, 14, 15, 19, 20, 22, 25, 26, 37, 39, 45, 46, 56, 67, 69, 70, 73, 77, 84, 87, 88,

Index

90, 93, 98, 101, 102, 105, 108, 120, 123, 126, 129, 131, 133, 134, 137, 138, 143, 144, 157, 161, 167, 175, 177, 194, 199, 202, 203, 205, 213, 221, 227, 231, 239, 240, 241, 242, 243, 244, 245, 246, 248, 253, 254, 262, 264, 269
Bullett M 156, 234
Bunting L 231
Burke Richard 138
Burke Rosemary 138, 139, 153, 161, 171, 175
Burness G K 31
Burnham on Sea Motor Club 189
Burton J L 18
Buxton 9, 58, 96, 125, 126, 158
Byrom J C 73, 76, 77, 96, 97

C

Cadwell Park 143, 164, 172, 181, 219, 236
Caesar Special 78, 117
Calthorpe 88
Cambridge University Automobile Club 59, 60, 61
Cameron Millar 178
Cardy T 188
Carr G 239
Carson Margery 134, 139, 175
Carson Mrs F 27, 32
Carson Special 12
Carson T 98
Carson (Tim) T W 9, 11, 12, 13, 15, 16, 17, 19, 24, 28, 31, 33, 35, 37, 42, 43, 46, 54, 63, 67, 78, 86, 101, 107, 161, 212, 247, 262
Castle Combe 112, 148
Cattell 158, 172
Chambers M 263
Charterhouse 20, 129, 133, 158
Chelford, Cheshire 52
Cherrett Allan 178
Cherrett Angela ix, 212
Chiltern Trials 8
"Chitty-Chitty-Bang-Bang" 116
Choate C 35, 46
Choate Margery 101
City and Guilds Motor Club 25
Clapham D 16, 25, 30
Clarke B 98, 99, 118, 120, 154, 157, 167, 173, 180, 184, 226, 231, 266
Clarke J 35
Clarke R 60

Clark P 61
Club badge 6
Club Committee 88
Club's objects and rules 6
Clutton Lt Col J 4, 12, 15, 19, 28, 35, 38
Clutton (Sam) Cecil 4, 5, 6, 8, 9, 10, 12, 13, 15, 16, 18, 19, 20, 22, 23, 24, 26, 27, 28, 31, 33, 35, 37, 38, 39, 40, 41, 44, 45, 46, 56, 60, 61, 67, 73, 75, 76, 77, 81, 84, 88, 90, 93, 101, 102, 103, 106, 108, 110, 111, 112, 116, 127, 134, 141, 149, 161, 178, 185, 205, 213, 240, 242, 244, 245, 261, 262
Clyno 87, 88, 245
Cobb P G 186
Cobden R 224, 225
Cognac Special 78, 147, 151, 171, 172, 188, 218
Colerne 148, 149, 150, 164, 172, 175, 187, 188, 189, 193, 194, 223, 236
Colledge H 192
Collings B 185
Collings R ix, 116, 148, 149, 165, 172, 179, 188, 215, 242
Collins P 114
Connaught 112, 116, 117, 148, 170, 171
Cook W A L 68
Cooper Bristol 114, 117, 144
Cooper Climax 185
Cope Sir Denzil and Lady 17
Cork T ix, 203, 233
Cornbury Park Sprint 195
Corner N 112, 114, 117, 127, 140, 143, 147, 170, 184, 196
Corsa della Mendola 131
Cotswold Trial 233
Cottam A 117, 169
Couper A ix, 233
Cove 159
Crabbe C 127, 146, 183
Craven A 237
Cream Cracker MG 231
Croix-en-Ternois 187
Croome M 237
Crouch D ix, 233
Crowther J M 115
Croydon Spped Trials 28
Crystal Palace 2, 26, 39, 59, 131
Cwm Whitton 229

D

Daimler 38, 39, 59, 165, 166, 172, 231, 244
Dancer J C 68
Dancers End 33, 59
Daniels G 103, 141, 161, 166, 172, 232, 257
Darbyshire Mrs Sue 224
Darracq 88
Davenport B 112
Davis (Sammy) S C H 13, 15, 18, 19, 30, 46, 185, 261
Dawkins H W 15
Dawkins R C 15
Day D 189, 190
Dean C 189
De Dion Bouton 52, 257
Defford 235
Delage 26, 40, 45, 52, 62, 68, 73, 75, 76, 77, 112, 114, 116, 140, 142, 143, 147, 169, 189, 225
Delahaye 22, 48
Delaney (Tom) C T 185
de Nevers G 115
Denne R V 84
Denyer A L 25
Diffey J 218, 226
Discoed 83, 128
Dixon D L 58
Dixon F H 46
Dixon P H 54
Dodge 171
Donington Park 2, 16, 20, 27, 30, 31, 33, 35, 36, 40, 41, 42, 59, 73, 77, 112, 113, 143, 146, 147, 150, 158, 164, 168, 171, 182, 184, 186, 195, 197, 218, 219, 220, 221, 223, 236, 249
Drumhouse 120, 153, 154
Dunham C G 64
Dunn A 120
Dunphy B C 124
Dutt R 73
Dye D 231
Dyer J 58

E

Eason-Gibson J 28
Eastbourne Rally 57
Eastern Rally 79, 86, 99, 122, 125, 133, 158, 164, 166, 173, 195, 202, 236
Edwardian and Light Car Rally 79

Index

Edwardians 12, 16, 17, 26, 44, 50, 57, 59, 61, 71, 74, 79, 80, 81, 82, 83, 86, 89, 90, 92, 93, 96, 99, 100, 110, 128, 129, 142, 149, 163, 164, 165, 168, 185, 186, 192, 249
Elcot Night Navigation Rally 157
Elder Malcolm ix, 159, 198, 203, 234
Elder Mark 234
Eligibility 47, 50, 180, 243, 250, 251, 253, 254, 255
Ellis R 215, 217, 239
Elsom M 240
Elstree Speed Trials 53
Elvington 235
Eminson A F 77, 112
Enstone 159, 160, 164, 173, 203, 233
ERA/ERAs 8, 30, 32, 45, 52, 62, 64, 69, 73, 76, 77, 79, 96, 97, 98, 112, 113, 114, 115, 116, 134, 139, 140, 144, 145, 146, 147, 168, 169, 171, 172, 178, 183, 185, 187, 188, 189, 190, 197, 209, 221, 223, 224, 225, 254, 257
Evans H B 23
Everett J 222
Ewen Dr G A 35, 45, 52, 58, 112

F

Fafnir 4, 12, 15, 24, 28, 35, 38, 45, 84, 100
Fairman J E G 62, 244
Fane A F P 16, 17
Felton R 171, 189, 200
ffrench-Mullen D A 244
Fiat 28, 33, 35, 39, 40, 41, 105, 197, 231
Filsell D vii, 88, 157, 200, 226
Firkins D 97
Fitzpatrick D 39
Footitt G R 78, 147, 148, 151, 169, 171, 172, 188, 263
Ford 23, 158, 173, 231
Ford R D 247
Foster B 222
Fox A 233
Franklin D 178, 215, 217
Frazer Nash 9, 10, 12, 13, 15, 16, 25, 26, 28, 35, 39, 41, 58, 61, 66, 68, 71, 74, 77, 80, 86, 92, 93, 94, 95, 96, 99, 100, 118, 120, 129, 131, 142, 144, 147, 152, 153, 154, 168, 169, 174, 177, 181, 186, 187, 191, 197, 198, 201, 214, 224, 225, 226, 227, 228, 237, 245
Frazer-Nash Archie 191
Freikaiserwagen 35
Fry J 35

G

Garfitt M ix, 201, 226
Gerard (Bob) F R 32, 45, 64, 113, 190, 197
Gibson Jarvie 262
Gibson R 229, 262
Gilbey S 245
Giles (Col) G M 13, 18
Gillies M 225
Gill J 226, 233, 235, 264
Giron L 52
Gloucester Trial 16, 30, 233
Glover P 173, 179
GN 12, 13, 16, 33, 34, 112, 118, 151, 165, 168, 187, 188, 189, 197, 221, 231, 234
Goodwood 55, 84, 87, 100, 107, 129, 133, 158, 163, 164, 172, 194, 195, 201, 204, 233, 236, 239
Gosh J 187
Gransden Lodge 59, 60, 61, 62, 64
Grant-Peterkin M 161, 164, 183, 198
Gray B 150, 166, 171, 187, 188
Green Andrea 161
Green W H 9, 144
Griffiths G 33
Griffiths (Tony) J A ix, 132, 263, 264, 266
Grimshaw T S 31, 35
Guildford trial 11
Guyatt J 222
Gwynne 95

H

Habershon R P R 62, 68
Hagley and District Car Club 80
Halford B 144, 170, 183, 196
Hambleton Rally 126, 133, 138
Hamilton C J 76
Hamilton J Duncan 69, 76, 266, 267
Hampton C W P 25, 27, 31
Hancock C J 197
Harcourt-Smith B 177, 178, 262
Hardy Special 150, 171, 187, 188
Harewood 235

Harper S 169
Harris (Dr) D P 86, 96, 118, 131, 154
Harris J F 167
Harris John 200, 236
Harris M J 97
Harrogate 93, 235, 236, 270
Harrow Car Club 30
Hartwell G 73, 113
Harvey S 202
Hawthorn J M 117, 145
Hayes R 90, 117
Heal A S 15, 18, 27, 30, 31, 33, 35, 39, 40, 41, 46, 58, 60, 63, 105, 108, 167, 213, 262
Heston 87, 129
Heyford (Upper) 204
Heyward C W A 73
Hickling H 171
Hill K viii, 65, 147, 165, 266, 267
Hill M viii, 65, 130, 199, 270
Hill (Mrs) J 89, 266
Hine H P 142
Hispano Suiza 93, 100
Hodkin D 60, 61
Holmes S 178, 215
"Homes and Gardens" 234, 235, 237
Horton J 112, 174
Houlgate R 237
Howard-Orchard D vii
Howard-Orchard Mrs G 232
Howe Earl 30
HRG 22, 48, 56, 154, 157, 167, 203, 222
Hughes B 158, 202, 226
Hulbert M 225
Hull D 114
Hull P vii, 38, 133, 141, 147, 150, 159, 161, 168, 174, 175, 177, 178, 179, 192, 213, 215, 245
Humber 82, 87, 96, 97, 99, 116, 118, 120, 135, 149, 154, 160, 166
Hunt J 115
Hutton TT 93
Hytten Dr F 177

I

Instone R 12
Invicta 9, 12, 84, 100, 247
Isotta Fraschini 87
Itala 16, 18, 26, 28, 33, 35, 39, 40, 41, 58, 59, 60, 61, 68, 73, 74, 76, 77, 93, 96, 99,

Index

101, 102, 103, 111, 112, 113, 116, 134, 142, 143, 149, 170, 218, 220, 221, 225, 232, 270
Itala Trophy 61, 73, 74, 76, 77, 96, 112, 113, 143, 170, 218, 220, 221, 225

J

Jackson D 27
Jaguar 91, 161, 196, 219
Jane J 71, 263
Jarvis K 69
Jeal L 217
Jeavons P 231
Jeddere-Fisher A 87, 88
Jenkinson D 131, 144, 166, 179, 184, 189, 241
Jewell S 221
John P R 58
Johnson B W 96
Johnson L 68
Jolley R 197
Jones A 157, 172, 226, 237, 264
Jones R 234
Jones T 266
Joseland M 179
Jowett 55, 99, 120
J T Williamson 142

K

Kain B 112, 117, 143, 147
Karslake K 37, 48, 91, 105, 108
Kentish Rally 195
King F 30
Kingsclere House 134
Kirkham D 16, 30
Knill-Jones P 234

L

Lagonda 22, 48, 85, 87, 88, 100, 115, 166, 167, 173, 188, 210, 228, 245
Lanchester 74, 93
Lancia 25, 30, 35, 48, 71, 93, 95, 98, 238
Lasham 129
Lea Francis 25, 26, 30, 39, 58, 87, 99, 118
Lee K 237
Lees P 31
Levy G G 25
Lewes Speed Trials 32, 33, 40, 57
Lewis (Ned) E T 4, 5, 8, 15, 19, 23, 24, 29, 31, 101, 262
Light Car and Edwardian Section 87, 89, 96, 163, 166, 194, 195, 198, 232, 236, 237, 256
Light Car, The 2, 3, 5, 8, 26, 41, 44, 45, 49, 52, 79, 87, 88, 89, 96, 129, 133, 137, 163, 164, 166, 169, 172, 187, 192, 198, 232, 256, 266, 269, 270
Lindsay (Hon) P 114, 116, 117, 144, 146, 149, 169, 170, 171, 183
Littlestone Speed Trials 18, 148, 205
Llandow 142, 143
Llandrindod Wells 89, 123
Llewellyn D 143, 147
Llewellyn T 169, 183, 218
Lockhart F 97, 117
Loire Tour 160
London to Brighton 7
Lorenzato R V 124
Lorraine Dietrich 26, 32, 39
Luton Hoo Speed Trials 63, 64, 69, 78
Lycett F 18, 19, 26, 30, 31, 33, 35, 37, 46, 54, 61, 63, 67, 73, 100, 103, 104, 171, 262
Lycett Northern Trophy 31
Lycett Trophy 28, 31, 37, 39, 53, 54, 71, 104, 120, 132, 184, 185, 226, 262, 263

M

Mackenzie L C 39
Madresfield 57, 58, 59, 67, 69, 70, 71, 78, 79, 98, 99, 129, 130, 131, 133, 164, 173, 193, 195, 204, 228, 229, 236, 248, 249
Majzub J 170, 218, 225
Mallory Park 185, 186, 195, 197, 236
Malyan J 214, 217
Mann C 170
Map reading 11, 26, 36
Marendaz Special 16
Marlow Trial 52
Marshall B 13
Marshall W 246
Maserati 40, 69, 73, 79, 113, 115, 116, 117, 137, 144, 145, 149, 170, 171, 178, 183, 245
Mason N 170, 183
Mathew D 35
May A 61
Mayman A 183, 188, 196
Mays R 112, 168
McDonald G 97
Measham The 79, 80, 95, 99, 118, 123, 124, 125, 133, 142, 154, 156, 172, 194, 201, 202, 206, 226, 227, 232, 236, 245
"Mellaha" 51, 102
Membership 36, 218, 253, 256
Mendip Night Rally 163, 172
Mercedes Benz 25, 27, 30, 31, 38, 48, 61, 66, 71, 94, 104, 113, 114, 116, 146, 165, 188, 218, 224, 248
Merrick T 117
MG 9, 10, 11, 12, 31, 48, 51, 53, 56, 80, 154, 204, 222, 224, 231
Midland Section 58, 80, 107
Mid Surrey Club 30
Millais Sir R 183
Mitchell A 222
Moffatt H 85, 88, 112, 114, 119, 126, 143, 147, 149, 150, 153, 161, 167, 171, 200, 234, 263
Monkhouse P 53
Montagu Trophy 131
Morley P 143, 147, 169, 171
Morris 2, 22, 23, 37, 48, 68, 96, 97, 154
Morris D 225
Morris Goodall 27
Morris M 114, 146, 147, 168, 169, 172, 224
Moss Mrs A 16
Moss S 16
Moss W 114
Motor Cycling Club 9, 58, 200
Motor Sport 3, 10, 19, 25, 26, 28, 39, 40, 53, 59, 61, 63, 88, 160, 219, 242, 269
Motor, The 269
Munro D 9, 12, 13
Murray N ix, 178, 189, 204, 215, 217, 239
Murray S 112

N

Naish Hill Climb 44
Napier 147, 169, 171, 189, 225
Nash R G J 39
Neve K 23, 28, 29, 30, 31, 43, 107, 116, 135, 149, 150, 179, 261
Newsletter 10, 67, 78, 96, 108, 110, 116, 118, 120, 122,

276

Index

136, 156, 159, 160, 161, 180, 192, 202, 212, 239
New Year's Day 160, 194, 252
Nicholson B H 3, 4, 9, 45
Nicholson C P L 3, 4, 5, 6, 9, 262
Nidderdale Trial 71, 78, 84, 86, 99, 118, 171, 172
N McCaw 46
Norris J B 68
Norris Special 73
Northern Committee 31
Northern Section 107
Northern Trial 30, 37, 79, 99, 118, 120
North S 215, 217

O

Odiham 99, 129
OM 87, 96, 99, 100, 125, 235
Oulton Park 79, 97, 104, 111, 113, 114, 115, 133, 142, 143, 144, 146, 164, 167, 171, 182, 186, 193, 196, 219, 220, 226
Owen (Geraint) G W 264

P

Panhard Levassor 149
Parker GN 187, 188, 189
Parnell R 40, 41, 77, 80
Passini J 13, 17
Patten D 202
Peacop J 169
Pearce D 226
Peerless B 191, 192
Pembrey 186, 195, 197, 220, 221, 223
Peterborough 237, 238, 256, 257
Peterborough Motor Club 122
Peters I 18
Peugeot 45, 87, 220
Phelps A 46
Phillips S 170
Phillips S F 144
Phoenix Green Garage 13, 37, 47
Phoenix Inn 13, 37, 108
Phoenix Special 34
Pickett F 191
Pilleth 151, 152, 199, 229
Pitts A G 113
Plowman T 18
Pole J S 16
Pomeroy Laurence 46, 51, 63, 67, 73, 79, 82, 83, 89, 90, 91, 92, 93, 95, 99, 101, 103, 104, 117, 125, 126, 127, 133, 163, 174, 194, 211, 212, 213, 223, 226, 227, 228, 236, 261
Pomeroy Laurence (Senior) 90
Pomeroy Memorial Trophy 79, 90, 91, 126, 127, 228
Poore R D 62, 69, 75, 76, 79, 113
Potter J M 158, 166, 202, 226, 263
Powell H P 9, 13, 15
Powys-Lybbe A 10
Prescott vii, 30, 33, 34, 40, 42, 45, 54, 59, 62, 67, 68, 73, 78, 79, 89, 93, 98, 99, 104, 111, 117, 133, 134, 135, 142, 148, 150, 161, 164, 167, 172, 178, 184, 187, 193, 195, 197, 211, 223, 233, 236, 237, 249
Presteigne ii, 37, 38, 39, 81, 84, 95, 98, 119, 128, 129, 131, 133, 151, 152, 199, 229, 232
Price G ix, 237
Price S 89
Pringle (Stuart) S A M 239, 262
Pugh A T 74, 75
PVT 81, 92, 123, 173, 179, 219, 226, 231, 249, 250, 252, 254, 265
Pyrenean Challenge 233

Q

Quorum Print Services Ltd iv, ix, 242, 243

R

Radnorshire Arms ii, 37, 38, 81, 84, 152, 199
Railton 48
Reece P B 80
Rees Flt/Lt J L 74
Renault 16, 39, 233
Rhydspence Inn 152, 173, 199
Ribblesdale Road Rally 86
Ridings Rally 235
Riley 9, 27, 32, 41, 48, 58, 66, 67, 77, 80, 84, 86, 87, 95, 110, 118, 124, 133, 154, 158, 166, 168, 171, 172, 173, 198, 204, 207, 211, 221, 224, 225, 232, 237
Risley A E 197
Rivers Fletcher A F 46, 52, 53, 68, 168
Riviere de la Sally 161
Roberts J 98
Rolls Royce 83
Rolt Mrs S 187
Rolt (Tom) L T C 13, 17, 33, 36, 37, 68, 94, 104, 111, 257
Rover Special 117, 145
Rowley J 58, 73, 81, 87, 107, 120, 124, 126, 157
Rushton F 120
Russell Road v, 139, 141, 161, 163, 175, 177, 178, 214, 215, 217, 253

S

Salmon D 253
Salvadori R 62
Samuelson Sir F 99
Sant R 168
Sarum Hill Garage, Basingstoke 42, 102
Schellenberg K 77, 98, 147
Scottish Trial 156, 163, 195, 236
Scott-Moncrieff (Mrs) A 144
Seaman R 73
Seaman Trophy 49, 73, 76, 77, 79, 146, 147, 169, 171, 182, 183, 219
Sears J 76, 92, 98, 99, 100, 171
Sears S E 57
Semmence special 33
Seth-Smith J 38
Sets-racing 222
Sewell D 180
Shawe-Taylor B 79
Shaw G 9
Shelsley Walsh 33, 112, 148, 150, 151, 164, 168, 187, 195, 223, 236
Shetliffe G ix, 200, 229, 234
Shipham Quarries 154
Shobdon 237
Shoosmith A 167, 198
Showell A W 71
Shrivenham 129
Silverstone 50, 67, 68, 72, 73, 74, 75, 76, 78, 79, 90, 91, 92, 95, 96, 97, 98, 99, 112, 113, 115, 116, 127, 129, 133, 139, 142, 143, 144, 145, 147, 148, 159, 163, 164, 165, 168, 169, 170, 172, 174, 182, 184, 185, 186, 194, 195, 196, 197, 206, 209, 210, 211, 213, 218, 219, 220, 221, 227, 236
Singer 154, 180
Sizaire-Naudin 38, 110
Skelton D 231

277

Index

Skinner S J 82, 99, 241
Skirrow J V 100
Slough Rally 79, 84, 85, 95, 129
Smatcher (The) 39, 83, 128, 151, 152, 200, 229
Smith D W G 125
Smith E 171, 175, 177, 178
Smith G 125, 169, 171, 187
Smith P 118
Snelling (Geoff) G N 29
Snetterton 169, 220, 221
Snow J L 80
Southern Rally 79
Southon A 47
Southport sand races 29
Spence H 87, 96, 99, 118, 120, 154
Spencer-Brooks Special 12
Spero H C 79, 113, 115
"Spider" 112, 168
Spollon B 261, 265
Sports-Car Club of America 63
Stanford J 241
Stanley Cup 16, 39
Stanley steamer 57, 93
Stapleton 38, 81, 82, 83, 128
Staveley J R C vii, 243, 262
Stephens A K ix, 168, 187, 188, 224, 261
Stevenson P 232
Stimson K 173
Stocken P 118
Stout W H 57
Stretton L 165, 194, 241
Stripe (Mike) M G vii, ix, 249, 253, 262
Stuart J T 113, 115
Stubberfield P 68, 78, 114, 117
Stutz 94
Sumner G 26
Sumner-JAP 16
Sumner R A C 16
Sunbeam 31, 56, 60, 71, 76, 86, 92, 93, 98, 100, 105, 112, 114, 116, 126, 143, 147, 183, 192, 202, 215, 228
Surrey Trial 9, 30
Surtees J 218
Sussex trial 16
Swainson J 37
Swift 154
Symondson R C 111

T

Talbot 43, 61, 87, 88, 93, 127, 166, 185, 222
Talbot Lago 185

Taylor (Dr) W A 78
Tebbett M ix, 198
Tebbett (Mrs) C ix, 229, 234
Tebbett P ix, 229
Theophile Schneider 149, 168
Thirlby D 131, 177, 194, 203, 241, 243
Threlfall (Mrs) D 267
Threlfall T 149, 158, 161, 168, 173, 227, 241, 266
Thruxton 112, 133, 139, 140, 142, 143, 148, 158
Toone R 181, 186
Toulmin M 10
Triangle Special 62
Triumph 228
Trojan 96, 118, 237
Tubbs B 45
Tubbs Bunny 45
"Turtle Drilling Company" Special 170
Twenty-first Birthday Party 99

U

Union Special 32

V

Vaughan C 41
Vauxhall 4, 9, 12, 13, 15, 16, 23, 28, 30, 31, 37, 38, 61, 63, 82, 90, 91, 92, 93, 94, 99, 100, 101, 108, 110, 120, 124, 154, 157, 168, 172, 178, 186, 187, 198, 231, 237
Venables-Llewellyn J 171
Verstage (Printers) 241
Verzons Hotel 160, 194, 200, 252
Veteran Car Club 5, 44, 105
Veteran class 17
Veteran Cycle Club 192, 241
Veteran Motor Car Club of America 93
Viggles. Squadron Leader 158, 166, 173
Vintage Sports Car Exchange 64

W

Waggon and Horses 29
Walker M ix, 187, 188, 189
Walker (Mrs) J A 188
Walker N 215, 217, 218
Walker P 69
Waller P 265
Wall F 114, 127, 143, 147
Warburton J 177, 227, 242, 243, 262

Watkins-Nash 45
Watkins Pitchford R 262
Watkins R 44, 262
Watt B 229, 248
Welsh Rally 37, 40, 79, 81, 133, 230, 232
Welsh Trial 119, 129, 152, 199, 236
Welsh Weekend (see Welsh Trial and Rally)
Wessex Trial 154
Westcott 204, 233, 236, 239
Weston-Super-Mare 189
"Whale, The" 79, 147
Whiddington A 24
Whincop A C 244
White G 200
Whitehead G 76, 77
Whitfield 235
Whitfield Semmence 32
Whitworth R H 31
Whyman J 138, 139, 161
Whyte G 221
Wickham L J 171, 184, 263
Wigglesworth S 215, 239
Wike P 27, 29, 31, 118
Wilby (Miss) V M 18, 26, 28, 35, 41
Wil-de-Gose R 62, 112
Wilkinson R ix, 237
Williams C 147, 225
Williamson I 231
Williamson J 76, 77, 96, 99, 113
Williamson John T 169
Wimmer R ix, 217, 239
Winchester R ix, 239
Winder C 120
Winder L 30, 97, 99, 118, 120, 231, 266
Windsor-Richards C 16, 25, 28, 37, 38, 39, 40, 46, 263, 264
Winn A 205
Wiscombe 150, 164, 168, 171, 184, 187, 194, 197, 210, 223, 224
Witley 84, 129
Witley "Rally" 129
Wolseley 48, 93, 154, 229, 237
Wright K 243
Wrigley E 22, 26

Z

Züst 116